Ukrainians in North America

A Select Bibliography

Compiled by Halyna Myroniuk and Christine Worobec

Immigration History Research Center
University of Minnesota, St. Paul

Multicultural History Society of
Ontario, Toronto

The Immigration History Research Center wishes to thank the National
Endowment for the Humanities for its generous assistance in the
preparation of this manuscript.

The Multicultural History Society is grateful for the support of
Ontario's Ministry of Culture and Recreation.

ISBN 0-919045-04-9

CONTENTS

PREFACE

This bibliography is a joint effort of the Immigration History Research Center of the University of Minnesota and the Multicultural History Society of Ontario. It came about because the two institutions discovered that they had undertaken, almost simultaneously, major surveys of their resources in Ukrainian North American studies. Since the greater Toronto area and the Center in the Twin Cities are, along with Edmonton, Alberta and Cambridge, Massachusetts, the major depositories of materials on Ukrainians in North America, it seemed possible to combine our work to maximum advantage for researchers.

This guide describes the Ukrainian Americana holdings at the Immigration History Research Center in St. Paul and books and printed materials on Ukrainian life in the U.S. and Canada at various libraries and depositories in Toronto including: the University of Toronto library system, the Metropolitan Toronto Public Library system, the Ukrainian National Federation's libraries and St. Vladimir Institute.

Halyna Myroniuk, senior library assistant with the IHRC, compiled and organized the part of the collection that deals with the United States. Christine Worobec, University of Toronto, did the work at the various Canadian libraries and depositories. Both women have shown a very high order of scholarship and research skills in their work. Wendy Jacobs has edited and reconciled the two compilations, an enormous task done with much skill. Darlene Zeleney assisted in the editing and with the many difficult linguistic problems.

We thought that the sort of guide most appropriate for the two institutions and most useful to the researchers needed a precise focus in ethnic and immigration studies. This bibliography, then, is not meant to be a general listing of material about Ukraine, but rather about the Ukrainian immigrants and all aspects of their history in North America. It includes only incidentally--as part of its general definition of ethnic political and cultural life--materials written in North America about Ukraine. On the other hand, the entries reflect all aspects of the Ukrainian ethnoculture in North America from history, economic life, cultural and religious life, organizational life to language maintenance, emigré literature of every genre and Ukrainian ethnic art, from the fine arts through iconography to folklore.

The result is a volume with nearly 2,000 titles. It is a work that, like a good <u>catalogue raisonné</u> of an art exhibit, has several purposes. It introduces researchers to the resources of the IHRC and of the greater Toronto area, and it also serves as a general bibliography on Ukrainians in North America.

        We would like to thank the compilers for their excellent and
patient work; we also thank Andrew Gregorovich, President of
the Ukrainian Librarians Association of Canada, and Anne McCarthy
and Janet Hamilton of the Multicultural History Society of Ontario
who prepared the manuscript and supervised production. Above all,
we wish to acknowledge the cooperation of the Ukrainian communities
in Canada and the United States. Their commitment to their
heritage and understanding of the importance of library and archives
preservation have made this guide possible.

        Copies of the bibliography are available in Canada through
the Multicultural History Society of Ontario and in the United
States through the Immigration History Research Center at the
University of Minnesota.

                        Robert F. Harney
                        Academic Director
                        Multicultural History Society of Ontario

                        Rudolph Vecoli
                        Director
                        Immigration History Research Center

USER'S GUIDE

So that the bibliography may be accessible with limited knowledge of Ukrainian, most publication information has been given in English. Titles of works published in Ukrainian have, of course, been left in the original.

Each entry lists the name of the author (or editor, compiler, translator); the number of volumes and/or edition; series title (if applicable); place of publication; publisher; number of pages (in most cases); and where the entry is held.

Most entries are in alphabetical order. In some sections, however, works published <u>by</u> an organization or individual are listed before those <u>about</u> the organization or individual and are given in chronological order.

Wherever possible, the English names of publishers have been used, e.g., Trident Press rather than Tryzub. An exception is the Ukrainian Free Academy of Sciences/Ukrains'ki Vil'ni Akademii Nauk, for which the Ukrainian acronym, UVAN, has been used throughout.

<u>Transliteration</u>: We have followed a modified Library of Congress system and have not used any diacritical marks. Apostrophes are used to indicate soft signs.

<u>Titles of series</u>: If an item in a Ukrainian and English-language series has been published in Ukrainian, the series title is first given in Ukrainian and the English title follows in parentheses.
If the item has been published in English, only the English-language series title is listed.
If a series publishes only Ukrainian-language works, the Ukrainian title only is given.

<u>Cross-listings</u>: Some entries pertain to more than one subject heading. Such works may be listed in more than one section, and in such cases full publication information is given.

<u>Children's literature</u>: The Metropolitan Toronto Library has extensive holdings; Minnesota, St. Vladimir and UNO listings are incomplete.

LOCATION INFORMATION

Metro: Metropolitan Toronto Library
                789 Yonge Street
                Toronto, Ontario   M4W 2G8

Minn.:   Immigration History Research Center
                University of Minnesota
                826 Berry Street
                St. Paul, Minnesota   55114

St. Vlad.:   St. Vladimir Institute Library
                620 Spadina Avenue
                Toronto, Ontario   M5S 2H4

UNO: Ukrainian National Federation Library
                297 College Street
                Toronto, Ontario   M5T 1S2

U of T: University of Toronto Libraries
                Main catalogue and book depository located at:
                    Robarts Library
                    St. George Street
                    Toronto, Ontario   M5S 1A1

I. BIBLIOGRAPHIES AND GENERAL REFERENCE MATERIAL

Antonovych-Rudnyts'ka, Maryna

FRANKIIANA V AMERYKANS'KYKH I KANADIIS'KYKH BIBLIOTEKAKH.
Winnipeg: Shevchenko Foundation, 1957. 32 p. (U of T)

Bachyns'kyi, Leonid

UKRAINS'KI DRUKOVANI VYDANNIA V KLIVLENDI. Ukrains'kyi muzei-
arkhiv u Klivlendi, no. 2. Cleveland: Ukrainian Museum-Archives,
1958. 46 p. (Minn.; U of T)

Bohdan, F.

BIBLIOTEKA TOVARYSTVA VZAIMNOI POMOCHI I UKRAINS'KA KNYZHKA
V VANKUVERI. 2 vols. Litopys UVAN (Chronicles), no. 17.
Winnipeg: Ukrainian Fraternal Society, Vancouver branch, 1959.
32 p. (Minn.; St. Vlad.; U of T)

Chaplenko, Nataliia, comp. and ed.

BIBLIOHRAFIIA VYDAN' ZHINOCHOI TVORCHOSTY POZA MEZHAMY UKRAINY.
Philadelphia: Ukrainian National Women's League of America,
1974. 53 p. (Metro; St. Vlad.; U of T)

Dorotich, Daniel, comp. and ed.

A BIBLIOGRAPHY OF CANADIAN SLAVISTS, 1951-1971. Canadian
Association of Slavists. Saskatoon: University of Saskatchewan
Press, 1972. 32 p. (St. Vlad.; U of T)

Fedyns'kyi, Oleksander

BIBLIOHRAFICHNYI POKAZHCHYK UKRAINS'KOI PRESY POZA MEZHAMY
UKRAINY. Ukrains'kyi muzei-arkhiv u Klivlendi, nos. 11- .
Cleveland: Ukrainian Museum-Archives, 1967- . (Minn.: 1967,
1968, 1970; St. Vlad.: 1972, 1975; U of T: 1967-75)

Fisk, Margaret et al., eds.

ENCYCLOPEDIA OF ASSOCIATIONS. Vol. 1. Detroit: Gale, 1975.
(U of T)

Franko-Kliuchko, Anna

RUKOPYSY IVANA FRANKA V KANADI: LYST IZ LIPIKA, IUHOSLAVII, TA
INSHE. UVAN Slavistica Series, no. 28. Winnipeg: UVAN, 1957.
16 p. (Minn.)

Gregorovich, Andrew Sviatoslav

BOOKS ON UKRAINE AND THE UKRAINIANS. Toronto: Studium Research Institute, 1963. 29 p. (Metro)

———.

CANADIAN ETHNIC GROUPS BIBLIOGRAPHY: A SELECTED BIBLIOGRAPHY OF ETHNO-CULTURAL GROUPS IN CANADA AND THE PROVINCE OF ONTARIO. Toronto: Ontario Department of the Provincial Secretary and Citizenship, 1972. 208 p. (U of T)

———.

UKRAINE AND UKRAINIAN CANADIANS: BOOKS FOR HIGH SCHOOL, COLLEGE AND PUBLIC LIBRARIES. Toronto: Ucrainica Research Institute, 1977. 41 p. (UNO)

Horbay, Z. and O. Woycenko, comps.

UKRAINICA CANADIANA, 1970. UVAN Bibliography Series, no. 18. Winnipeg: D. Lobay Foundation at UVAN, 1971. 32 p. (St. Vlad.)

Klymasz, Robert Bohdan

A BIBLIOGRAPHY OF UKRAINIAN FOLKLORE IN CANADA, 1902-1964. Anthropology Papers, no. 21. Ottawa: National Museum of Canada, 1969. 53 p. (Metro)

Magocsi, Paul R.

CARPATHO-RUTHENIANS IN NORTH AMERICA. Balch Institute Historical Reading Lists, no. 31. Philadelphia: Balch Institute, 1976. 6 p. (U of T)

Mandryka, Mykyta Ivanovych

BIO-BIBLIOGRAPHY OF J.B. RUDNYC'KYJ. UVAN Ukrainian Scholars Series, no. 10. Winnipeg: UVAN, 1961. 72 p. (Metro; Minn.; U of T)

Muchin, J.S., comp.

SLAVIC COLLECTION OF THE UNIVERSITY OF MANITOBA LIBRARIES. Winnipeg: University of Manitoba Libraries and UVAN, 1970. 71 p. (Minn.; U of T)

Onufriichuk, Fedir, comp.

KNYHOZBIRNIA MYTROPOLYTA ILARIONA. Winnipeg: Christian Press, 1963. 28 p. (U of T)

Ovechko, Ivan

BIBLIOHRAFICHNYI POKAZHCHYK ZHURNALISTYCHNYKH I LITERATURNYKH
PRATS' NA EMIGRATSII, 1950-1967. n.p., n.d. (Minn.)

Procko, Bohdan P.

UKRAINIANS IN NORTH AMERICA. Balch Institute Historical
Reading Lists, no. 5. Philadelphia: Balch Institute, 1974.
4 p. (U of T)

Romanenchuk, Bohdan

BIBLIOHRAFIIA VYDAN' UKRAINS'KOI EMIHRATSIINOI LITERATURY,
1945-1970. Biblioteka ukrains'koi knyhy, no. 2. Philadelphia:
Kyiv Publishing, 1974. 96 p. (U of T)

Rudnyts'kyi, Iaroslav Bohdan

A BIBLIOGRAPHY OF WRITINGS, 1933-1963. Winnipeg, 1964. 96 p.
(U of T)

______, comp.

SLAVICA CANADIANA: SELECTED BIBLIOGRAPHY OF SLAVIC BOOKS AND
PAMPHLETS PUBLISHED IN OR RELATING TO CANADA. UVAN Slavistica
Series, nos. 15- . Winnipeg: UVAN, 1950- . (Minn.: nos. 15, 18,
27, 30, 33, 36, 42, 45, 55; St. Vlad.: no. 63; UNO: nos. 15- ;
U of T: nos. 15, 21)

______.

SLAVISTYKA V KANADI V 1950r. UVAN Slavistica Series, no. 9.
Winnipeg: UVAN, 1950. 44 p. (Minn.; St. Vlad.)

______, et al., comps.

UKRAINICA CANADIANA, 1953- . UVAN Bibliography Series, nos. 1-
Winnipeg: Ukrainian Canadian Committee, 1954- . (Metro: 1955,
1960; Minn.: 1953-64; St. Vlad.: 1955-57, 1961-64, 1969; UNO:
1957, 1966; U of T: 1953-72)

______.

UKRAINICA IN THE LIBRARY OF CONGRESS: A PRELIMINARY SURVEY.
Washington, 1956. 94 p. (U of T)

———.

Z PODOROZHI PO AMERYTSI, 1956. Kliub pryiateliv ukrains'koi
knyzhky, vol. 29. Winnipeg: Ivan Tyktor, 1956. 128 p. (St. Vlad.;
UNO; U of T)

Stefaniuk, Myroslav

UKRAINIAN-AMERICANS IN THE UNITED STATES: AN ANNOTATED
BIBLIOGRAPHY AND GUIDE TO RESEARCH FACILITIES. Occasional
Papers in Ethnic Studies, no. 5. Ethnic Studies Division of
the Center for Urban Studies. Detroit: Wayne State University,
1977. (U of T)

Suchowersky, C.N., comp. and ed.

A CATALOGUE OF THE LIBRARY OF OREST STARCHUK. Edmonton:
University of Alberta library, 1972. 180 leaves. (U of T)

UKRAINIAN BOOKS. UKRAINS'KI KNYZHKY. Regina: Saskatchewan
Provincial Library, Bibliographic Services, 1972. 33 p. (U of T)

Voitsenko, Ol'ha

MATERIIALY DO FRANKIIANY V KANADI, 1910-1956. Winnipeg:
Shevchenko Foundation, 1957. 64 p. (U of T)

———, et al., comps. and eds.

SCRIPTA MANENT...: A BIO-BIBLIOGRAPHY OF J.B. RUDNYC'KYJ.
2 vols. Readings in Slavic Literature, nos. 13-13a. Winnipeg,
1975. (Metro: vol. 1; UNO: vol. 1; U of T: vols. 1-2)

———.

SLAVIC ARCHIVES IN CANADA: UVAN COLLECTIONS IN WINNIPEG. UVAN
Slavistica Series, no. 71. Winnipeg: UVAN, 1971. 24 p. (St. Vlad.)

Weres, Roman

DIRECTORY OF UKRAINIAN PUBLISHING HOUSES, PERIODICALS, BOOKSTORES,
LIBRARIES AND LIBRARY COLLECTIONS OF UKRAINICA IN THE DIASPORA.
Ukrainian Reference Series, no. 2. Chicago: Ukrainian
Bibliographical-Reference Center, 1976. 56 p. (Metro; U of T)

________, comp.

INDEX OF UKRAINIAN ESSAYS IN COLLECTIONS PUBLISHED OUTSIDE THE
IRON CURTAIN, 1951-1962. Ukrainian Bibliography. Microfilm
Series. Chicago: Ukrainian Bibliographical-Reference Center,
n.d. (U of T)

________, comp.

INDEX OF UKRAINIAN ESSAYS IN COLLECTIONS PUBLISHED OUTSIDE THE
IRON CURTAIN, 1963-1964. Ukrainian Bibliography. Microfilm
Series. Chicago: Ukrainian Bibliographical-Reference Center,
1967. (Minn.)

________.

UKRAINE: SELECTED REFERENCES IN THE ENGLISH LANGUAGE.
Kalamazoo: Western Michigan University, 1961. 233 p. (Metro;
UNO; U of T)

2nd enl. ed.: Ukrainian Reference Series, no. 1. Chicago:
Ukrainian Research and Information Institute, 1974. 312 p.
(St. Vlad.; UNO; U of T)

________.

UKRAINIKA DIIASPORIIANA ZA ROKY 1973, 1974, 1975: BIBLIOHRAFIIA.
Ukrains'ki dovidkovi materialy (Ukrainian Reference Series),
no. 3. Chicago: Ukrainian Bibliographical-Reference Center,
1977. 63 p. (U of T)

Wynar, Lubomyr Roman

ENCYCLOPEDIC DIRECTORY OF ETHNIC NEWSPAPERS AND PERIODICALS IN
THE UNITED STATES. Littleton, Colo.: Libraries Unlimited, 1972.
260 p. (U of T)

________, et al.

ENCYCLOPEDIC DIRECTORY OF ETHNIC ORGANIZATIONS IN THE UNITED
STATES. Littleton, Colo.: Libraries Unlimited, 1975. 414 p.
(U of T)

II. UKRAINIANS IN CANADA

History

Bilets'kyi, Leonid

UKRAINS'KI PIONERY V KANADI, 1891-1951. Winnipeg: Ukrainian
Canadian Committee, 1951. 128 p. (Minn.; UNO)

Bilon, Petro

SPOHADY. 2 vols. Pittsburgh: Do svitla, 1952, 1956. (Minn.;
St. Vlad.; UNO; U of T: vol. 2)

Borovs'kyi, Mykhailo Leontiievych

PLANTS FROM UKRAINE IN CANADA. UVAN Natural Sciences Series.
Winnipeg: UVAN, 1975. 46 p. (Metro; U of T)

————.

ROSLYNY PERESLENI Z UKRAINY DO KANADY: "IEVSHAN ZILLIA".
Winnipeg: Ukrainian Women's Association of Canada, Manitoba
provincial executive, 1967. 48 p. (Minn.; St. Vlad.)

Borovyk, Mykhailo

UKRAINS'KO-KANADS'KA PRESA TA II ZNACHENNIA DLIA UKRAINS'KOI
MENSHYNY V KANADI. Ucrainica diasporiana, vol. 2. Munich:
Ukrainian Free University, 1977. 341 p. (U of T)

Bozhyk, Panteleimon

KANADIIS'KA MUZA. Yorkton, Sask.: Redeemer's Voice, 1936.
189 p. (Minn.; U of T)

Bryk, Alexander S.

MOI ZHYTTIEVI STUDII. Winnipeg: Trident Press, 1956. 528 p.
(Minn.; St. Vlad.; UNO; U of T)

Buck, Tim

SHCHO VYBERE KANADA, OB'IEDNANNIA CHY KHAOS? Toronto: Progressive
Labour Party, 1944. 47 p. (UNO)

Burke, Marguerite B.

THE UKRAINIAN CANADIANS. Multicultural Canada Series. Toronto:
Van Nostrand Reinhold, 1978. 64 p. (Metro; St. Vlad.)

Bychyns'kyi, Zynovii

ISTORIIA KANADY. With an introduction by Ch.V. Hordon.
Winnipeg, 1928. 222 p. (UNO)

Chorneiko, Mykhailo

SHCHOB NE ZABUTY I DENNI PODII. Saskatoon: Globe Printers,
1964. 131 p. (Metro)

Chumer, Vasyl' A.

SPOMYNY PRO PEREZHYVANNIA PERSHYKH UKRAINS'KYKH PERESELENTSIV
V KANADI, 1892-1942. Edmonton, 1942 (?). 188 p. (Metro; Minn.;
St. Vlad.; UNO; U of T)

Darcovich, William

UKRAINIANS IN CANADA: THE STRUGGLE TO RETAIN THEIR IDENTITY.
Ottawa: Ukrainian Self-Reliance League of Canada, 1967. 38 p.
(Minn.; U of T)

Davidson, G.A.

THE UKRAINIANS IN CANADA: A STUDY IN CANADIAN IMMIGRATION.
Montreal, 1947. 23 p. (U of T)

Davies, Raymond Arthur

THIS IS OUR LAND: UKRAINIAN CANADIANS AGAINST HITLER. Toronto:
Progress Publishers, 1943. 158 p. (Metro; St. Vlad.; U of T)

Dmytriv, Nestor

KANADIIS'KA RUS': PODOROZHNI SPOMYNY. Dzherela do istorii
ukraintsiv Kanady, no. 1. Winnipeg: UVAN, 1972. 56 p. (Metro;
St. Vlad.; UNO; U of T)

Ewach, Honore

TSIKAVI OPOVIDANNIA Z DAVN'OI ISTORII KANADY. Kul'tura i
osvita, no. 5. Winnipeg: Ukrainian Cultural and Educational
Centre, 1944. 38 p. (U of T)

Ewanchuk, Michael

SPRUCE, SWAMP AND STONE: A HISTORY OF THE PIONEER UKRAINIAN
SETTLEMENTS IN THE GIMLI AREA. Winnipeg: published by the
author, 1977. 320 p. (St. Vlad.)

Fry, Olivia Rose

MY HERITAGE FROM THE BUILDERS OF CANADA. New York: Carlton
Press, Hearthstone Books, 1967. 183 p. (Metro; U of T)

Gregorovich, Andrew Sviatoslav

CHRONOLOGY OF UKRAINIAN CANADIAN HISTORY. Toronto: Ukrainian
Canadian Committee, 1974. 64 p. (Metro; Minn.; U of T)

______

UKRAINIANS IN CANADA. 4 vols. Maps by Fred Nakoneczny. Toronto:
Ukrainian National Federation, 1974-75. (Metro)

______, ed.

THE UKRAINIANS IN CANADA. Toronto: Ukrainian National Youth
Federation of Canada, 1964. 8 p. (U of T)

Gregorovich, J.B., ed.

IMMIGRATION UKRAINIAN-CANADIAN. Papers and proceedings of the
immigration conference, June 7, 1975, sponsored by the Ukrainian
Canadian Committee, Ontario Council and the Canadian Ukrainian
Immigrant Aid Society. Toronto: Orelets Press, 1976. 98 p.
(U of T)

Hardwick, Francis C., ed.

TO THE PROMISED LAND: CONTRIBUTIONS OF UKRAINIAN IMMIGRANTS AND
THEIR DESCENDANTS TO CANADIAN SOCIETY. Research by Adam Kozak.
Canadian Culture Series, no. 3. Vancouver: Tantalus Research,
1973. 62 p. (Metro; UNO)

Havrysh, Vasyl'

MOIA KANADA I IA: SPOHADY I ROZPOVIDI PRO UKRAINS'KYKH PIONERIV
U KANADI. Edmonton: published by the author, 1974. 349 p.
(Metro; UNO; U of T)

Hermaniuk, Maksym, Metropolitan

SHKIL'NE PYTANNIA MANITOBY: PASTYRS'KE POSLANNIA. Winnipeg, 1964.
(Minn.)

HISTORY OF OURS: FRENCH, GERMAN, HUNGARIAN, ITALIAN, POLISH AND
UKRAINIAN. Brantford: Brantford and District Citizenship Council,
1967. (St. Vlad.)

Hlynka, Isydore

GRADUATES AND THE UKRAINIAN COMMUNITY: ADDRESS BY DR. ISYDORE HLYNKA. Ukrainian Voice English Series, no. 2. Winnipeg: Ukrainian Voice, 1964. (Minn.)

Horokhovych, T.

BAT'KY I DITY. Winnipeg: Ukrainian Women's Association of Canada, 1965. 136 p. (Metro; Minn.; U of T)

House of Commons. Official Report

SPEECHES OF MR. ANTHONY HLYNKA AND MR. W.A. TUCKER ON DISPLACED PERSONS IN EUROPE: SPEAKING ON THE ADDRESS IN REPLY TO THE SPEECH FROM THE THRONE. Delivered in the House of Commons on Monday, September 24, 1945 and Wednesday, September 26, 1945. Ottawa: Edmond Cloutier, 1945. 7 p. (St. Vlad.; UNO)

Humeniuk, Peter

HARDSHIPS AND PROGRESS OF UKRAINIAN PIONEERS: MEMOIRS FROM STUARTBURN COLONY AND OTHER POINTS. Winnipeg: published by the author, 1977. 236 p. (St. Vlad.; UNO)

Hunchak, N.J.

POPULATION. Canadians of Ukrainian Origin Series, no. 1. Winnipeg: Ukrainian Canadian Committee, 1945. 164 p. (UNO; U of T)

Hutsuliak, Mykhailo

UKRAINETS'- SPIVTVORETS' KORDONIV KANADY I ALIASKY. Biblioteka ukrainoznavstva, no. 24. Vancouver-Toronto: Shevchenko Scientific Society, 1967. 132 p. (Minn.; UNO; U of T)

Iasenchuk, Iosyf

KANADYIS'KYI KOBZAR. Edmonton: Ukrains'ka knyharnia, 1918. 64 p. (St. Vlad.)

Iasinchuk, Lev

ZA OKEIANOM: OSOBYSTI POMICHENNIA I PEREZHYVANNIA ZA CHAS ODNORICHNOHO POBUTU V AMERYTSI. Lviv: Ridna Shkola, 1930. 255 p. (Minn.; UNO; U of T)

Iasnovs'kyi, Pylyp

PID RIDNYM I PID CHUZHYM NEBOM. Buenos Aires: Julian Serediak, 1961. 330 p. (Minn.; U of T)

Inter-University Committee on Canadian Slavs

SLAVS IN CANADA. Proceedings of the second national conference on Canadian Slavs, June 9-11, 1967. Ottawa: University of Ottawa, 1968. 286 p. (St. Vlad.)

Isaiv, Vsevolod V., ed.

UKRAINTSI V AMERYKANS'KOMU TA KANADS'KOMU SUSPIL'STVAKH: SOTSIOLOHICHNYI ZBIRNYK. Ukrains'kyi sotsiolohichnyi instytut, Pratsi (Works of the Ukrainian Sociological Institute), vol. 1. Jersey City, N.J.: M.P. Kots', 1976. 360 p. (St. Vlad.; UNO; U of T)

ISTORIIA UKRAINS'KOI EMIGRATSII V KANADI ZA CHAS VID 1890 DO 1903 ROKU. Winnipeg: Narodna drukarnia, 1930. (Minn.)

Ivanchuk, Mykhailo

ISTORIIA UKRAINS'KOHO POSELENNIA V OKOLYTSI GIMLI. Winnipeg: Trident Press, 1975. 335 p. (St. Vlad.; UNO; U of T)

Jaenen, C.J.

SOME THOUGHTS ON THE MANITOBA MOSAIC. Ukrainian Voice English Series, no. 4. Winnipeg: Ukrainian Voice, 1964. (Minn.)

Kalbach, Warren E. and Wayne W. McVey, Jr.

THE UKRAINIAN POPULATION IN CANADA AND ALBERTA SINCE WORLD WAR ONE. Toronto, n.d. (Minn.)

Kardash, William A.

HITLER'S AGENTS IN CANADA: A REVEALING STORY OF POTENTIALLY DANGEROUS FIFTH COLUMN ACTIVITIES IN CANADA AMONG UKRAINIAN CANADIANS. Toronto: Morris printing, 1942. 32 p. (Metro; U of T)

Kaye-Kysilevs'kyi, Vladimir J.

EARLY UKRAINIAN SETTLEMENTS IN CANADA, 1895-1900: DR. JOSEF OLESKIW'S ROLE IN THE SETTLEMENT OF THE CANADIAN NORTHWEST. Canadian Centennial Series, no. 1. Ukrainian Canadian Research Foundation. Toronto: University of Toronto Press, 1964. 420 p. (Metro; Minn.; St. Vlad.; UNO; U of T)

————.

PARTICIPATION OF UKRAINIANS IN THE POLITICAL LIFE OF CANADA. Ottawa, 1957. 24 p. (U of T)

————.

POCHATKY POSELENNIA UKRAINTSIV U KANADI. First in a series of cultural, historical and sociological research projects of the Ukrainian Canadian Research Foundation. Toronto, 1963. 4 p. (Minn.; UNO).

————.

SLAVIC GROUPS IN CANADA. UVAN Slavistica Series, no. 12. Winnipeg: UVAN, 1951. 30 p. (Minn.; St. Vlad.)

Kelebay, Yarema Gregory

THE UKRAINIAN COMMUNITY IN MONTREAL. M.A. dissertation, Concordia University, 1975. 109 p. (Metro)

Keywan, Zonia

GREATER THAN KINGS. Montreal: Harvest House, 1977. 165 p. (Metro; St. Vlad.; U of T)

Kirkconnell, Watson

OUR UKRAINIAN LOYALISTS. Winnipeg: Ukrainian Canadian Committee, 1943. 28 p. (St. Vlad.; U of T)

————.

THE UKRAINIAN CANADIANS AND THE WAR. World Affairs Series, C-3. Toronto: Oxford University Press, 1940. 30 p. (Metro; Minn.; U of T)

————.

VIINA-TA UKRAINS'KI KANADIITSI. World Affairs Series. Toronto: Oxford University Press, 1940. 30 p. (Minn.; St. Vlad.; UNO)

Kobzei, Toma

NA TERNYSTYKH TA KHRESHCHATYKH DOROHAKH. 2 vols. Scranton, Pa.: Narodna volia, 1972-73. (UNO; U of T)

Kosikovs'kyi, Oleksa

MII VYNDSORS'KYI LITOPYS: SPOHADY I ZAPYSKY. Michigan:
published by the author, 1974. 113 p. (Metro; UNO; U of T)

Kostash, Myrna

ALL OF BABA'S CHILDREN. Edmonton: Hurtig, 1977. 414 p. (Metro;
St. Vlad.; UNO; U of T)

Kovalchuk, Pavlo

CRIMINAL HIRELINGS. Trans. by George Semeniuk. Kiev: Ukraina
Society, 1975. 32 p. (U of T)

Koziak, Methodius

UKRAINIAN IN SASKATCHEWAN SCHOOLS: A BRIEF HISTORY. Foreword by
C.H. Andrusyshen. Toronto: Basilian Press, 1976. 66 p. (UNO)

Krawchuk, Peter

IVAN FRANKO SERED KANADS'KYKH UKRAINTSIV. Lviv: Kameniar, 1966.
76 p. (U of T)

_______.

NA KANADS'KII ZEMLI. Lviv: Knyzhkovo-zhurnal'ne vyd-vo, 1963.
394 p. (U of T)

_______.

NA NOVII ZEMLI: STORINKY Z ZHYTTIA, BOROT'BY I TVORCHOI PRATSI
KANADS'KYKH UKRAINTSIV. Toronto: Association of United
Ukrainian Canadians, 1958. 391 p. (Minn.; St. Vlad.; UNO;
U of T)

_______.

P'IATDESIAT ROKIV SLUZHINNIA NARODU: DO ISTORII UKRAINS'KOI
NARODNOI PRESY V KANADI. Toronto: Ukrains'ke zhyttia, 1957.
248 p. (U of T)

_______.

PID PROVODOM BLAHORODNYKH IDEI: V.I. LENIN I UKRAINS'KA
PROHRESYVNA HROMADS'KIST' U KANADI. Toronto: Kobzar, 1969.
143 p. (U of T)

______.

TARAS SHEVCHENKO V KANADI. Ed. by Ie.P. Kyryliuk. Kiev:
Derzhavne vydavnytstvo khudozhn'oi literatury, 1961. 211 p.
(Metro; U of T)

______.

THE UKRAINIANS IN WINNIPEG'S FIRST CENTURY. Trans. by Mary
Skrypnyk. Toronto: Kobzar, 1974. 70 p. (Metro; U of T)

______.

UKRAINTSI V ISTORII VINNIPEHA. Toronto: Kobzar, 1974. 168 p.
(Metro; UNO; U of T)

______.

VAZHKI ROKY. Toronto: Kobzar, 1968. 110 p. (St. Vlad.; UNO;
U of T)

Kudryk, Vasyl'

CHUZHA RUKA ABO KHTO ROZ'IEDNUIE UKRAINS'KYI NARID. Winnipeg:
Visnyk, 1935. 208 p. (Minn.; UNO)

KUDY NAM ITY? Yorkton, Sask.: Redeemer's Voice, n.d. (Minn.)

Kyrylenko, Orest

UKRAINTSI V AMERYTSI. Vienna: Souiz vyzvolennia
Ukrainy, 1916. 40 p. (Minn.)

Lupul, Manoly Robert

THE ROMAN CATHOLIC CHURCH AND THE NORTHWEST SCHOOL QUESTION:
A STUDY IN CHURCH-STATE RELATIONS IN WESTERN CANADA, 1875-1905.
Toronto: University of Toronto Press, 1974. 292 p. (St. Vlad.;
U of T)

______, ed.

UKRAINIAN CANADIANS, MULTICULTURALISM, AND SEPARATISM: AN
ASSESSMENT. Proceedings of a conference sponsored by the
Canadian Institute of Ukrainian Studies, Edmonton, September
9-11, 1977. Edmonton: University of Alberta Press, 1978. 177 p.
(St. Vlad; U of T)

Lysenko, Vera

MEN IN SHEEPSKIN COATS: A STUDY IN ASSIMILATION. Toronto:
Ryerson Press, 1947. 312 p. (Metro; St. Vlad.; U of T)

MacGregor, James Grierson

VILNI ZEMLI. FREE LANDS: THE UKRAINIAN SETTLEMENT OF ALBERTA.
Toronto: McClelland and Stewart, 1969. 274 p. (Metro; Minn.;
UNO; U of T)

Mandryka, M.I.

SHLIAKH UKRAINS'KOHO ROBITNYTSTVA V NOVIM KRAIU. Biblioteka
pravdy i voli, no. 1. Winnipeg, 1929. 43 p. (UNO; U of T)

———.

THE UKRAINIAN QUESTION. Winnipeg: Canadian Ukrainian Educational
Association, 1940. 57 p. (St. Vlad.; U of T)

Marunchak, Mykhailo H.

AMONG UKRAINIAN PIONEERS OF ALBERTA. 2nd ed. Ukrainian
Canadian Pioneer's Library, no. 6. Winnipeg, 1965. 88 p.
(Metro)

———.

ISTORIIA PRESY, LITERATURY I DRUKU PIONERS'KOI DOBY. 2nd ed.
Winnipeg: UVAN, 1969. 284 p. (Metro; U of T)

———.

ISTORIIA UKRAINTSIV KANADY. 2 vols. Winnipeg: UVAN, 1968-74.
(Metro: vol. 1; St. Vlad.; U of T)

———.

KANADIIS'KA TEREBOVLIA. Litopys UVAN (Chronicles), no. 25.
Winnipeg: UVAN, 1966. (Metro; Minn.; UNO; U of T)

———.

KANADIIS'KA TEREBOVLIA: MISTSE PERSHOI UKRAINS'KOI SLUZHBY
BOZHOI V KANADI. Winnipeg: Zahal'na biblioteka UKT, 1964. 40 p.
(Minn.; UNO)

———.

SHOTLIANDS'KI POSELENTSI TA UKRAINS'KA HROMADA V POINT DOGLES. Studii do istorii ukraintsiv Kanady, vol. 1. Winnipeg: UVAN, 1964-65. 255 p. (Metro)

———.

STUDII DO ISTORII UKRAINTSIV KANADY. Winnipeg, 1970. (Minn.; U of T)

———.

THE UKRAINIAN CANADIANS: A HISTORY. Winnipeg: UVAN, 1970. 792 p. (Metro; Minn.; St. Vlad.; UNO; U of T)

———.

V ZUSTRICHI Z UKRAINS'KYMY PIONERAMY AL'BERTY. Winnipeg: Zahal'na biblioteka UKT, 1964. 88 p. (Minn.; UNO)

2nd ed.: Biblioteka pionera, no. 6. Winnipeg, 1965. (Minn.; U of T)

NASHA KANADA. Toronto: Department of Education, Community Programs Branch, n.d. 94 p. (Minn.; St. Vlad.)

Nimchuk, Ivan

UKRAINTSI V BRYTIIS'KII KOLIUMBII. Edmonton: H. Bratkov, 1953. 20 p. (U of T)

O SHCHO KHODYT'?: KIL'KA DUMOK NA TEMU NADKHODIACHYKH VYBORIV. Saskatoon: Ukrains'ka liberal'na orhanizatsiia, n.d. 14 p. (UNO)

Oles'kiv, Osyp

PRO VIL'NI ZEMLI. Dzherela do istorii ukraintsiv Kanady, no. 11. Winnipeg: UVAN, 1975. 38 p. (St. Vlad.; UNO)

Olynyk, Roman

NE IAK STORONNIA LIUDYNA. Winnipeg: Trident Press, 1965. 11 p. (U of T)

Onufrijchuk, Theodore T.

  THE HISTORY OF R.M. OF SLIDING HILLS. Mikado, Sask., 1967.
  109 p. (Minn.)

OSNOVNI VIDOMOSTY PRO KANADU. Ottawa: Ministry of the Secretary
  of State, Citizenship Branch, 1947. 37 p. (Minn.; UNO)

Paluk, William

  CANADIAN COSSACKS: ESSAYS, ARTICLES AND STORIES ON UKRAINIAN-
  CANADIAN LIFE. Winnipeg: Canadian Ukrainian Review, 1943. 130 p.
  (Metro; St. Vlad.; UNO; U of T)

Panchuk, John

  BUKOWINIAN SETTLEMENTS IN SOUTHERN MANITOBA: GARDENTOWN AREA.
  Battle Creek, Mich.: published by the author, 1971. 86 p.
  (Minn.; St. Vlad.; UNO)

Paximadis, Mary

  LOOK WHO'S COMING: THE WACHNA STORY. Illus. by William Kurelek.
  Oshawa: Wachna Foundation, 1976. 124 p. (St. Vlad.)

Petrivs'kyi, Mykhailo

  MRII SL'OZAMY OBLYTI: OPOVIDANNIA Z ZHYTTIA UKRAINS'KYKH PIONERIV
  I IMIHRANTIV V KANADI. Winnipeg, 1973. 167 p. (Metro; St. Vlad.;
  UNO; U of T)

  2nd ed.: Buenos Aires, Julian Serediak, 1977. 205 p. (UNO)

Piniuta, Harry

  LAND OF PAIN, LAND OF PROMISE: FIRST PERSON ACCOUNTS BY UKRAINIAN
  PIONEERS, 1891-1914. Saskatoon: Western Producer Prairie Books,
  1978. 225 p. (Metro; St. Vlad.; U of T)

Pitiura, Michael, comp.

  ANTI-KOSYGIN DEMONSTRATION IN TORONTO, OCTOBER 25, 1971: A
  PUBLIC INQUIRY. n.p., n.d. 105 p. (UNO)

Poltorats'kyi, Oleksii Ivanovych

  BRATY DALEKI I RIDNI. Kiev: Znannia, 1967. 47 p. (U of T)

Poniatenko, P.

KUL'TURA, NATSIONAL'NIST' TA ASYMILIATSIIA. Winnipeg: Ukrains'ka
vydavnycha spilka, 1917. 50 p. (St. Vlad.; UNO; U of T)

Potrebenko, Helen

NO STREETS OF GOLD: A SOCIAL HISTORY OF UKRAINIANS IN ALBERTA.
Vancouver: New Star Books, 1977. 311 p. (Metro; St. Vlad.; UNO;
U of T)

PRERIIA: KANADIIS'KYI AL'MANAKH. Winnipeg: Tovarystvo opiky nad
ukrains'kymy pereselentsiamy im. sv. Rafaila v Kanadi, 1928.
124 p. (U of T)

Presunka, Peter

CANADA'S CHOICE: BICULTURAL RETREAT OR PLANNED NATIONHOOD. 2nd ed.
n.p., 1967. 64 p. (St. Vlad.; U of T)

PROMOVA POSLA O. ZHEREBKA. Speech before the Saskatchewan
Provincial Legislature, Regina, on March 7, 1940. Regina:
Saskatchewan Liberal Association, n.d. 13 p. (UNO)

PROPAMIATNA KNYHA Z NAHODY ZOLOTOHO IUVILEIU POSELENNIA UKRAINS'KOHO
NARODU V KANADI. Yorkton, Sask.: The Episcopal Ordinariate,
1941. 338 p. (UNO; U of T)

Royick, Alexander

UKRAINIAN SETTLEMENTS IN ALBERTA. Reprinted from Canadian
Slavonic Papers, vol. 10, no. 3 (1968). (Minn.; St. Vlad.)

Rudnyts'kyi, Iaroslav Bohdan

KANADIIS'KI MISTSEVI NAZVY UKRAINS'KOHO POKHODZHENNIA. 2nd ed.
UVAN Seriia Nazvoznavstvo (Onomastica Series), no. 2. Winnipeg:
Ukrainian National Home, 1951. 88 p. (Metro; Minn.; UNO; U of T)

3rd ed.: Winnipeg, Ukrainian National Home, 1957. 96 p. (Metro)

______, comp.

MANITOBA, MOSAIC OF PLACE NAMES. Introd. by Watson Kirkconnell.
Winnipeg: Canadian Institute of Onomastic Sciences, 1970.
221 p. (UNO; U of T)

———.

MOSAIC OF WINNIPEG STREET NAMES. Winnipeg: Canadian Institute
of Onomastic Sciences, 1974. 333 p. (Metro; U of T)

Sawkey, John Andrew

THOSE WERE THE DAYS: THE HISTORY OF MACNUTT, CALDER, DROPMORE
AND THE SURROUNDING DISTRICTS, PIONEER TO PRESENT. n.p., 1972.
293 p. (UNO; U of T)

Semenyna, Ivan

ZBEREZHENI HOSPODOM: SPOMYNY PROPOVIDNYKA. Doroha pravdy, no. 11.
Toronto-Chicago: Doroha pravdy, 1958. (Minn.)

Sharyk, Mykhailo

Z VIDDALI PIATDESIAT LIT: BOROT'BA ZA NASHE OBLYCHCHIA I VOLIU
UKRAINS'KOHO NARODU. Biblioteka Proboiem, nos. 8, 12. Toronto:
Proboiem, 1969- . (Metro; Minn.; UNO; U of T)

Sheffe, Norman

MANY CULTURES, MANY HERITAGES. Toronto: McGraw Hill-Ryerson,
1975. 544 p. (St. Vlad.)

Sheptyts'kyi, Mytropolyt Andrii, Graf

KANADYSKYM RUSYNAM (sic). Zhovkva, Ukraine: Pechatnia oo.
Vasylyian, 1911. 93 p. (Minn.; U of T)

Sherbinin, Michael A.

THE GALICIANS DWELLING IN CANADA AND THEIR ORIGIN. Transactions
of The Historical and Scientific Society of Manitoba, no. 71.
Winnipeg: The Manitoba Free Press, 1906. 11 p. (Metro)

SHISTDESIAT LIT U KANADI, 1891-1951: IUVILEINI SVIATKUVANNIA.
Toronto, 1951. 64 p. (St. Vlad.; UNO)

Shpytkovs'kyi, Ihor, comp.

    AL'MANAKH KANADIIS'KYKH UKRAINS'KYKH VOIAKIV. Winnipeg:
Buduchnist' natsii, 1946. 239 p. (UNO)

Simpson, George Wilfrid

    THE BLENDING OF TRADITIONS IN WESTERN CANADIAN SETTLEMENT.
Canadian Historical Association Annual Report, pp. 46-52. 1944.
(Metro)

Slavutych, Yar

    COLLECTED PAPERS ON UKRAINIAN SETTLERS. Edmonton: Shevchenko
Scientific Society, 1973. (Minn.)

    ——————.

    ZAKHIDN'OKANADS'KYI ZBIRNYK. Pt. 1. Edmonton: Shevchenko
Scientific Society, 1973. 206 p. (Metro; St. Vlad.; UNO; U of T)

Stechyshyn, Iüliian

    ISTORIIA POSELENNIA UKRAINTSIV U KANADI. Edmonton: Ukrainian
Self-Reliance League of Canada, 1975. 351 p. (Metro; UNO;
U of T)

    ——————.

    MIZH UKRAINTSIAMY V KANADI. Saskatoon: Ukrainian Self-Reliance
League of Canada, 1953. 47 p. (Metro; Minn.; St. Vlad.; UNO;
U of T)

    ——————.

    NASHI DOSIAHNENNIA V KANADI I NASHE MAIBUTNIE. Toronto:
Ukrainian Self-Reliance League of Canada, 1967. 28 p. (St. Vlad.)

Swenarchuk, Janet, ed.

    FROM DREAMS TO REALITY: A HISTORY OF THE UKRAINIAN SENIOR
CITIZENS OF REGINA AND DISTRICT, 1896-1976. Winnipeg: Trident
Press, 1977. 194 p. (Metro; UNO; U of T)

Swyripa, Frances

    UKRAINIAN CANADIANS: A SURVEY OF THEIR PORTRAYAL IN ENGLISH-
LANGUAGE WORKS. Canadian Institute of Ukrainian Studies.
Edmonton: University of Alberta Press, 1978. 169 p. (Metro;
St. Vlad.; U of T)

Swystun, Wasyl

UKRAINS'KA DERZHAVA V SVITLI ISTORII I TRADYTSII. Lecture
delivered at Memorial Hall, Edmonton, Alberta, on Sunday,
September 12, 1945. Toronto: Morris Printing, 1945 (?) (Minn.)

______.

"UKRAINS'KYI PATRIOTYZM" V KANADI: NA SLOVAKH I NA DILI.
Winnipeg: Tovarystvo kul'turnoho zv'iazku z Ukrainoiu, 1957.
111 p. (Minn.; St. Vlad.; UNO)

Terlytsia, Marko

PRAVNUKY POHANI. Kiev: Radians'kyi pys'mennyk, 1960. 305 p.
(U of T)

Teslia, Ivan

ROZSELENNIA UKRAINTSIV V KANADI. Ottawa, 1957. 31 p. (UNO)

______.

UKRAINS'KE NASELENNIA KANADY: POSELENNIA I DEMOHRAFICHNA
KHARAKTERYSTYKA. Shevchenko Scientific Society of Canada.
Zbirnyk (Collected papers), no. 9. Toronto: Ukrainian Echo,
1968. 68 p. (Minn.; UNO; U of T)

______, and Paul Yuzyk

UKRAINTSI V KANADI: IKH ROZVYTOK I DOSIAHNENNIA. Munich:
Ukrainian Husbandry Academy, 1968. 78 p. (Metro; UNO; U of T)

THIS BOGEY OF THE TOWER OF BABEL. Ukrainian Voice English Series,
   no. 3. Winnipeg: Ukrainian Voice, 1964. (Minn.)

TRIBUTE TO OUR UKRAINIAN PIONEERS IN CANADA'S FIRST CENTURY.
   Proceedings of the Special Convention of the Association of
   United Ukrainian Canadians and the Workers' Benevolent Association
   of Canada. Winnipeg: AUUC and WBAC, 1966. 100 p. (Metro;
   St. Vlad.)

TSE--KANADA: KYSHEN'KOVYI PROVIDNYK PO KANADI. n.p.: Ministry of
   Mines and Natural Resources and the Canadian Association for
   Adult Education, 1949. 131 p. (Minn.; St. Vlad.)

UKRAINIAN CANADIANA. Edmonton: Ukrainian Women's Association of
Canada, 1976. 96 p. (St. Vlad.)

Ukrainian Canadian Research Foundation, Toronto

REVIEWS AND LETTERS ON EARLY UKRAINIAN SETTLEMENTS IN CANADA,
1895-1900: DR. OLESKIW'S ROLE IN THE SETTLEMENT OF THE
CANADIAN NORTHWEST, BY VLADIMIR J. KAYE. Canadian Centennial
Series. Toronto: University of Toronto Press, 1965. 14 p.
(U of T)

Ukrainian Fraternal Society, Vancouver branch

BRYTIIS'KA KOLUMBIIA I UKRAINTSI. Winnipeg, 1957. 200 p.
(Minn.; U of T)

Ukrainian National Youth Federation of Canada

CANADA'S CULTURE: VIEWS OF CANADIAN YOUTH OF UKRAINIAN ORIGIN.
Brief submitted to the Royal Commission on Bilingualism and
Biculturalism, Toronto, June 1964. Toronto, 1966. 24 p.
(Metro; UNO)

Ukrainian Pioneers Association of Alberta

THE UKRAINIAN PIONEERS IN ALBERTA, CANADA. Edmonton, 1970.
384 p. (Metro; UNO; U of T)

———.

UKRAINIANS IN ALBERTA. Edmonton, 1975. 564 p. (Metro; St. Vlad.;
UNO; U of T)

UKRAINIAN YEARBOOK. Winnipeg, 1944- . (Minn.: vol. 5 (1948-49);
vols. 7-10 (1950-54); St. Vlad.: vols. 9-11 (1952-55); UNO:
vol. 4 (1947-48), vols. 6-7 (1949-51), vol. 9 (1952-53),
vol. 11 (1954-55); U of T: vol. 1 (1944))

VELYKI ROKOVYNY. Winnipeg, 1938. (Minn.)

Voitsenko, Ol'ha

CANADA'S CULTURAL HERITAGE: UKRAINIAN CONTRIBUTION. Litopys
UVAN (Chronicles), no. 22. Winnipeg: UVAN, 1964. 16 p. (U of T)

______.

DO ISTORII UKRAINTSIV U BRYTANS'KII KOLIUMBII. Litopys UVAN
(Chronicles), no. 7. Winnipeg: UVAN, 1972. 46 p. (St. Vlad.;
U of T)

______.

LITOPYS UKRAINS'KOHO ZHYTTIA V KANADI. 5 vols. Winnipeg:
Trident Press, 1961- . (Metro; Minn.; St. Vlad.; UNO; U of T)

______.

THE UKRAINIANS IN CANADA. Ottawa, 1967. 278 p. (Minn.; St. Vlad.;
U of T)

2nd rev. ed.: Winnipeg, Trident Press, 1968. 271 p. (Metro;
St. Vlad.; UNO; U of T)

Volynets', M.

ZHOVTOBLAKYTNA DOLAROKHAPNA PEREZVA: IAK LIDERY UKRAINS'KYKH
ZHOVTOBLAKYTNYKH ORGANIZATSII V KANADI "RIATUVALY" STARYI KRAI
I "DOPOMAHALY SYROTAM." Winnipeg: Robitnycho-farmers'ke
vydavnyche tovarystvo, 1932. 256 p. (UNO)

Young, Charles H.

THE UKRAINIAN CANADIANS: A STUDY IN ASSIMILATION. Ed. by Helen
R.Y. Reid. Toronto: Thomas Nelson & Sons, 1931. 327 p. (Metro;
Minn.; U of T)

Yuzyk, Paul

FOR A BETTER CANADA. A collection of selected speeches delivered
in the Canadian Senate and at banquets and conferences across
Canada. Toronto: Ukrainian National Association, 1973. 352 p.
(Metro; St. Vlad.; UNO; U of T)

______.

LES CANADIENS-UKRAINIENS: LEUR PLACE ET LEUR RÔLE DANS LA VIE
CANADIENNE. French translation by Bernard Nicolau. Winnipeg,
1967. 99 p. (Metro)

______.

SENATOR YUZYK'S MAIDEN SPEECH. Ukrainian Voice English Series,
no. 5. Winnipeg: Ukrainian Voice, 1964. (Minn.)

————.

   THE UKRAINIANS IN MANITOBA: A SOCIAL HISTORY. The Historical
   and Scientific Society of Manitoba. Toronto: University of
   Toronto Press, 1953. 232 p. (Metro; UNO; U of T)

————.

   UKRAINIAN CANADIANS: THEIR PLACE AND ROLE IN CANADIAN LIFE.
   Toronto: Ukrainian Canadian Business and Professional
   Federation, 1967. 104 p. (Minn.; St. Vlad.; UNO; U of T)

ZA KRASHCHU KANADU: BORIT'SIA, PRATSIUITE, HOLOSUITE.
   Election program of the Progressive Labour Party. Winnipeg:
   Universal Printers, 1945. 31 p. (UNO)

ZBIRKA PRATS' CHLENIV MOLODIZHNOI SEKTSII SPILKY UKRAINS'KYKH
   ZHURNALISTIV KANADY. Ed. by Mykola Lypovets'kyi. Toronto:
   Association of Ukrainian Journalists in Canada, 1973. 73 p.
   (UNO; U of T)

ZVERNENNIA VOIUIUCHOI UKRAINY DO VSIIEI UKRAINS'KOI EMIGRATSII.
   Toronto: Na Varti, 1953. 16 p. (UNO)

Autobiographies/Biographies

General

Kaye, Vladimir Julian

DICTIONARY OF UKRAINIAN CANADIAN BIOGRAPHY: PIONEER SETTLERS
OF MANITOBA, 1891-1900. Foreword by W.L. Morton. Toronto:
Ukrainian Canadian Research Foundation, 1975. 249 p. (UNO;
U of T)

Krawchuk, Petro, comp.

ZHINOCHI DOLI. Toronto: Kobzar, 1973. 503 p. (UNO; U of T)

Shtohryn, Dmytro M., ed.

UKRAINIANS IN NORTH AMERICA: A BIOGRAPHICAL DIRECTORY OF
NOTEWORTHY MEN AND WOMEN OF UKRAINIAN ORIGIN IN THE UNITED
STATES AND CANADA. Champaign, Ill.: Association for the
Advancement of Ukrainian Studies, 1975. 424 p. (Metro; UNO;
U of T)

Individual

Kateryna Mykhailivna Antonovych

________.

Z MOIKH SPOMYNIV. 5 vols. Winnipeg: UVAN, 1965-73. (Metro:
vol. 3; Minn.: 1970; U of T: vols. 1-2)

Leonid Bilets'kyi

Mandryka, M.I.

LEONID BILETS'KYI. UVAN Seriia Ukrains'ki vcheni (Ukrainian
Scholars Series), no. 6. Winnipeg: UVAN, 1957. (Minn.; UNO;
U of T)

Toma Bilous

Rudnyts'kyi, Iaroslav Bohdan

TOMA BILOUS: OSTANII NARODNYI SOPILKAR U KANADI. 2 vols.
Biblioteka pionera, no. 3. Winnipeg: Biblioteka pionera, 1960.
32 p. (Minn.; U of T)

Mykhailo Leontiievych Borovs'kyi

Rozhin, Ivan

  M.L. BOROVS'KYI: BIBLIOHRAFICHNYI NARYS ZHYTTIA, HROMADS'KOI
  I NAUKOVOI PRATSI Z NAHODY 70-RICHCHIA IUVILEIU. Reprint.
  Winnipeg: Volhynian Research Institute, 1962. 47 p. (Minn.;
  St. Vlad.)

Bishop Kyr Nykyta Budka

Bala, Osyp

  PERSHYI UKRAINS'KYI IEPYSKOP KANADY KYR NYKYTA BUDKA. Vol. 1.
  Winnipeg: Tsentralia ukraintsiv katolykiv Manitoby, 1952- .
  (Minn.; U of T)

Mykhailo Dodiak

  ______.

  KNYHA MUDROSTY HUTSULA SAMOUKA. Toronto: Prut Printing, 1976.
  364 p. (St. Vlad.; UNO; U of T)

Zosym Donchuk

PRATSIA I NAHORODA ZOSYMA DONCHUKA. Philadelphia: Vlasna khata,
  1973. 376 p. (Metro; U of T)

Honore Ewach

  ______.

  UKRAINS'KE IEVSHAN-ZILLIA V KANADI: IUVILEINA ZBIRKA TVORIV O.
  IVAKHA V 40-LITTIA IOHO PRATSI PEROM, 1920-1960. Winnipeg:
  Trident Press, 1960. 31 p. (St. Vlad.)

Petro Havrysyshyn

Marunchak, Mykhailo Hryhorii

  PETRO HAVRYSYSHYN: PIONER-BUDIVNYCHYI SHASHKEVYCHIVS'KOI
  DIL'NYTSI (POINT DOGLES) U VINNIPEGU. Biblioteka pionera,
  no. 4. Winnipeg: Biblioteka pionera, 1962-3. 110 p. (Minn.;
  UNO; U of T)

Kyrylo Henyk

Krawchuk, Peter

    KANADS'KYI DRUH IVANA FRANKA. Toronto: Kobzar, 1971. 110 p.
    (U of T)

Ivan Humeniuk

________.

    MOI SPOMYNY: DO ROZVYTKU ORHANIZOVANOHO ZHYTTIA UKRAINTSIV U
    SKHIDNII KANADI. Toronto: Trident Press, 1957. 60 p. (Metro;
    Minn.; St. Vlad.; UNO; U of T)

Stefan Iarema

________.

    URYVKY ZI SPOMYNIV PRO MOIU SKROMNU ORHANIZATSIINU PRATSIU V
    SKHIDNII KANADI. Toronto, 1957. 63 p. (St. Vlad.; U of T)

Ilarion, Metropolitan of Winnipeg and All Canada

IUVILEINA KNYHA NA POSHANU MYTROPOLYTA ILARIONA U 75-LITTIA IOHO
    ZHYTTIA I PRATSI, 1882-1957. Winnipeg: Jubilee Committee, 1958.
    318 p. (Minn.; St. Vlad.; U of T)

LIUDYNA PRATSI: DESIATYLITTIA ARKHYPASTYRS'KOI PRATSI MYTROPOLYTA
    ILARIONA. Winnipeg: Jubilee Committee, 1950. 72 p. (St. Vlad.;
    UNO)

Nesterenko, A.

    MYTROPOLYT ILARION: SLUZHYTEL' BOHOVI I NARODOVI: BIOHRAFICHNA
    MONOHRAFIIA. Winnipeg, 1958. 150 p. (Metro)

Anna Ionkers

Knysh, Irena

    PATRIOTYZM ANNY IONKER. Winnipeg: Ukrainian Canadian Committee,
    Women's Council, 1964. 192 p. (Minn.; St. Vlad.; UNO; U of T)

Myroslav Irchan

Vlasenko, V.P. and Peter Krawchuk

    MYROSLAV IRCHAN. Kiev: Radians'kyi pys'mennyk, 1960. (U of T)

Vasyl' Kudryk

MUZH IDEI I PRATSI: V 50-LITTIA HROMADS'KO-ZHURNALISTYCHNOI TA
    TSERKOVNOI PRATSI O.V. KUDRYKA. Winnipeg: Jubilee Committee,
    1958. 126 p. (Minn.; St. Vlad.)

Vasyl' Kushnir

NA VIRNII SLUZHBI BOHOVI I NARODOVI. Winnipeg, 1959. (Minn.)

Illia Kyriiak

Marunchak, Mykhailo H.

    ILLIA KYRIIAK TA IOHO TVORCHIST'. Winnipeg: UVAN, 1973. 79 p.
    (Metro; St. Vlad.; UNO; U of T)

Svyryd Lomachka

__________.

    SVYRYD LOMACHKA V KANADI: FEILETONY. Toronto: V. Usatiuk, 1951.
    101 p. (Metro; St. Vlad.)

Michael Luchkovich

__________.

    A UKRAINIAN CANADIAN IN PARLIAMENT: MEMOIRS OF MICHAEL LUCHKOVICH.
    Ed. by John Gregorovich. Canadian Centennial Series, no. 2.
    Toronto: Ukrainian Canadian Research Foundation, 1965. (Minn.;
    UNO; U of T)

Hanna Mandryka

HANNA MANDRYKA: VYBRANE. Ed. by Stefaniia Bubniuk and Teodora
    Havrysyshyn. Introd. by Ol'ha Voitsenko. Winnipeg: Ukrainian
    Canadian Committee, Women's Council, 1962. 104 p. (UNO)

Mykyta I. Mandryka

Marunchak, Mykhailo, ed.

MYKYTA IVANOVYCH MANDRYKA: IUVILEINYI ZBIRNYK U VIDZNACHENNIA
85-RICHCHIA IOHO ZHYTTIA TA 65-RICHCHIA IOHO POETYCHNOI,
SUSPIL'NO-POLITYCHNOI I KUL'TURNO-NAUKOVOI DIIAL'NOSTI, 1886-
1971. Winnipeg, 1973. 151 p. (U of T)

Volynets', Stepan

M.I. MANDRYKA. Winnipeg, 1949. 16 p. (U of T)

Tymofei Mats'kiv

______.

Z-NAD DNISTRA NA KANADS'KI PRERII. Edmonton: Ukrainian News,
1963. 208 p. (Metro; Minn.; UNO; U of T)

Michael, Archbishop of Toronto and Eastern Canada

Minenko, Tymofii, ed.

IUVILEINA KNYHA NA POSHANU IOHO VYSOKOPREOSVIASHCHENSTVA,
VYSOKOPREOSVIASHCHENNISHOHO MYKHAILA, ARKHYIEPYSKOPA TORONTA
I SKHIDNOI KANADY, Z NAHODY IOHO 80-LITTIA ZHYTTIA I 45-LITTIA
SVIASHCHENSTVA. Toronto: Jubilee Committee, 1965. 148 p.
(Minn.; St. Vlad.; UNO)

Iuliian Pavlykovs'kyi

Kachor, Andrii

TRYDTSIAT'-P'IAT' LIT NA SLUZHBI NARODU: PAM'IATI INZH. IU.
PAVLYKOVS'KOHO. Speech delivered at the commemorative meeting
of the Winnipeg Credit Union on April 17, 1950. Winnipeg:
Credit Union, 1950. 31 p. (Minn.)

William J. Perepeliuk

Kohus'ka, Natalia L., comp.

NEW ROADWAYS OF LIFE: A BIOGRAPHICAL SKETCH OF WILLIAM J.
PEREPELIUK. n.p., n.d. (Minn.)

______, comp.

NOVYMY DOROHAMY: BIOHRAFICHNYI NARYS PRO VASYLIA PEREPELIUKA.
Winnipeg, 1972. 242 p. (Metro; Minn.; St. Vlad.; UNO; U of T)

Vasyl' Plaskonis

______.

Z RIDNOHO SELA V SHYROKYI SVIT: SPOHADY. St. Catharines, Ont.:
published by the author, 1975. 256 p. (Metro; Minn.; UNO;
U of T)

Avgustyn Romaniuk

______.

MOI PIONIRS'KI PRYHODY V KANADI. Winnipeg: published by the
author, 1958. 228 p. (Minn.; St. Vlad.; U of T)

______.

TAKING ROOT IN CANADA: AN AUTOBIOGRAPHY. Illus. by Gordon Dale.
Winnipeg: Columbia Press, 1954. 283 p. (Minn.; St. Vlad.; UNO;
U of T)

Iuliia Rudnyts'ka

Voitsenko, Ol'ha

ZHYTTIA VELYCHNE I STRADAL'NE...: PAM'IATI IULII RUDNYTS'KOI.
Biblioteka pionera, no. 5. New York-Montreal-Winnipeg: Biblioteka
pionera, 1964. 16 p. (Minn.; U of T)

Iaroslav Bohdan Rudnyts'kyi

______.

Z PODOROZHI PO KANADI, 1949-1959. Kliub pryiateliv ukrains'koi
knyzhky, vol. 33. Winnipeg: Ivan Tyktor, 1959. (Metro; Minn.;
UNO; U of T)

Mandryka, Mykyta Ivanovych

BIO-BIBLIOGRAPHY OF J.B. RUDNYC'KYJ. UVAN Ukrainian Scholars Series,
no. 10. Winnipeg: UVAN, 1961. 72 p. (Metro; Minn.; U of T)

Slavutych, Iar et al.

PROFESSOR J.B. RUDNYC'KIJ, SEXAGENARIUS, 1910-1970. Winnipeg,
1971. 96 p. (St. Vlad.; U of T)

______.

TVORETS' UKRAINS'KOI NAUKY V KANADI TA INSHI STATTI I MATERIIALY
Z PRYVODU 60-RICHCHIA IAROSLAVA RUDNYTS'KOHO. Winnipeg, 1971.
96 p. (U of T)

Voitsenko, Ol'ha et al., comps. and eds.

SCRIPTA MANENT...: A BIO-BIBLIOGRAPHY OF J.B. RUDNYC'KYJ.
2 vols. Readings in Slavic Literature, nos. 13-13a. Winnipeg,
1975. (Metro: vol. 1; UNO: vol. 1; U of T: vols. 1, 2)

Vitalii Sahaidakivs'kyi

______.

PRAVDY NE VTOPYTY: SPOHADY Z 50-TY RICHCHIA PASTYRSTVA, 1927-
1977. Toronto, 1977. 360 p. (St. Vlad.)

Mykhailo Sharyk

______.

Z VIDDALI P'IATDESIAT LIT. 2 vols. Biblioteka Proboiem, nos.
8, 12. Toronto: Proboiem, 1969. (Metro; Minn.; UNO; U of T)

Volodymyr Sikevych

______.

STORINKY IZ ZAPYSNOI KNYZHKY. 7 vols. Winnipeg: Ukrainian
Riflemen's Society, 1941-51. (Minn.: vols. 2-3, 5-7;
St. Vlad.: vols. 1-2, 5-6; UNO: vols. 1-3, 5, 7; U of T: vols.
3, 5)

Iuliian V. Stechyshyn

Udod, Hryhorii

JULIAN W. STECHISHIN: HIS LIFE AND WORK. Saskatoon: Petro
Mohyla Ukrainian Institute, 1978. 118 p. (St. Vlad.)

Mariia Strutyns'ka

______.

DALEKE ZBLYZ'KA. Winnipeg: Trident Press, 1975. 246 p. (U of T)

Petro Svarych

______.

SPOMYNY: 1877-1904. Winnipeg: Trident Press, 1976. 239 p.
(St. Vlad.; UNO)

Ivan Tyktor

TRYDTSIATLITTIA VYDAVNYCHOI DIIAL'NOSTY IVANA TYKTORA, 1923-1953.
Winnipeg: Kliub pryiateliv ukrains'koi knyzhky, 1953. (Minn.)

Ol'ha Voitsenko

Kohus'ka, Natalia Levenets'

NA STOROZHI KUL'TURY: O. VOITSENKO. Winnipeg: Ukrainian Women's
Association of Canada, 1947. 128 p. (St. Vlad.)

Economic Life

Bellegay, Michael M.

NAUKA PRO UPRAVU ZEMLI: ABO, IAK UPRAVLIATY ZEMLIU V KANADI I STEITAKH PISLIA NAINOVIISHOI SYSTEMY I DOS'VIDU. Edmonton: Prosvita, n.d. (Minn.; St. Vlad.)

______.

NAUKA PRO UPRAVU ZEMLI: ABO SHCHO KOZHDOMU CHOLOVIKOVY TREBA ZNATY DO USPISHNOHO FARMOVANIA V KANADI. Edmonton: Prosvita, n.d. 128 p. (St. Vlad.)

Dominion Shorthorn Breeders' Association

SHORTHORNY PODVIINOI TSILY. Winnipeg, 1920. 23 p. (UNO)

Kachor, Andrii

DVADTSIATYRICHCHIA KOOPERATYVNOI HROMADY U VINNIPEGU, 1949-1969. A short history of the "Kooperatyvna hromada" and of Ukrainian cooperatives in Winnipeg. Winnipeg: Kooperatyvna hromada, 1971. 112 p. (Minn.)

Karabut, M.

SADIVNYTSTVO V ZAKHIDNII KANADI. An illustrated handbook. Winnipeg: Ukrainian Booksellers and Publishers, 1939. (Minn.)

Mazurok, Osyp

AL'BOM UKRAINS'KOI MOLOCHARS'KOI KOOPERATSII "MASLOSOIUZ", 1902-1944. Edmonton: published by the author, 1969. 79 p. (Minn.; U of T)

______.

AL'BOM UKRAINS'KYKH MOLOCHARS'KYKH PRATSIVNYKIV SHCHO VIDIISHLY U VICHNIST'. Edmonton: Hurtok b. maslosoiuznykiv im. Andriia Paliia, 1962. (Minn.)

Mersy, Mary

IAK FARMER MOZHE DISTATY VES' PLID SVOIEI PRATSI. Winnipeg: Ukrains'ki robitnychi visti, 1920. (Minn.)

Okhrym, Oleksander P.

UKRAINS'KI KREDYTOVI KOOPERATYVY V TORONTI V 1957r. Toronto:
Ukrainian Credit Unions of Toronto, Coordinating Committee,
1958. 14 p. (UNO)

Onufriichuk, Fedir

ZAHAL'NA ISTORIIA NAIHOLOVNISHYKH KHLIBNYKH ROSLYN. With a
resume in English by Dr. P. Matsenko. Yorkton, Sask.: published
by the author, 1972. (Minn.)

STATUT KREDYTOVYKH KOOPERATYV U PROVINTSII ONTARIO, KANADA.
    Toronto: Ukrainian Credit Unions of Toronto, Coordinating
    Committee, 1958. 12 p. (UNO)

Topol'nyts'kyi, V.

DE POMICH DLIA NAS: ABO, SHCHADNYCHO-KREDYTOVI SPILKY.
Winnipeg: Kul'tura i osvita, 1944. 32 p. (Minn.; UNO)

U DVADSIAT' PIAT'-RICHCHIA...SHCHADNYCHO-KREDYTOVOI SPILKY
    "NOVA HROMADA." Yorkton, Sask.: Nova hromada Credit Union,
    1964. 40 p. (U of T)

Ukrainian (Toronto) Credit Union

DO VASHYKH POSLUH. Jubilee edition commemorating the 25th
anniversary of the Ukrainian Credit Union, 1944-1969. Ed. by
Vasyl' Veryha. Toronto: Kiev Printers, 1970. 112 p. (St. Vlad.;
UNO; U of T)

————.

IUVILEINA PAM'IATKA DESIATYRICHCHIA OSNUVANNIA UKRAINS'KOI
KREDYTOVOI SPILKY U TORONTI, 1944-1954. Toronto: Basilian
Press, n.d. 31 p. (UNO)

————.

STATUT UKRAINS'KOI (TORONTO) KREDYTOVOI SPILKY Z OBMEZHENOIU
VIDPOVIDAL'NISTIU. n.p., n.d. (UNO)

———.

UKRAINS'KA KREDYTOVA SPILKA V TORONTI, 1976. n.p., n.d. 28 p.
(UNO)

ZHYVYI SKOT NA FARMI: I SHCHO KOZHDOMU FARMEROVY TREBA ZNATY DO
USPISHNOHO FARMEROVANNIA V KANADI. Winnipeg: Ukrainian
Booksellers and Publishers, n.d. (Minn.)

Religious Life

General

Bozhyk, Panteleimon

TSERKOV UKRAINTSIV V KANADI, 1890-1927. Winnipeg: Kanadyis'kyi
ukrainets', 1927. 335 p. (Minn.; St. Vlad.; UNO)

Ukrainian Evangelical-Baptist Church

Kindrat, Petro

UKRAINS'KYI BAPTYSTS'KYI RUKH U KANADI: SPOHADY PRO PIONERS'KU
DUKHOVNU PRATSIU V KANADI. Doroha pravdy, no. 48. Toronto-
Winnipeg, 1972. 170 p. (Minn.; UNO; U of T)

Ukrainian Orthodox Churches*

ARKHYIEREIS'KA LITURHIIA I ARKHYIEREIS'KA VIZYTATSIIA.
   Winnipeg: Ukrainian Greek Orthodox Church in Canada, 1954.
   80 p. (St. Vlad.)

DIRECTORY OF EASTERN ORTHODOX CHURCHES: UNITED STATES, CANADA
   AND MEXICO. Detroit: Council of Eastern Orthodox Youth Leaders
   of the Americas, n.d. (Minn.)

DOGMATYCHNO-KANONICHNE STANOVYSHCHE UKRAINS'KOI HREKO-PRAVOSLAVNOI
   TSERKVY V KANADI. n.p., n.d. (Minn.)

DOKINCHIMO BUDOVU VSEKANADIIS'KOI KATEDRY. Winnipeg: Holy Trinity
   Ukrainian Greek Orthodox Cathedral, 1961. 31 p. (Minn.; St. Vlad.)

Holy Trinity Ukrainian Orthodox Church, Canora, Sask.

   DEDICATION: SEPTEMBER 29, 1963. Canora, 1963. (Minn.)

Holy Trinity Ukrainian Greek Orthodox Church, Vancouver

   DVADTSIAT' PIATYLITNII IUVILEI UKRAINS'KOI PRAVOSLAVNOI HROMADY
   PRESVIATOI TROITSI, VANKUVER, B.K., 1937-1962. Vancouver, 1962.
   (St. Vlad.)

---

* Includes the Ukrainian Greek Orthodox Church in Canada (Ukrains'ka
   hreko-pravoslavna tserkva v Kanadi) and the Ukrainian Orthodox
   Church in Canada (Ukrains'ka pravoslavna tserkva v Kanadi).

Holy Trinity Ukrainian Greek Orthodox Cathedral, Winnipeg

PIV STOLITTIA UKRAINS'KOI HREKO-PRAVOSLAVNOI TSERKVY V KANADI,
1918-1968. Winnipeg, 1968. 32 p. (Minn.; St. Vlad.)

————.

UKRAINS'KA HREKO-PRAVOSLAVNA KATEDRA PRESVIATOI TROITSI U
VYNYPEGU (sic). Winnipeg, 1949. (St. Vlad.)

————.

UROCHYSTE VIDKRYTTIA MYTROPOLYCHOI VSEUKRAINS'KOI KATEDRY PRESV.
TROITSI UKRAINS'KOI HREKO-PRAVOSLAVNOI TSERKVY V KANADI, 8-ho
LYPNIA, 1962, VINNIPEG, MAN. Winnipeg: Trident Press, 1962.
126 p. (Minn.; St. Vlad.)

————.

VIDKRYTTIA KATEDRY PRESVIATOI TROITSI: UKRAINS'KOI HREKO-
PRAVOSLAVNOI TSERKVY V KANADI, 8-ho CHERVNIA 1952. Winnipeg:
Trident Press, 1952. 64 p. (Minn.; St. Vlad.; UNO)

Panchuk, John

PERSHA UKRAINS'KA TSERKVA V KANADI: ISTORYCHNYI NARYS.
Winnipeg: published by the author, 1974. 35 p. (Minn.; UNO;
U of T)

Pihuliak, I.M.

UKRAINS'KA PRAVOSLAVNA TSERKVA V RUMUNS'KIM IARMI I BUKOVYNTSI
V KANADI. Winnipeg: Ukrainian Publishing Co. of Canada, 1927.
32 p. (Minn.; UNO)

Savchuk, S.V.

OSNOVNI ZASADY UKRAINS'KOI HREKO-PRAVOSLAVNOI TSERKVY V
KANADI. Winnipeg: Trident Press, 1950. 15 p. (Minn.; St. Vlad.)

————.

P'IATNAITSIAT' (sic) LIT PRATSI UKRAINS'KOI HREKO-PRAVOSLAVNOI
TSERKVY V KANADI. Winnipeg: Consistory of the Ukrainian Greek
Orthodox Church in Canada, 1933. (Minn.)

St. Demetrius Ukrainian Orthodox Church, Long Branch, Ont.

UROCHYSTE VIDKRYTTIA UKRAINS'KOHO PRAVOSLAVNOHO KHRAMU SV.
DYMYTRIIA, NEDILIA 11 TRAVNIA 1958r. n.p., 1958. (St. Vlad.)

St. John's Ukrainian Orthodox Cathedral, Edmonton

PAMIATKA Z POSVIACHENNIA UHOL'NOHO KAMENIA UKRAINS'KOI
PRAVOSLAVNOI KATEDRY, 31-ho SERPNIA 1952. Edmonton: Alberta
Printing, 1952. 104 p. (Minn.; St. Vlad.)

St. Vladimir's Cathedral, Toronto

V PAM'IAT' POSVIACHENNIA UKRAINS'KOI PRAVOSLAVNOI KATEDRY SV.
VOLODYMYRA V TORONTO, 22 TRAVNIA 1955r. Toronto: St. Vladimir's,
1955. 160 p. (Minn.; St. Vlad.)

St. Vladimir Ukrainian Greek Orthodox Church, Hamilton, Ont.

PAM'IATKA POSVIACHENNIA IKONOSTASU UKRAINS'KOI HREKO-PRAVOSLAVNOI
TSERKVY SV. VOLODYMYRA, HAMYLTON, ONT., NEDILIA 22 LYPNIA, 1962r.
Hamilton, 1962. 27 p. (St. Vlad.)

______.

P'IATDESIATYLITTIA: KOROTKYI NARYS, 1926-1976. Hamilton,
1976. 244 p. (St. Vlad.)

St. Vladimir's Ukrainian Orthodox Church, Toronto

OTVORENNIA UKRAINS'KOI PRAVOSLAVNOI TSERKVY SV. VOLODYMYRA,
NEDILIA 7-ho LYSTOPADA 1948. Winnipeg: Ukrainian Publishing Co.
of Canada, 1948. 63 p. (St. Vlad.)

Swystun, Wasyl

AVTOKEFALIIA: CHY ZALEZHNIST' VID CHUZHYKH? An analysis of the
dogmatic and canonical position of the Ukrainian Greek Orthodox
Church in Canada. Winnipeg, 1935. 46 p. (Minn.; St. Vlad.)

______.

DOGMATYCHNO-KANONICHNE STANOVYSHCHE UKRAINS'KOI HREKO-PRAVOSLAVNOI
TSERKVY V KANADI. Winnipeg, 1935. 36 p. (St. Vlad.; UNO)

______.

KRYZA V UKRAINS'KII PRAVOSLAVNII (AVTOKEFAL'NII) TSERKVI.
Winnipeg, 1947. 128 p. (Minn.; St. Vlad.; UNO)

Trosky, Odarka Savella

THE UKRAINIAN GREEK ORTHODOX CHURCH IN CANADA. Winnipeg, 1968.
87 p. (St. Vlad.; U of T)

Udod, Hryhorii

UKRAINS'KA HREKO-PRAVOSLAVNA KATEDRA PRESVIATOI TROITSI V
SASKATUNI, 1918-1971. Saskatoon: Holy Trinity Ukrainian Greek
Orthodox Cathedral, 1973. 211 p. (St. Vlad.; UNO; U of T)

UHODA UKRAINS'KOI AVTOKEFAL'NOI PRAVOSLAVNOI TSERKVY Z ZHUKIVTSIAMY
ABO TAK ZVANI "TEZY", Z 6-ho BEREZNIA 1935r. Winnipeg, 1944.
(Minn.)

Ukrainian Greek Orthodox Church in Canada

CHARTER I STATUT. Winnipeg: Consistory of the Ukrainian Greek
Orthodox Church, 1931. (Minn.)

______.

CHARTER I STATUT. Winnipeg: Consistory of the Ukrainian Greek
Orthodox Church, 1937. (Minn.)

______.

CHOTYRNADTSIATYI SOBOR UKRAINS'KOI HREKO-PRAVOSLAVNOI TSERKVY
V KANADI, VINNIPEG, MANITOBA, 30 I 31 LYPNIA TA I 2 SERPNIA
1970r: MATERIIAL DLIA DUKHOVENSTVA I DELEHATIV. Winnipeg, 1970.
108 p. (St. Vlad.)

______.

PIATNADTSIATYI SOBOR UKRAINS'KOI HREKO-PRAVOSLAVNOI TSERKVY V
KANADI, 2-6 LYPNIA 1975r. Winnipeg: Consistory of the
Ukrainian Greek Orthodox Church, 1975. 132 p. (St. Vlad.)

______.

PROPAMIATNA KNYHA UKRAINS'KOI HREKO-PRAVOSLAVNOI TSERKVY V
KANADI..Winnipeg: Consistory of the Ukrainian Greek Orthodox
Church, 1938, 64 p. (St. Vlad.)

______.

PROTOKOL NADZVYCHAINOHO SOBORU UKRAINS'KOI HREKO-PRAVOSLAVNOI
TSERKVY V KANADI, 1951r. Winnipeg: Consistory of the Ukrainian
Greek Orthodox Church, 1951. 102 p. (Minn.; St. Vlad.)

______.

PROTOKOL ODYNADTSIATOHO SOBORU UKRAINS'KOI HREKO-PRAVOSLAVNOI
TSERKVY V KANADI, 1955r. Winnipeg: Consistory of the Ukrainian
Greek Orthodox Church, 1955. 136 p. (Minn.; St. Vlad.)

______.

PROTOKOL SEMOHO SOBORU UKRAINS'KOI HREKO-PRAVOSLAVNOI TSERKVY
V KANADI, 1935r. Winnipeg: Consistory of the Ukrainian Greek
Orthodox Church, 1935. 90 p. (Minn.; St. Vlad.)

______.

STATUT I PRAVYLA UKRAINS'KOI HREKO-PRAVOSLAVNOI TSERKVY V
KANADI, PRYINIATI NADZVYCHAINYM SOBOROM UHPTs V KANADI, 1951r.
Winnipeg: Consistory of the Ukrainian Greek Orthodox Church,
1952. (Minn.)

______.

STATUT UKRAINS'KOI HREKO-PRAVOSLAVNOI TSERKVY V KANADI, 1950r.
Winnipeg: Consistory of the Ukrainian Greek Orthodox Church,
1950. 44 p. (St. Vlad.)

______.

VELYKE ROKOVYNY. 3 parts. Winnipeg: Consistory of the Ukrainian
Greek Orthodox Church, 1938. 224 p. (Minn.; St. Vlad.)

______.

ZBIRNYK MATERIIALIV Z NAHODY IUVILEINYKH SVIATKUVAN' U 50-LITTIA
UKRAINS'KOI HREKO-PRAVOSLAVNOI TSERKVY V KANADI. Winnipeg:
Consistory of the Ukrainian Greek Orthodox Church, 1968. 328 p.
(St. Vlad.)

Ukrainian Orthodox Brotherhood of St. Vladimir, Toronto

SOROKLITTIA UKRAINS'KOHO PRAVOSLAVNOHO BRATSTVA SV. VOLODYMYRA
V TORONTI. Ed. by M. Mukha and T. Khokhitva. Toronto: Ukrainian
Orthodox Brotherhood of St. Vladimir, 1978. 64 p. (St. Vlad.)

______.

V OBORONI VIRY. 4 vols. Toronto: Ukrainian Orthodox Brotherhood
of St. Vladimir, 1955-9. (Metro: vols. 1-4; Minn.: vols. 1-4;
St. Vlad.: vols. 1-4; UNO: vols. 1-3; U of T: vol. 1)

Ukrains'ka hreko-pravoslavna tserkva sv. Apostola Andriia
Pervozvannoho, Toronto

   IUVILEINA KNYHA DVADTSIATYP'IATYRICHCHIA UKRAINS'KOI PRAVOSLAVNOI
   TSERKVY SV. APOSTOLA ANDRIIA PERVOZVANNOHO V TORONTI. Toronto:
   Ukr. pravoslavna tserkva sv. Ap. Andriia, 1975. 186 p. (St. Vlad.)

Ukrains'ka hreko-pravoslavna tserkva sv. Iuriia Peremozhtsia,
Lachine, Que.

   IUVILEINA KNYHA UKRAINS'KOI HREKO-PRAVOSLAVNOI TSERKVY SV.
   IURIIA PEREMOZHTSIA LIASHIN, KVEBEK: Z NAHODY 25-LITTIA
   ISNUVANNIA PARAFII, 1945-1970; 25-LITTIA POSVIACHENNIA TSERKVY,
   1946-1971. Lachine: Jubilee Committee, 1971. 64 p. (St. Vlad.)

Ukrains'ka hreko-pravoslavna tserkva sv. Ivana, Oshawa

   DVADTSIATYLITNII IUVILEI UKRAINS'KOI HREKO-PRAVOSLAVNOI TSERKVY
   SVIATOHO IVANA V OSHAVI, ONTARIO, 1935-1955. n.p., n.d. 71 p.
   (St. Vlad.)

Ukrains'ka hreko-pravoslavna tserkva sv. Petra i Pavla, Niagara Falls, Ont.

   PAM'IATKA 10-LITN'OHO IUVILEIU UKRAINS'KOI HREKO-PRAVOSLAVNOI
   TSERKVY SV. PETRA I PAVLA, NEDILIA 25 LYSTOPADA, 1962r.
   Hamilton: Vira, 1962. 17 p. (St. Vlad.)

Ukrains'ka pravoslavna hromada sv. Ivana, Edmonton

   IUVILEI SOROKOLITTIA, 1923-1963. Edmonton: Ukrains'ka pravoslavna
   hromada sv. Ivana, 1963. (Minn.)

Ukrains'ka pravoslavna hromada sv. Ivana, Oshawa

   SOROKOLITNII IUVILEI, 1935-1975. Toronto: Harmony Printing,
   1975. 125 p. (St. Vlad.)

Ukrains'ka pravoslavna hromada sv. Volodymyra, Toronto

   PAMIATNA KNYHA SVIATA-OTVORENNIA 1938r. Toronto, 1950. 20 p.
   (St. Vlad.)

————.

   STATUT I CHLENS'KA KNYZHOCHKA. Toronto, n.d. 14 p. (St. Vlad.)

Ukrains'ka pravoslavna hromada sv. Volodymyra, Windsor

PROPAMIATNA KNYHA: Z NAHODY POSVIACHENNIA UHOL'NOHO KAMENIA I
VIDKRYTTIA NOVOI TSERKVY DNIA 6-ho ZHOVTNIA 1963r. Winnipeg:
Trident Press, 1963. 144 p. (St. Vlad.)

Ukrains'ka pravoslavna hromada svv. Petra i Pavla, Brooksby, Sask.

P'IATDESIAT-LITTIA. n.p.: Jubilee Committee, 1976. 40 p.
(St. Vlad.)

Ukrains'ka pravoslavna tserkva Rizdva Presviatoi Bohorodytsi,
Oshawa

OTVORENNIA UKRAINS'KOI PRAVOSLAVNOI TSERKVY RIZDVA PRESVIATOI
BOHORODYTSI, 1953r. Winnipeg: Trident Press, 1953. 23 p.
(St. Vlad.)

Ukrains'ka pravoslavna tserkva sv. Iuriia Peremozhtsia, Grimsby,
Ont.

IUVILEINA KNYHA: Z NAHODY 25-LITTIA ISNUVANNIA PARAFII, 1943-
1968. Ed. by Tymofii Minenko. Grimsby: Harmony Printing, 1968.
100 p. (St. Vlad.)

Ukrains'ka pravoslavna tserkva sv. Sofii, Montreal

DVADTSIAT'-LIT: 1926-1951. n.p., n.d. 112 p. (Minn.; St. Vlad.)

Ukrains'kyi pravoslavnyi sobor sv. Pokrovy, Winnipeg

SOROKLITTIA UKRAINS'KOHO PRAVOSLAVNOHO SOBORU SV. POKROVY.
Winnipeg: Christian Press, 1965. (St. Vlad.)

Ukrainian Catholic (Uniate) Church

Baran, Anna Mariia

UKRAINS'KI KATOLYTS'KI TSERKVY SASKACHEVANU. With an English
translation by Chrystyna T. Pastershank. Saskatoon: Ukrainian
Catholic Council of Saskatchewan, 1977. 389 p. (Metro; St. Vlad.)

Barclay, Clayton

THE ROLE OF THE UKRAINIAN CATHOLIC CHURCH IN THE FREE WORLD
TODAY. Reprint. Winnipeg: Ukrainian Catholic Youth Organization
of Manitoba, 1966. (Minn.)

Basilian Fathers, Vancouver

    DVADTSIAT'RICHCHIA OTTSIV VASYLIIAN U VANKUVERI, 1937-1957.
Edmonton, 1957. 96 p. (Minn.; U of T)

Bélanger, L.F.

    LES UKRAINIENS CATHOLIQUES DU RIT GRÈC-RUTHÈNE AU CANADA.
Quebec: L'Université Laval, 1945. 56 p. (U of T)

Beskyd, Iuliian, ed.

    CHVERT'STORICHCHIA NA VLADYCHOMU PRESTOLI TORONTONS'KA
EPARKHIIA, 1948-1973. Toronto: Nasha meta, 1975. 816 p. (UNO)

_____, ed. and comp.

    U KHRYSTOVIM VYNOHRADNYKU: AL'MANAKH TORONTONS'KOI EPARKHII.
Toronto: Toronto Eparchy of the Ukrainian Catholic Church,
1964. 752 p. (Minn.; UNO)

Committee for Defense of Rites and Traditions of the Ukrainian
Catholic Church in Canada

    CHUZHYNETS' V OBORONI UKRAINS'KOI TSERKVY. Toronto, 1966. 8 p.
(St. Vlad.)

Fedoriv, Iurii

    NA SVIATYKH MISTSIAKH: DNEVNYK UKRAINS'KOHO PALOMNYTSTVA Z
KANADY DO SVIATOI ZEMLI VID 8-ho DO 27-ho SERPNIA 1960.
Toronto: Dobra knyzhka, 1962. 162 p. (Metro; UNO)

Gerych, Iu.

    SUCHASNA SYTUATSIIA V NASHI TSERKVI I IAKYI VYKHID. Toronto:
Toronto Eparchy of the Ukrainian Catholic Church, 1976. 27 p.
(UNO)

Hladyshevs'kyi, M.

    IUVILEINA PAM'IATKA V 50-LITTIA ISNUVANNIA UKRAINS'KOI
KATOLYTS'KOI PARAFII V KALGARAKH, ALBERTA. Calgary, 1962.
166 p. (Minn.; U of T)

IUVILEINA KNYHA ZHROMADZHENNIA SESTER SLUZHEBNYTS'. Edmonton:
    Sisters Servants of Mary Immaculate, 1942. 207 p. (U of T)

Ivashko, Volodymyr, ed.

SHEMATYZM SASKATUNS'KOI UKRAINS'KOI KATOLYTS'KOI EPARKHII.
Yorkton, Sask.: Redeemer's Voice, 1961. 115 p. (U of T)

Katrii, Iuliian

PIZNAI SVII OBRIAD: LITERATURNYI RIK UKRAINS'KOI KATOLYTS'KOI
TSERKVY. Ukrains'ka dukhovna biblioteka. Toronto: Basilian
Press, 1976. (U of T)

Kazymyra, Bohdan Z.

MYTROPOLYT ANDRII SHEPTYTS'KYI. METROPOLITAN ANDREW SHEPTYCKYJ
AND THE UKRAINIANS IN CANADA. Toronto: Basilian Press, 1954.
149 p. (U of T)

______.

PERSHI OSTAHY. Yorkton, Sask.: Redeemer's Voice, 195(?). 28 p.
(U of T)

______.

RELIHIINO-HROMADS'KE ZHYTTIA V UKRAINS'KII KATOLYTS'KII
MYTROPOLII V KANADI. Toronto: Basilian Press, 1965. 102 p.
(U of T)

Kohut, Iosyf

NARYS ISTORII UKRAINS'KOI KATOLYTS'KOI TSERKVY SV. TROITSI V
STIUARTBURN, MANITOBI: MOI SPOMYNY. Yorkton, Sask.: Redeemer's
Voice, 1958. 31 p. (St. Vlad.; UNO)

Kuzyk, Dmytro

ZA UKRAINS'KU MOVU V NASHII TSERKVI. Trenton, N.J.: published
by the author, 1964. 47 p. (UNO)

Maloney, George

WHAT DOES IT MEAN TO BE A UKRAINIAN CATHOLIC AND UKRAINIAN
CATHOLIC AUTONOMY. Weston, Ont.: St. Demetrius Ukrainian Catholic
Church, 197(?). 35 p. (St. Vlad.)

Marunchak, Mykhailo H.

ZMAHANNIA ZA NEZALEZHNIST' UKRAINS'KOI TSERKVY V KANADI: ROLIA
KATEDRY SV. VOLODYMYRA I OL'HY U VINNIPEGU. Winnipeg: Cathedral
of Ss. Vladimir and Olga, 1966-7. 99 p. (Metro; U of T)

MONDER UCHORA I S'OHODNI: IZ PRYVODU BLAHOSLOVENNIA NOVOI TSERKVY
SV. VERKHOVNYKH APOSTOLIV PETRA I PAVLA, MONDER, ALBERTA,
29 CHERVNIA 1969. Monder, Alta.: Basilian Fathers, 1969. 232 p.
(UNO; U of T)

Nimchuk, Ivan

DIV PAPS'KI ENTSYKLIKY V SOTSIAL'NYKH SPRAVAKH: REFERAT
VYHOLOSHENYI U SERII "SOTSIIAL'NYKH DNIV" B.U.K. V EDMONTONI
14 HRUDNIA 1951r. Biblioteka katolyts'koi aktsii, no. 6.
Edmonton, 1951. 32 p. (St. Vlad.)

OBRIAD SVIACHENNIA NA IEPYSKOPA I ARKHIIEREIS'KA SLUZHBA BOZHA
PREOSVIASHCHENNOHO NILIA NYKOLAIA SAVARYNA, ChSVV. Toronto,
1943. 97 p. (UNO)

Olen'chuk, Mykhailo

TSERKOVNO-RELIHIINI ZAVDANNIA UKRAINTSIV KATOLYKIV U KANADI.
Biblioteka katolyts'koi aktsii, no. 3. Edmonton, 1951. 22 p.
(St. Vlad.)

PERSHA UKRAINS'KA KATOLYTS'KA MYTROPOLIIA V KANADI, 12 LIUTOHO 1957.
Winnipeg: Metropolitan Ordinariate, 1957.

Popowich, Claudia Helen

TO SERVE IS TO LOVE: THE CANADIAN STORY OF THE SISTERS SERVANTS
OF MARY IMMACULATE. Foreword by Vladimir J. Kaye. Toronto:
Sisters Servants of Mary Immaculate, 1971. 344 p. (UNO; U of T)

PROPAM'IATNA KNYHA: O.O. VASYLIIAN U KANADI: 50 LIT NA SLUZHBI
BOHOVI T NARODOVI, 1902-1953. Toronto: Basilian Press, 1953.
432 p. (Minn.; St. Vlad.; U of T)

PROPAMIATNA KNYHA Z NAHODY ZOLOTOHO IUVILEIU POSELENNIA UKRAINS'KOHO
NARODU V KANADI. Yorkton, Sask.: Episcopal Ordinariate, 1941.
338 p. (UNO; U of T)

Redemptorist Fathers of the Eastern Rite, Yorkton, Sask.

IUVILEINA KNYHA, 1906-1956. Yorkton, Sask., 1956. (Minn.)

Ruthenian Greek Catholic Church in Canada

STATUT RUSKOI HREKO-KATOLYTS'KOI TSERKVY V KANADI. Winnipeg:
West Canada, 1913. (Minn.)

Scott, William Louis

EASTERN CATHOLICS: WITH SPECIAL REFERENCE TO THE RUTHENIANS IN
CANADA. Toronto: Catholic Truth Society of Canada, 1923. 47 p.
(Metro)

————.

THE UKRAINIANS: OUR MOST PRESSING PROBLEM. Toronto: Catholic
Truth Society of Canada, n.d. 64 p. (U of T)

Semchuk, Stepan

CENTENNIAL OF CANADA AND 75 YEARS OF THE UKRAINIAN CATHOLIC
CHURCH. Winnipeg, 1967. 7 p. (U of T)

————.

KOROTKA ISTORIIA NASHOI TSERKVY. Nashi vydannia, nos. 13-14.
Yorkton, Sask.: Ukrainian Catholic Brotherhood of Canada,
1944. 40 p. (UNO; U of T)

————.

NASHA KHOLMSHCHYNA. Monder, Alta.: Basilian Fathers, 1948.
30 p. (U of T)

Sisters Servants of Mary Immaculate

IUVILEINI SPOMYNY, 1902-1952. Toronto: Apostolic Exarchate for
Eastern Canada, 1952. 288 p. (UNO)

Ukrainian Catholic (Uniate) Church in Canada

PERSHA UKRAINS'KA KATOLYTS'KA MYTROPOLIIA V KANADI. Winnipeg:
Metropolitan Ordinariate, 1957. 183 p. (St. Vlad.; UNO)

Ukrainian Holy Ghost Parish, Sydney, N.S.
  1912-1972. n.p., n.d. 48 p. (St. Vlad.)

_____.

  THE UKRAINIAN CATHOLIC HOLY GHOST PARISH: FIFTIETH ANNIVERSARY,
  1913-1963. n.p., n.d. unpaged. (St. Vlad.)

Vavryk, Vasyl'
  "IDITE DO IOSYFA": V KANADIIS'KIM LIURDI. Slovo dobroho
  pastyria, vol. 5, nos. 3-4. New York: Basilian Fathers in the
  U.S.A., 1954. (Minn.)

Z RYMOM CHY PROTY RYMU? Edmonton: Ukrainian News, 1935. 30 p.
  (St. Vlad.)

Cultural and Intellectual Life: Learned Societies, Academies,
Universities, Museums

Antonovych, Kateryna Mykhailivna

ROLIA UKRAINS'KOI ZHINKY V PRATSI UVU. Litopys UVAN (Chronicles),
no. 11. Winnipeg: UVAN, 1953. 16 p. (Minn.; UNO)

Association of Ukrainian Educators in Canada

RIDNA SHKOLA: PROHRAMY NAVCHANNIA I VYKHOVANNIA. Toronto:
Basilian Press, 1952. 61 p. (UNO; U of T)

Baran, O., O.V. Gerus and Ia. Rozumnyi, comps.

IUVILEINYI ZBIRNYK UKRAINS'KOI VIL'NOI AKADEMII NAUK V KANADI.
M. Marunchak et al., eds. Winnipeg: UVAN, 1976. 657 p. (U of T)

Bezushko, Volodymyr and Iaroslav B. Rudnyts'kyi

VYDANNIA UVAN U PERSHOMU DESIATYLITTI, 1945-1955. Litopys UVAN
(Chronicles), no. 13. Winnipeg: UVAN, 1955. 22 p. (Minn.; U of T)

Bida, Konstantyn

SUSPIL'NO-NATSIONAL'NA FUNKTSIIA UKRAINS'KOI KUL'TURY V DIIASPORI.
Reprint. Toronto-New York: Association of Ukrainian Educators in
Canada and Educational Council of the Ukrainian Congress Committee
of America, 1965. 11 p. (UNO)

————.

VYKHOVNI NAPRIAMY DLIA NAVCHAL'NYKH PROHRAM V UKRAINS'KYKH
RIDNYKH SHKOLAKH I NA UKRAINO-ZNAVCHYKH KURSAKH. Toronto:
Severyn Vindyk, 1962. 11 p. (UNO)

Boiko, Max

KUL'TURNA PRATSIA VOLYNIAN U PIVNICHNII AMERYTSI. Pratsi Oseredka
bibliohrafii Volyni, no. 13. Bloomington, Ind.: Society of Volyn
in Toronto, 1978. 213 p. (U of T)

BUDIVEL'NA KAMPANIIA KOLEGII SV. VASYLIIA VELYKOHO. Toronto,
1959. (Minn.)

CHOMU BUDUIEMO PAM'IATNYK TARASOVI SHEVCHENKOVI V KANADI?
Winnipeg: Ukrainian Canadian Committee, 1960. 15 p. (UNO)

Danyliw, W. George

THE UKRAINIAN STUDENT AND HIS ORGANIZATIONS IN THE WORLD.
Toronto: Toronto Free Press, 1959. 26 p. (St. Vlad.)

Dontsov, Dmytro

ZAPOVIT SHEVCHENKA: DOPOVID' VYHOLOSHENA NA SHEVCHENKIVS'KII
AKADEMII V TORONTI 9 BEREZNIA 1950r. Toronto: Ukrainian Youth
Association (SUM), 1950. 16 p. (St. Vlad.; UNO)

Doroshenko, Dmytro

ROZVYTOK UKRAINS'KOI NAUKY PID PRAPOROM SHEVCHENKA. Litopys
UVAN (Chronicles), no. 10. Winnipeg: UVAN, 1949. 11 p. (Minn.;
St. Vlad.; UNO; U of T)

Gregorovich, Andrew, comp.

UKRAINIAN TORONTO: A GUIDE AND DIRECTORY TO UKRAINIAN ARTS
AND CULTURAL GROUPS, ORGANIZATIONS AND INSTITUTIONS IN TORONTO.
Prepared for the Second World Congress of Free Ukrainians,
November 1-4, 1973. Toronto: Ukrainian Canadian Committee, 1973.
33 p. (UNO)

2nd ed.: Toronto, Ukrainian Canadian Committee, 1976. 64 p.
(Metro; U of T)

Harvard University Ukrainian Studies Fund, Canadian Committee

TSENTR UKRAINS'KYKH STUDII HARVARDS'KOHO UNIVERSYTETU I UKRAINTSI
KANADY. Ed. by Vasyl' Veryha. Toronto, 1976. 30 p. (UNO)

Holubnychyi, Vsevolod, ed.

SUT' UKRAINS'KOI KUL'TURY I UKRAINS'KA KUL'TURA V DIIASPORI:
DOPOVID' NA PIDHOTOVCHII SESII DLIA SPRAV KUL'TURY V TORONTI,
30-ho BEREZNIA 1964r. Toronto: Association of Ukrainian
Educators in Canada and the Educational Council of the Ukrainian
Congress Committee of America, 1965. 51 p. (UNO)

Hryhorii Skovoroda Ukrainian School, Toronto

VIDHOMIN ROKIV AL'MANAKH. Ed. by Ivan Luchkiv. Toronto:
H. Skovoroda Ukrainian School, 1976. 118 p. (St. Vlad.)

Hryhorijiv, N., ed.

    ZAVDANNIA UKRAINS'KOHO SHKIL'NYTSTVA V KANADI. Saskatoon:
Tsentralia ukrains'koho shkil'nytstva v Kanadi, n.d. 61 p.
(St. Vlad.)

Isaiv, Ivan, ed.

    PROPAMIATNA KNYHA: UKRAINS'KYI KATOLYTS'KYI SOIUZ, UKRAINS'KYI
NARODNYI DIM, 1906-1965. Edmonton, 1966(?) (Minn.)

KNYHA MYSTTSIV I DIIACHIV UKRAINS'KOI KUL'TURY: UCHASNYKIV PERSHOI
    ZUSTRICHI UKRAINS'KYKH MYSTTSIV AMERYKY I KANADY Z HROMADIANSTVOM
    U DNIAKH 3-5 LYPNIA 1954. Toronto: Basilian Press, 1954. 312 p.
    (Metro; St. Vlad.; UNO; U of T)

Knysh, Irena

    VIDHUKY CHASU. Collected sketches, articles, memoirs. Winnipeg:
published by the author, 1972. 404 p. (Metro; UNO; U of T)

KOLEGIIA MALA SEMINARIIA SV. VOLODYMYRA. ST. VLADIMIR'S COLLEGE
    MINOR SEMINARY. Roblin, Man. (St. Vlad.)

Lupul, Manoly Robert

    THE ROMAN CATHOLIC CHURCH AND THE NORTHWEST SCHOOL QUESTION:
A STUDY IN CHURCH-STATE RELATIONS IN WESTERN CANADA, 1875-1905.
Toronto: University of Toronto Press, 1974. 292 p. (St. Vlad.;
U of T)

Mandryka, M.I., comp.

    PIVSTOLITTIA PRATSI UKRAINS'KOHO TOVARYSTVA CHYTAL'NI PROSVITY
U VINNIPEGU. Winnipeg: Prosvita Reading Association, 1958.

————.

    SYMON PETLIURA. Speech delivered in memory of S.V. Petliura,
June 3, 1957, at the Holy Trinity Ukrainian Greek Orthodox
Cathedral in Winnipeg. n.p., n.d. 12 p. (St. Vlad.)

Matsenko, Pavlo

    DUMKY PRO VEDENNIA KUL'TURNO-OSVITNOI PRATSI PO FILLIIAKH UNO
V KANADI. Saskatoon: Ukrainian National Federation, 1940. 29 p.
(Minn.; UNO)

Mats'kiv, Tymofei

    Z-NAD DNISTRA NA KANADS'KI PRERII. Edmonton: Ukrainian News, 1963. 208 p. (Metro; Minn.; UNO; U of T)

MUZEI T.H. SHEVCHENKA V PALERMO: LEKTSIA-EKSKURSIIA. Toronto: Association of United Ukrainian Canadians, 1954. 61 p. (St. Vlad.)

Mykhailo Hrushevsky Ukrainian Institute

    IUVILEINA KNYHA: 25-LITTIA INSTYTUTU IM. MYKHAILA HRUSHEVS'KOHO V EDMONTONI. Edmonton: M. Hrushevsky Institute, 1943. (Minn.)

NARYS ISTORII MATIRNOHO TOVARYSTVA PROSVITY I OHLIAD PROSVITNYKH TOVARYSTV U KANADI. Winnipeg: Prosvita, 1968. 309 p. (Metro; Minn.; U of T)

Nykoliak, Dmytro A., ed.

    KOROTKYI ISTORYCHNYI NARYS UKRAINS'KOHO NARODNOHO DOMU V TORONTO. Toronto: Ukrainian National Home, 1953. 36 p. (Metro; Minn.; UNO; U of T)

Olynyk, Roman

    NA POROZI DRUHOHO PIVSTOLITTIA. Winnipeg: Trident Press, 1970. 61 p. (Minn.; St. Vlad.)

OSEREDOK UKRAINS'KOI KUL'TURY I OSVITY. Winnipeg: Kul'tura i osvita, 1945. 23 p. (Minn.; UNO)

OSEREDOK UKRAINS'KOI KUL'TURY I OSVITY: 1944-1954. Winnipeg: Novyi shliakh, n.d. (Minn.; UNO)

PAMIATKA DEVIATYKH UKRAINS'KYKH LITNIKH KURSIV, 1948, 1955: PRY KOLIEGII SV. ANDREIA V VINNIPEGU. Winnipeg, 1955. (Minn.)

Petro Mohyla Ukrainian Institute, Saskatoon

    IUVILEINA KNYHA 25-LITTIA INSTYTUTU IM. PETRA MOHYLY V SASKATUNI. Winnipeg: Ukrainian Voice, 1945. 429 p. (Minn.; St. Vlad.; UNO; U of T)

————.

   KAMENIARI: 1950-51, 1951-52, 1952-53. Student yearbook. Winnipeg:
Trident Press, 1953. (Minn.)

Prosvita, Fort William, Ont.

   ZOLOTYI IUVILEI. Essays and memoirs commemorating the fiftieth
anniversary of the Prosvita Society in Fort William, 1906-1956.
Winnipeg: Prosvita (Fort William), 1956. 93 p. (Metro; Minn.;
St. Vlad.; U of T)

Prosvita, Port Arthur, Ont.

   ZOLOTI VOROTA. Jubilee edition commemorating the fiftieth
anniversary of the Prosvita Society in Port Arthur. Port Arthur,
1960. 328 p. (St. Vlad.; UNO)

Prosvita, Montreal

   ZOLOTYI IUVILEI TOVARYSTVA PROSVITA IM. T. SHEVCHENKA V
MONTREALI-POINT ST. CHARLZ. Ed. by Mariia Davydovych. Montreal,
1964. 294 p. (UNO)

Prykhodko, Viktor

   PID SONTSEM PODILLIA: SPOHADY. Vol. 1. 4th ed. New York:
Krynytsia, 1967. (St. Vlad.)

Rudnyts'kyi, Iaroslav Bohdan

   BIBLIOTEKA CHYTAL'NI "PROSVITY" U VINNIPEGU. 2nd ed. Litopys
UVAN (Chronicles), no. 14. Winnipeg: Prosvita, 1956. 30 p.
(Minn.; UNO; U of T)

————.

   BIBLIOTEKA OSEREDKU UKRAINS'KOI KUL'TURY I OSVITY V KANADI,
1944-1954. Winnipeg: Kul'tura i osvita, 1955. 32 p. (Minn.; UNO;
U of T)

————.

   BIBLIOTEKA TOVARYSTVA PROSVITY U FORT VILLIIAMI, ONTARIO. 2nd
ed. Litopys UVAN (Chronicles), no. 15. Winnipeg: Prosvita, 1957.
32 p. (Minn.; U of T)

——————.

BIBLIOTEKA TOVARYSTVA PROSVITA V PORT ARTURI, ONTARIO. 2nd ed.
Litopys UVAN (Chronicles), no. 19. Winnipeg: Prosvita, 1961.
16 p. (Minn.; U of T)

——————.

SLAVIC AND BALTIC UNIVERSITIES IN EXILE. UVAN Slavistica Series,
no. 4. Winnipeg: UVAN, 1949. 16 p. (Minn.; St. Vlad.)

Shevchenko Scientific Society of Canada

BIULETEN': MATERIIALY IV-oi NAUKOVOI KONFERENTSII NTSh-TORONTO.
No. 1. Toronto: Homin Ukrainy, 1953. 163 p. (UNO)

——————.

COLLECTED PAPERS FROM THE CONFERENCES OF THE SHEVCHENKO SCIENTIFIC
SOCIETY OF CANADA. No. 6. Toronto: Homin Ukrainy, 1962. 123 p.
(UNO)

——————.

KHRONIKA NAUKOVOHO TOVARYSTVA IM. SHEVCHENKA ZA RIK 1963.
Toronto, 1963- . (Minn.)

——————.

ZBIRNYK: MATERIIALIV V-oi NAUKOVOI KONFERENTSII NTSh-TORONTO.
No. 1. Toronto: Homin Ukrainy, 1954. 192 p. (Minn.; UNO)

——————.

ZBIRNYK: MATERIIALIV NAUKOVYKH KONFERENTSII KANADS'KOHO NTSh.
No. 6. Toronto: Homin Ukrainy, 1962. 123 p. (Minn.; UNO)

——————.

ZBIRNYK: MATERIIALIV NAUKOVOI KONFERENTSII KANADS'KOHO NTSh:
V OBORONI UKRAINS'KOI KUL'TURY I NARODU. No. 7. Toronto:
Homin Ukrainy, 1966. 183 p. (Metro; Minn.; UNO)

——————.

ZBIRNYK NAUKOVYKH PRATS' NA POSHANU IEVHENA VERTYPOROKHA.
No. 12. Toronto: Homin Ukrainy, 1972. 314 p. (UNO)

Skwarok, Josaphat J.

THE UKRAINIAN SETTLERS IN CANADA AND THEIR SCHOOLS, WITH
REFERENCE TO GOVERNMENT, FRENCH CANADIAN AND UKRAINIAN
MISSIONARY INFLUENCES, 1891-1921. Edmonton, 1959. 157 p.
(Metro; St. Vlad.; U of T)

Stechyshyn, Iuliian

LOVTSI DUSH: ABO KOLIEGIIA SV. IOSYFA V IORKTONI V SVITLI
FAKTIV. Saskatoon: published by the author, 1927. 35 p.
(Minn.; St. Vlad.)

_______.

UKRAINS'KYI INSTYTUT IM. P. MOHYLY V MYNULOMU I MAIBUTN'OMU.
Winnipeg: Trident Press, 1966. (Minn.)

St. Andrew's College, Winnipeg

KALENDAR I PROHRAMA NAVCHANNIA, 1973-1974. Winnipeg: Trident
Press, n.d. 32 p. (St. Vlad.)

_______.

KOLEGIIA SV. ANDREIA V VINNIPEGU. Winnipeg: St. Andrew's, 1962.
(St. Vlad.)

_______.

OFITSIINE VIDKRYTTIA KOLEHII SV. ANDREIA V VINNIPEGU NA
PLOSHCHI MANITOBS'KOHO UNIVERSYTETU 4-5 LYPNIA 1964r. Reprint.
Winnipeg: Trident Press, 1964. 80 p. (St. Vlad.)

_______.

PROMIN'. Yearbook of the St. Andrew's College students' club.
Winnipeg. (Minn.: 1946-51; St. Vlad.: 1949-50)

_______.

SLOVO: SVIATOCHNE VYD. STUDENTIV-BOHOSLOVIV V DEN' SVOHO
PATRONA SV. APOSTOLA ANDRIIA PERVOZVANNOHO. Winnipeg, 1957.
(Minn.)

St. John's Institute, Edmonton

RICHNYK STUDENTS'KOHO KRUZHKA PRY UKRAINS'KIM INSTYTUTI SV.
IVANA I VIDDILU SOIUZU UKRAINS'KOI MOLODI KANADY TA SOIUZU
UKRAINOK KANADY. 5 vols. Edmonton, 1950-54. (Minn.)

———.

RICHNYK STUDENTS'KOHO KRUZHKA PRY UKRAINS'KYM INSTYTUTI SV.
IVANA V EDMONTONI, 1963-1964. Edmonton, n.d. (Minn.)

———.

SOROKOLITTIA INSTYTUTU SV. IVANA V EDMONTONI, 1959. Edmonton:
Alberta Printing, 1959. 266 p. (Minn.; St. Vlad.)

St. Vladimir Institute, Toronto

PERED BRAMOIU: NARYS ISTORIŤ INSTYTUTU SV. VOLODYMYRA V TORONTI.
Toronto: St. Vladimir Instivute, 1969. 126 p. (St. Vlad.)

———.

TYKHYI IAR, 1958-1962. Hamilton, Ont.: Komitet litnikh kursiv
ukrainoznavstva, n.d. 22 p. (St. Vlad.)

Svirs'kyi, Nykon N.

TUDY LYNUT' NASHI SERTSIA: ISTORIIA MONDERS'KOHO MANASTYRIA.
Monder, Alta.: Basilian Fathers, 1963. (Minn.)

Taran'ko, Mykhailo, ed.

"Zi shkil'noho rukhu v Kanadi." In UCHYTEL': PEDAGOGICHNO-
NAUKOVYI ZBIRNYK. Vol. 1. Lviv: Uchytel's'ka organizatsiia, 1925.
(Minn.)

Tsentralia ukrains'koho shkil'nytstva v Kanadi

ZAVDANNIA UKRAINS'KOHO SHKIL'NYTSTVA V KANADI. Collection of
lectures and materials commemorating the 30th anniversary of
the P. Mohyla Institute in Saskatoon. Saskatoon, 1947. (Minn.)

Ukrainian Canadian Foundation of Taras Shevchenko

CHOTYRNADTSIATYI RICHNYI ZVIT NA DEN' 31 BEREZNIA, 1977. n.p.,
n.d. 64 p. (UNO)

———.

DEV'IATYI RICHNYI ZVIT NA DEN' 31 BEREZNIA, 1972. n.p., n.d.
38 p. (UNO)

———.

P'IATYI RICHNYI ZVIT NA DEN' 31-ho BEREZNIA, 1968. Winnipeg:
Ukrainian Canadian Foundation, 1968. (Minn.)

————.

VOS'MYI RICHNYI ZVIT NA DEN' 31-ho BEREZNIA, 1971. n.p., n.d.
36 p. (UNO)

UKRAINIAN CANADIANA. Edmonton: Ukrainian Women's Association of
Canada, 1976. 96 p. (St. Vlad.)

Ukrainian Free Academy of Sciences, Canada (UVAN)

LIST OF PUBLICATIONS OF THE UKRAINIAN FREE ACADEMY OF SCIENCES-UVAN
OF CANADA, INC. Winnipeg: UVAN, n.d. 15 p. (UNO)

Ukrainian National Federation

RIDNA SHKOLA: PLIAN I PROHRAMY. Winnipeg: Ukrainian National
Federation, Executive Committee, 1950. 23 p. (UNO)

Ukrainian National Home Association, Winnipeg

LITOPYS UKRAINS'KOHO-KANADIIS'KOHO 60-LITTIA: PROPAM'IATNA
KNYHA UKRAINS'KOHO NARODNOHO DOMU V VINNIPEGU, MAN. Winnipeg:
Ukrainian National Home, 1951. 38 p. (St. Vlad.)

————.

PROPAMIATNA KNYHA UKRAINS'KOHO NARODNOHO DOMU V VINNIPEGU.
Comp. by Semen Kovbel'. Ed. by D. Doroshenko. Winnipeg:
Ukrainian National Home, 1949. 863 p. (Metro; St. Vlad.; UNO;
U of T)

————.

SVIATKUVANNIA SOROKOLITTIA UKRAINS'KOHO NARODNOHO DOMU V
VINNIPEGU. Winnipeg: Ukrainian National Home, 1953. 57 p.
(Minn.; St. Vlad.)

UKRAINS'KA KNYZHKA I II POCHATKY V BRYTANS'KII KOLUMBII. Vancouver:
Ukrainian Fraternal Society, 1968. 64 p. (St. Vlad.; UNO)

Ukrainian Orthodox Church in Canada

Z DIIAL'NOSTY RADY UKRAINS'KOI SHKOLY ZA 1964-5 NAVCHAL'NYI RIK:
DOSHKILLIA, UKRAINS'KI SHKOLY I KURSY UKRAINOZNAVSTVA. Toronto,
1966. 44 p. (St. Vlad.)

UKRAINS'KE DOSHKILLIA: ZBIRNYK VYKHOVNYKH MATERIIALIV DLIA
UKRAINS'KYKH RODYN I DYTIACHYKH SADKIV. Ed. by Iaroslav Chumak.
Toronto: Dobra knyzhka, 1977. 471 p. (Metro)

UKRAINS'KI PROFESIONALISTY V AMERYTSI I V KANADI, 1935. Winnipeg:
Promin', 1935. (Minn.)

Voitsenko, Ol'ha, ed.

UKRAINA KENORS'KA: IUVILEINA KNYHA CHYTAL'NI TOVARYSTVA PROSVITA
IM. T. SHEVCHENKA ZA PERSHE 50-RICHCHIA, 1915-1965. Kenora, Ont.:
Prosvita, 1965. 296 p. (Minn.; St. Vlad.)

VYSHCHI OSVITNI KURSY. Winnipeg: Ukrainian National Federation,
Culture and Education Commission, 1944. 33 p. (Minn.; UNO)

Zelenyi, Zenon

PRATSIA UKRAINS'KYKH PEDAHOHIV U KANADI: U 20-RICHCHIA OUPK.
Toronto: Association of Ukrainian Educators in Canada, 1969.
45 p. (UNO)

Zhars'kyi, Edvard

UKRAINS'KA KUL'TURA I UKRAINS'KA VYKHOVNA SYSTEMA. Paper
presented at conference on Ukrainian culture in Toronto, March 29,
1964. Toronto-New York: Association of Ukrainian Educators in
Canada and the Educational Council of the Ukrainian Congress
Committee of America, 1964. 16 p. (UNO)

Organizations

Association of United Ukrainian Canadians (AUUC)

Prokop, Peter

FIFTY YEARS, 1918-1968: ASSOCIATION OF UNITED UKRAINIAN
CANADIANS. Toronto: AUUC National Committee, 1968. 49 p.
(Metro; St. Vlad.)

Federation of Ukrainian Social Democracy in Canada (FUSD)

FEDERATSIA UKRAINS'KOI SOTSIIAL-DEMOKRATII V KANADI: KONSTYTUTSIIA.
Winnipeg: FUSD, 1912. 20 p. (St. Vlad.)

Organization of Ukrainian Nationalists (OUN)

Kvitkovs'kyi, D., comp.

U 40-RICHCHIA OUN. Papers from the conference of Ukrainians of
America and Canada held in Detroit, Mich., September 1-3, 1969.
New York-Toronto: Organization for the Rebirth of Ukraine and
the Ukrainian National Federation of Canada, 1970. 98 p. (UNO)

Plast

______, Edmonton branch

P'IATNADTSIAT'-LITTIA PLASTU V EDMONTONI. Edmonton: Plast,
1963. 62 p. (Minn.; U of T)

______.

SHLIAKHOM DESIATYRICHCHIA. Edmonton: Plast, 1959. 82 p. (Minn.;
U of T)

______, Montreal branch

NASH PRAPOR. Montreal: Plast, 1965. (Minn.)

______, Toronto branch

Z PERSPEKTYVY PIATNADTSIATY ROKIV: PAMIATKOVE VYDANNIA Z NAHODY
15-RICHCHIA PLASTOVOI STANYTSI V TORONTO. Ed. by Iurii
Piasets'kyi and Omelian Tarnavs'kyi. Toronto, 1963. 100 p. (UNO)

Nemylivs'kyi, Volodymyr

SHUKH-TUR-PLASTUN. Toronto, 1963. 40 p. (Minn.; St. Vlad.;
UNO)

Paliiv, Ts'opa

NAPRIAMNI DLIA RICHNOHO PLIANU PRATSI U PLASTOVYKH Z'IEDNANNIAKH.
Zapysky ukrains'koho plastuna, no. 22. New York-Toronto: Molode
zhyttia, 1954. (Minn.)

PLAST NA POROZI SVOIOHO 60-LITTIA. Munich: Molode zhyttia, 1970.
(Minn.)

POSIBNYK ZV'IAZKOVOHO DLIA VYKHOVNOI PRATSI V ULADI PLASTUNIV
IUNAKIV. New York-Toronto: Plast, 1970. 471 p. (St. Vlad.)

Tysovs'kyi, Oleksander

ZHYTTIA V PLASTI: POSIBNYK DLIA UKRAINS'KOHO PLASTOVOHO
IUNATSTVA. 2nd enl. ed. Toronto-Detroit, 1961. 545 p. (UNO)

Soiuz het'mantsiv derzhavnykiv Ameryky i Kanady

————.

ZA UKRAINU: PODOROZH VEL'MOZHIVOHO PANA HET'MANYCHA DANYLA
SKOROPADS'KOHO DO ZLUCHENYKH DERZHAV AMERYKY I KANADY. Comp.
by Ivan Isaiv. Edmonton: Soiuz het'mantsiv derzhavnykiv,
1938. 318 p. (UNO)

Soiuz ukrains'koi molodi Kanady (SUMK)

————.

PROHRAMA NA LYSTOPADOVE SVIATO. Saskatoon, n.d. (Minn.)

Kohus'ka, Natalia Levenets', comp.

IUVILEINA KNYZHKA SOIUZU UKRAINS'KOI MOLODI KANADY: Z NAHODY
25-LITTIA HROMADS'KOI PRATSI PERSHOI ORGANIZATSII UKRAINS'KOI
MOLODI V KANADI, 1931-1956. Winnipeg: SUMK, 1956. 222 p.
(Minn.; St. Vlad.)

"Ukraina" Sport Association, Toronto

Khorostil', Ia.

BORITESIA-POBORETE: OHLIAD DIIAL'NOSTY SPORTOVOHO TOVARYSTVA
UKRAINA V TORONTI, KANADA, ZA ROKY 1948-1949. Toronto:
"Ukraina" Sport Association, 1950. 91 p. (St. Vlad.; UNO)

Ukrainian Canadian Committee (UCC/KUK)

——————.

CHARTER OF THE UKRAINIAN CANADIAN COMMITTEE, JUNE 28, 1963.
n.p., n.d. 7 p. (UNO)

——————.

KONFERENTSIIA SHYRSHOI RADY KOMITETU UKRAINTSIV KANADY.
Winnipeg, 1947. 84 p. (UNO; U of T)

——————.

MATERIIALY PEREDKONGRESOVOI RICHNOI KONFERENTSII KUK TORONTO.
Held at St. Vladimir Institute, December 4-6, 1970. n.p.,
n.d. (UNO)

——————.

PRATSIA I PRAVDA PEREMOZHE: PRO REPREZENTATSIINYI KOMITET KANADY.
Saskatoon: UCC, n.d. 31 p. (UNO)

——————.

ZBIRNYK MATERIIALIV I DOKUMENTIV U DVADTSIATYP'IATYLITTIA
DIIAL'NOSTY KUK, 1940-1965. Winnipeg: UCC, 1965. 310 p.
(St. Vlad.; UNO; U of T)

——————.

ZVIDOMLENNIA EKZEKUTYVNOHO DYREKTORA KOMITETU UKRAINTSIV KANADY
D-RA S. IA. KAL'BY, 1968-1971. Winnipeg: UCC, 1971. (St. Vlad.)

Kokhan, Volodymyr

ZBIRNYK MATERIIALIV I DOKUMENTIV U 25-LITTIA DIIAL'NOSTY KUK,
1940-1965. Winnipeg: UCC, 1965. 310 p. (UNO)

Ukrainian Canadian Committee, Congresses

FIRST ALL-CANADIAN CONGRESS OF UKRAINIANS IN CANADA. Winnipeg:
UCC, 1943. 210 p. (Metro; UNO; U of T)

SECOND ALL-CANADIAN CONGRESS OF UKRAINIANS IN CANADA. Winnipeg:
UCC, 1946. 190 p. (U of T)

PERSHYI VSE-KANADIIS'KYI KONGRES UKRAINTSIV KANADY. Winnipeg:
UCC, 1943. 216 p. (Minn.; UNO; U of T)

DRUHYI VSE-KANADIIS'KYI KONGRES UKRAINTSIV KANADY. Winnipeg:
UCC, n.d. 197 p. (St. Vlad.; UNO; U of T)

TRETII VSE-KANADIIS'KYI KONGRES UKRAINTSIV KANADY. Held in
Winnipeg, February 7-9, 1950. Winnipeg: UCC, n.d. 158 p.
(St. Vlad.; UNO; U of T)

REZOLIUTSII SKHVALENI III-m KONGRESOM UKRAINTSIV KANADY. Held in
Winnipeg, February 7-9, 1950. n.p., n.d. (UNO)

CHETVERTYI VSE-KANADIIS'KYI KONGRES UKRAINTSIV KANADY. Held in
Winnipeg, July 8-10, 1953. Winnipeg: UCC, n.d. 163 p. (St. Vlad.;
UNO; U of T)

P'IATYI I SHOSTYI VSE-KANADIIS'KYI KONGRESY UKRAINTSIV KANADY.
Winnipeg: UCC, 1959. 240 p. (St. Vlad.; UNO; U of T)

S'OMYI KONGRES UKRAINTSIV KANADY. Held in Winnipeg, July 5-7, 1962.
Winnipeg: UCC, 1962. 158 p. (UNO; U of T)

VOS'MYI KONGRES UKRAINTSIV KANADY. Held in Winnipeg, October 9-11,
1965. n.p.: UCC, 1965. 196 p. (U of T)

DEV'IATYI KONGRES UKRAINTSIV KANADY. Held in Winnipeg, October 11-14,
1968. n.p.: UCC, 1968. 183 p. (St. Vlad.; U of T)

DESIATYI KONGRES UKRAINTSIV KANADY. Held in Winnipeg, October 8-11,
1971. n.p.: UCC, 1971. 237 p. (U of T)

ODYNADTSIATYI KONGRES UKRAINTSIV KANADY. Winnipeg: UCC, 1974.
247 p. (St. Vlad.)

Ukrainian Canadian Foundation of Taras Shevchenko

______.

STATUT I PRAVYL'NYK FUNDATSII IM. T. SHEVCHENKA PRY UKRAINS'KOMU
VIDDILI CH. 360, KANADIIS'KOHO LEGIONU. Comp. by Stepan Pavliuk.
Toronto: Kiev Printers, 1958. 32 p. (UNO)

Ukrainian Canadian Relief Fund

______.

RICHNYI ZVIT DILOVOI SEKRETARKY ZA RIK 1946 I NARYS PLANU
PRATSI NA RIK 1947. Winnipeg, 1947. (UNO; U of T)

______.

RICHNYI ZVIT FONDU DOPOMOHY UKRAINTSIV KANADY ZA RIK 1947,
Winnipeg: Ukrainian Canadian Relief Fund, n.d. 46 p. (UNO)

______.

RICHNYI ZVIT FONDU DOPOMOHY UKRAINTSIV KANADY ZA 1948 RIK.
Winnipeg: Ukrainian Canadian Relief Fund, 1948. 16 p. (Minn.;
UNO)

Ukrainian Catholic Women's League of Canada/Liga ukrains'kykh katolyts'kykh zhinok Kanady

______, Toronto branch

NACHERK ISTORII LIGY UKRAINS'KYKH KATOLYTS'KYKH ZHINOK KANADY
TORONTS'KOI EPARKHII, 1945-1975. Toronto: Basilian Press,
1975. 360 p. (Metro; UNO)

Voitkiv, Mykhailyna

PRYCHYNKY DO ISTORII LIGY UKRAINS'KYKH KATOLYTS'KYKH ZHINOK
KANADY. Biblioteka Katolyts'koi aktsii, no. 21. Edmonton:
Catholic Action, 1952. 24 p. (U of T)

Ukrainian Democratic Youth Association (ODUM)

______.

AL'MANAKH-ZBIRNYK ODUM-u, 1950-1965. Toronto-Chicago-New York:
Moloda Ukraina, 1965. 228 p. (Minn.)

Ukrainian Fraternal Society of Canada

______.

CHARTER AND BY-LAWS AS ADOPTED BY THE FIRST CONVENTION OF THE
SOCIETY. Held in Winnipeg, February 25-26, 1944. Winnipeg:
Ukrainian Publishing Co. of Canada, n.d. 149 p. (UNO)

______.

PROTOKOL TRET'OI KONVENTSII UKRAINS'KOHO TOVARYSTVA VZAIMNOI
POMOCHI V KANADI, 1950. Winnipeg: Trident Press, 1950. 62 p.
(St. Vlad.)

______.

PROTOKOL P'IATOI KONVENTSII UKRAINS'KOHO TOVARYSTVA VZAIMNOI
POMOCHI V KANADI. Held in Edmonton, June 28-29, 1956. Winnipeg:
Ukrainian Fraternal Society, 1957. 61 p. (UNO)

______.

PROTOKOL SHESTOI KONVENTSII UKRAINS'KOHO TOVARYSTVA VZAIMNOI
POMOCHI V KANADI. Held in Winnipeg, August 6-7, 1959.
Winnipeg: Ukrainian Fraternal Society, 1959. 63 p. (UNO)

______.

PROTOKOLY VOS'MOI I DEV'IATOI KONVENTSII UKRAINS'KOHO
TOVARYSTVA VZAIMNOI POMOCHI V KANADI, 1965-1968. Winnipeg:
Trident Press, n.d. 112 p. (St. Vlad.; UNO)

______, Vancouver branch

BRYTIIS'KA KOLUMBIIA I UKRAINTSI. Commemorating the 30th
anniversary of the Vancouver branch of the Ukrainian Fraternal
Society of Canada, 1927-1957. Vancouver, 1957. 200 p. (St. Vlad.;
UNO; U of T)

Batyts'kyi, V., comp.

IUVILEINA KNYZHKA UKRAINS'KOHO TOVARYSTVA VZAIMNA POMICH: Z
NAHODY 10 ROKIV VID ODERZHANNIA DOMINIIAL'NOHO CHARTERU, 1925-
1935. Winnipeg: Ukrainian Fraternal Society, 1935. 112 p.
(Minn.; St. Vlad.; UNO; U of T)

Ukrainian Labour-Farmer Temple Association

NARADY UKRAINS'KYKH ROBITNYCHO-FARMERS'KYKH MASOVYKH ORHANIZATSII,
IAKI VIDBULYSIA V UKRAINS'KIM ROBITNYCHIM DOMI U VINNIPEGU, V
PONEDILOK, 11-ho BEREZNIA 1935 ROKU. n.p., n.d. (St. Vlad.)

ZVIT I REZOLIUTSII TRYNADTSIATOHO Z'IZDU TOVARYSTVA UKRAINS'KYI
   ROBITNYCHO-FARMERS'KYI DIM SHCHO VIDBUVSIA V DNIAKH 11 I 12
   LYPNIA 1932 ROKU V UKR. ROB. DOMI U VINNIPEGU. Winnipeg:
   Ukrainian Labour-Farmer Temple Association, 1932. 63 p. (St. Vlad.)

Civil Liberties Union of Toronto

   THE CASE OF THE SEIZED PROPERTIES OF THE UKRAINIAN LABOUR-FARMER
   TEMPLE ASSOCIATION: AN APPEAL FOR JUSTICE. Toronto, 1944. 32 p.
   (Metro)

Ukrainian Liberation Fund of Canada/
Ukrains'kyi vyzvol'nyi fond Kanady

______.

   ZVIT ZA ROKY 1958-1959. n.p., n.d. 12 p. (UNO)

______.

   ZVIT KRAIOVOHO KOMITETU UKRAINS'KOHO VYZVOL'NOHO FONDU KANADY
   ZA CHAS VID ZHOVTNIA 1975 RIK DO ZHOVTNIA 1978 RIK. Toronto,
   1978. 17 p. (UNO)

Ukrainian National Democratic Union (UNDO)

Lypovets'kyi, Ivan and Pavlo Step, eds.

   DESIATYLITNII SHLIAKH. Toronto: published by the authors,
   1958. 96 p. (Minn.; St. Vlad.; U of T)

Ukrainian National Federation of Canada (UNO)

______.

   A PROGRAM AND A RECORD. Saskatoon: UNO, 1943. 32 p. (U of T)

______.

   DVAD'TSIAT P'IAT LITTIA UNO: VELYKYI MUZYCHNYI FESTIVAL'.
   Toronto, 1957. (UNO)

______.

   MEMORIIAL UKRAINS'KOHO NATSIONAL'NOHO OB'IEDNANNIA DO KOROLIVS'KOI
   KOMISII V OTTAVI DLIA SPRAV DVOMOVNOSTY I DVOKUL'TURNOSTY.
   Toronto, 1964. 14 p. (UNO)

______.

PAM'IATKOVA KNYHA 22-ho ZAHAL'NOHO Z'IZDU UNO, 1966r. 56 p.
(UNO)

______.

PAM'IATKOVA KNYHA 23-ho KRAIOVOHO Z'IZDU UNO, 1969r. Winnipeg,
1969. (Minn.)

______.

PAM'IATKOVA KNYHA IUVILEINA: XVI KRAIOVA KONFERENTSIIA UNO,
1952r. Winnipeg, 1952. (UNO)

______.

PRAVYL'NYK KONFERENTSII I ZBORIV UNO. n.p., n.d. 8 p. (UNO)

______.

PRAVYL'NYK UKRAINS'KOHO NATSIONAL'NOHO OB'IEDNANNIA KANADY.
Winnipeg: UNO, 1952. 43 p. (UNO)

______.

PROHRAMY ZANIAT' DLIA VYKHOVNYKIV DOROSTU UKRAINS'KOHO NATSIONAL'NOHO
OB'IEDNANNIA I BRATNIKH ORHANIZATSII. Toronto: UNO, 1962-63. (UNO)

______.

REGULIAMIN UKRAINS'KOHO NATSIONAL'NOHO OB'IEDNANNIA KANADY.
n.p., 1947. 31 p. (UNO)

______.

STATUT UKRAINS'KOHO NATSIONAL'NOHO OB'IEDNANNIA KANADY.
Winnipeg: Ukrainian National Publishing Co., 1946. 33 p. (UNO)

______.

STATUT I PRAVYL'NYK UKRAINS'KOHO NATSIONAL'NOHO OB'IEDNANNIA
KANADY. Toronto, 1956. 37 p. (UNO)

______.

STATUT UKRAINS'KOHO NATSIONAL'NOHO OB'IEDNANNIA KANADY. Toronto,
1965. 22 p. (UNO)

————.

ZBIRNYK DOPOVIDEI STADIINOI KONFERENTSII UNO-ODVU-ZAREVO, 1963r.
Toronto: UNO, 1963. 91 p. (Minn.; UNO)

————.

ZBIRNYK MATERIIALIV XXII KRAIOVOHO Z'IZDU UNO I BRATNIKH
ORHANIZATSII. Toronto, 1966. 88 p. (Minn.; UNO)

————.

ZVIT Z DIIAL'NOSTY UNO KANADY ZA RIK 1962. Toronto, n.d. 52 p.
(UNO)

————.

ZVIT Z DIIAL'NOSTY UNO KANADY ZA RIK 1963. Toronto, n.d. 59 p.
(UNO)

————.

ZVIT Z DIIAL'NOSTY UNO KANADY ZA RIK 1964. Toronto, 1964. 68 p.
(UNO)

————.

ZVIT Z DIIAL'NOSTY UNO KANADY ZA RIK 1965. Toronto, n.d. 44 p.
(UNO)

————.

ZVIT Z DIIAL'NOSTY UNO KANADY ZA 1966 I 1967rr. Toronto, n.d.
90 p. (UNO)

————.

ZVIT Z DIIAL'NOSTY UNO KANADY ZA RIK 1968. Toronto, n.d. 42 p.
(UNO)

————.

ZVIT Z DIIAL'NOSTY PREZYDII UNO KANADY: ZA CHAS VID 21 TRAVNIA
1956r. DO 31 TRAVNIA 1960r. Toronto, 1960. 30 p. (UNO)

————.

ZVIT Z DIIAL'NOSTY KRAIOVOI EKZEKUTYVY UNO KANADY ZA RIK 1950.
Winnipeg, 1951. 52 p. (UNO)

————.

ZVIT Z DIIAL'NOSTY KRAIOVOI EKZEKUTYVY UNO KANADY ZA RIK 1952.
Winnipeg, 1954. 27 p. (UNO)

————.

ZVIT Z DIIAL'NOSTY KRAIOVOI EKZEKUTYVY UNO KANADY ZA RIK 1953.
Winnipeg, 1954. 34 p. (UNO)

————.

ZVIT Z DIIAL'NOSTY KRAIOVOI EKZEKUTYVY UNO KANADY ZA RIK 1954.
Toronto, 1955. 37 p. (UNO)

————.

ZVIT Z DIIAL'NOSTY KRAIOVOI EKZEKUTYVY UNO KANADY ZA RIK 1955.
Toronto, 1956. 38 p. (UNO)

————.

ZVIT Z DIIAL'NOSTY KRAIOVOI EKZEKUTYVY UNO KANADY ZA RIK 1956.
Toronto, 1957. 30 p. (UNO)

————.

ZVIT Z DIIAL'NOSTY KRAIOVOI EKZEKUTYVY UNO KANADY ZA RIK 1957.
Toronto, 1958. 34 p. (UNO)

————.

ZVIT Z DIIAL'NOSTY KRAIOVOI EKZEKUTYVY UNO KANADY ZA RIK 1958.
Toronto, 1959. 33 p. (UNO)

————.

ZVIT Z DIIAL'NOSTY KRAIOVOI EKZEKUTYVY UNO KANADY ZA RIK 1959.
Toronto, 1960. 41 p. (UNO)

————.

ZVIT Z DIIAL'NOSTY KRAIOVOI EKZEKUTYVY UNO KANADY ZA RIK 1960.
Toronto, 1961. 43 p. (UNO)

______.

ZVIT Z DIIAL'NOSTY KRAIOVOI EKZEKUTYVY UNO KANADY ZA RIK 1961.
Toronto, 1962. 49 p. (UNO)

______.

ZVIT Z DIIAL'NOSTY KRAIOVOI EKZEKUTYVY UNO KANADY ZA RIK 1962.
Toronto, n.d. 52 p. (St. Vlad.; UNO)

______.

ZVIT Z DIIAL'NOSTY KRAIOVOI EKZEKUTYVY UNO KANADY ZA RIK 1969.
Toronto, n.d. 73 p. (UNO)

______.

ZVIT Z DIIAL'NOSTY KRAIOVOI EKZEKUTYVY UNO KANADY ZA 1970-71
ROKY. Toronto, n.d. 76 p. (UNO)

______.

ZVIT Z DIIAL'NOSTY KRAIOVOI EKZEKUTYVY UNO KANADY ZA 1975-76
ROKY. Toronto, 1977. 99 p. (UNO)

______, Sudbury branch

IUVILEINA KNYHA 25-RICHCHIA FILII UNO V SUDBURY. Sudbury: UNO,
1957. 104 p. (St. Vlad.; UNO)

______, Toronto branch

PROPAMIATNA KNYZHKA. Toronto, 1950. (U of T)

Kossar, Volodymyr

DLIA NASHOHO DOBRA. Winnipeg: Ukrainian National Printing Co.,
1944. 47 p. (Minn.; St. Vlad.; UNO; U of T)

Matsenko, Pavlo, comp.

DUMKY PRO VEDENNIA KUL'TURNO-OSVITNOI PRATSI PO FILIAKH UNO V
KANADI. Saskatoon: UNO Committee for Culture and Education,
1940. 29 p. (UNO)

Pavlychenko, T.K.

RUKH NATSIONAL'NOI IEDNOSTY. UNO jubilee conference. Winnipeg:
UNO, 1952. 30 p. (Minn.; St. Vlad.; UNO)

Plaviuk, Mykola

PROBLEMY SVITOVOHO KONGRESU UKRAINTSIV. Winnipeg-Toronto: UNO,
1965. 20 p. (UNO)

Ukrainian National Youth Federation of Canada (UNYF)

————.

CONSTITUTION OF THE UKRAINIAN NATIONAL YOUTH FEDERATION OF
CANADA. Toronto, 1965. 48 p. (UNO)

————.

SEVEN PRESIDENTS IN UNIFORM. Winnipeg, 1945. 16 p. (UNO; U of T)

————.

ZASPIVAIMO RAZOM, BRATTIA: SPIVANYK DLIA UKRAINS'KOI MOLODI.
Winnipeg: UNYF Dominion Executive, n.d. 26 p. (UNO)

Gregorovich, Andrew Sviatoslav, ed.

UKRAINIAN NATIONAL YOUTH FEDERATION OF CANADA, 1934-1964,
PRESENTS THE LIFE OF A POET. A tribute to Shevchenko, at the
O'Keefe Centre, October 11, 1964. Toronto: UNYF, 1964. 64 p.
(U of T)

Ukrainian Revolutionary Democratic Party (URDP)

Koval', V., ed.

NA SUD UKRAINS'KOI EMIGRATSII "NATSIONAL-KOMUNIZM"--KHVYL'OVYZM
TA IOHO PROPOGATORIV: MATERIIALY Z PEREVEDENOI AKTSII V SShA I
V KANADI. New York: URDP, 1959. 64 p. (Minn.; St. Vlad.; UNO)

Ukrainian Riflemen's Society in Canada/ Ukrains'ka strilets'ka hromada v Kanadi (USHK)

————.

AL'MANAKH, 1928-1938. Saskatoon: USHK, 1938. 160 p. (Minn.;
UNO)

———.

NACHERK PIDRUCHNYK DLIA UKRAINS'KYKH MOLODSHYKH STARSHYN I
PIDSTARSHYN. Saskatoon: USHK, 1938. 413 p. (Minn.; UNO)

———.

SOROKARICHCHIA UKRAINS'KOI STRILETS'KOI HROMADY, VIDDILU CH.3
U MONTREALI. n.p., 1968. (UNO)

———.

UKRAINS'KA STRILETS'KA HROMADA V KANADI, 1928-1938. Saskatoon:
USHK, 1938. 160 p. (UNO)

Knysh, Zynovii, ed.

ZA CHEST', ZA SLAVU, ZA NAROD: ZBIRNYK NA ZOLOTYI IUVILEI
UKRAINS'KOI STRILETS'KOI HROMADY V KANADI, 1928-1978. Toronto:
USHK, 1978. 639 p. (St. Vlad.; UNO)

Viking, (?)

OSNOVY STRILETS'KOHO SPORTU. Pt. 1. Sudbury: USHK, 1939. 48 p.
(Minn.; UNO)

Ukrainian Self-Reliance League of Canada (USRLC/SUS)

———.

NA POROZI NOVOI DOBY. Papers read at the USRLC conference in
Winnipeg, December 23-25, 1944. Winnipeg: USRLC, 1945. 80 p.
(Minn.; St. Vlad.)

Batyts'kyi, V.

SHCHO IE SOIUZ UKRAINTSIV SAMOSTIINYKIV TA IOHO SOIUZNI
ORHANIZATSII? Winnipeg: USRLC, 1942. 23 p. (St. Vlad.)

Burianyk, W.

SUS: ITS MEANING AND SIGNIFICANCE. Toronto: USRLC, 1967. 40 p.
(Minn.; U of T)

Lazarovych, P.I.

SOIUZ UKRAINTSIV SAMOSTIINYKIV I UKRAINS'KA VYZVOL'NA SPRAVA.
Winnipeg: USRLC, 1951. 32 p. (Minn.; St. Vlad.)

_______.

STRUKTURA SOUIZU UKRAINTSIV SAMOSTIINYKIV (SUS) TA ROLIA
TOVARYSTVA UKRAINTSIV SAMOSTIINYKIV (TUS). Edmonton: USRLC,
1959. 11 p. (St. Vlad.)

Stechyshyn, Myroslav

SAMOSTIINIST', SOBORNIST', FEDERATSIIA. Lecture delivered at
the USRLC conferences in Winnipeg, Edmonton and Saskatoon,
December 25, 1941-January 1, 1942. Winnipeg: USRLC, 1942. 24 p.
(Minn.; UNO)

_______.

SOIUZ UKRAINTSIV SAMOSTIINYKIV V KANADI I OB'IEDNANNIA
UKRAINS'KOHO NARODU. Lecture delivered at the national conventions
in Saskatoon and Edmonton, December, 1932. Winnipeg: USRLC,
1933. (Minn.)

Telychko, K.

NASHI ZAVDANNIA. Edmonton: USRLC, 1961. 28 p. (Minn.; St. Vlad.)

Ukrainian Sich Riflemen (USS) in Canada

Soltykevych, Iaroslav

SALIUT OSTANN'OI SOTNI. In commemoration of the 50th anniversary
of the Ukrainian Sich Riflemen. Toronto: Ukrainian Sich Riflemen,
1964. 64 p. (Minn.; St. Vlad.; UNO)

Ukrainian Women's Association of Canada (UWAC/SUK)

_______.

IUVILEINA KNYHA Z NAHODY 30-LITN'OI DIIAL'NOSTY ZHINOCHOHO
TOVARYSTVA PRY KATEDRI SV. IVANA V EDMONTONI. A history of the
Ukrainian Women's Association, Edmonton branch, 1926-56. Ed. by
D.E. Iandova. Edmonton: Alberta Printing, 1956. 216 p. (St. Vlad.)

NA STOROZHI KUL'TURY. In commemoration of the 20th anniversary of
cultural work conducted by the Ukrainian Women's Association of
Canada. Winnipeg: UWAC, 1947. (Minn.)

Knysh, Irena

PERSHI KROKY NA EMIGRATSII. Winnipeg: Kultura i osvita, 1955.
39 p. (Minn.; U of T)

Kohus'ka, Natalia Levenets'

CHVERT' STOLITTIA NA HROMADS'KII NYVI, 1926-1951: ISTORIIA
SOIUZU UKRAINOK KANADY. Winnipeg: UWAC, 1952. 540 p. (Metro;
St. Vlad.; UNO; U of T)

______.

DOROHAMY SOROKRICHCHIA. Hamilton: UWAC, 1967. 32 p. (St. Vlad.;
U of T)

______, comp.

FORTY YEARS IN RETROSPECT, 1926-1966. Trans. by Sonia Cipywnyk.
Hamilton: UWAC, 1967. (Metro)

<u>Ukrainian Women's Organization of Canada/
Orhanizatsiia ukrainok Kanady im. Ol'hy Basarab</u> (OUK)

______.

XX KRAIOVA KONFERENTSIIA ORHANIZATSII UKRAINOK KANADY, 10-12
TRAVNIA 1963 V TORONTI. n.p., n.d. (UNO)

______.

IUVILEINA KNYHA 35-LITTIA OUK, 1930-1965. Toronto, 1965. 76 p.
(UNO)

______.

IUVILEI 40-RICHCHIA OUK. Toronto: Kiev Printers, 1970. (UNO)

______.

STATUT ORHANIZATSII UKRAINOK KANADY IM. OL'HY BASARABOVOI:
SKHVALENYI KK OUK DNIA 28 CHERVNIA 1937r. Saskatoon: New
Pathway Publishers, 1939. 16 p. (UNO)

______.

ZVIT Z DIIAL'NOSTY ORHANIZATSII UKRAINOK KANADY IM. OL'HY
BASARAB ZA ROKY 1965-1968. Toronto, n.d. (Minn.)

Knysh, Irena, ed.

NA SLUZHBI RIDNOHO NARODU: IUVILEINYI ZBIRNYK ORHANIZATSII
UKRAINOK KANADY IM. OL'HY BASARAB U 25-RICHCHIA VID ZASNUVANNIA,
1930-1955. Winnipeg: OUK, 1955. 500 p. (Minn.; UNO; U of T)

Ukrainian Youth Association (SUM) of Canada

———.

15-RICHCHIA OSEREDKU SPILKY UKRAINS'KOI MOLODI V MONTREALI,
1950-1965. Montreal, 1966. (Minn.)

DVADTSIAT' P'IAT' ROKIV SUM KANADY, 1948-1973. Toronto: SUM, 1973.
414 p. (UNO)

World Congress of Free Ukrainians (WCFU)/
Svitovyi kongres vil'nykh Ukraintsiv

———.

PERSHYI MANIFEST DO UKRAINS'KOHO NARODU V UKRAINI I POZA II
MEZHAMY V SSSR TA V KRAINAKH MOSKOVS'KOHO BL'OKU, 16-19
LYSTOPADA. New York, 1967. (Minn.)

———.

REZOLIUTSII: 16-19 LYSTOPADA. New York: WCFU, 1967. (Minn.)

———.

PERSHYI SVITOVYI KONGRES VIL'NYKH UKRAINTSIV. Winnipeg-New York-
London: WCFU, 1969. 479 p. (Minn.; St. Vlad.; U of T)

———.

SVITOVA VYKHOVNO-OSVITNIA SESIIA, 11-12 LYSTOPADA 1967r. n.p.,
1967. 32 p. (UNO)

———.

ZVERNENNIA DO UKRAINTSIV POZA UKRAINOIU SUSHCHYKH, 16-19
LYSTOPADA. New York, 1967. (Minn.)

Figol', Atanas

SVITOVYI KONGRES VIL'NYKH UKRAINTSIV. Paris-Rome-Munich, 1965.
(Minn.)

III. UKRAINIANS IN THE UNITED STATES

History

Amerykans'ki ukraintsi

   PROPAMIATNA KNYHA, 1843-1943. Philadelphia: Basilian Fathers,
   1943. (Minn.)

AMERYKANS'KYI PROSVITIANYN. Lviv, 1932. (Minn.)

Bachyns'kyi, Iuliian

   UKRAINS'KA IMMIGRATSIIA V Z'IEDYNENYKH DERZHAVAKH AMERYKY.
   Ukrains'ka emigratsiia, vol. 1. Lviv: Iuliian Bachyns'kyi and
   Oleksander Harasevych, 1914. 492 p. (Minn.; UNO)

Balaban, Viktor and Bohdan Hirka

   UKRAINTSI V TEKSASI: MATERIIALY DO ISTORII 200-RICHCHIA ZSA I
   100-RICHCHIA UKRAINTSIV V AMERYTSI. Ed. by Ivan Ovechko.
   Houston: Viktor Balaban, 1976. 160 p. (UNO)

BERI I CHITAI: NAPYSAV TVERDYI RUSYN. New York, 1908. (Minn.)

Bol'shak, Vasyl' Hryhoriiovych

   HUSAK NA BRODVEI. Kiev: Dnipro, 1970. 333 p. (Minn.)

Bratush, James D.

   A HISTORICAL DOCUMENTARY OF THE UKRAINIAN COMMUNITY OF
   ROCHESTER, NEW YORK. Trans. by Anastasia Smerychynska. Rochester:
   Christopher Press, 1973. 581 p. (Minn.; St. Vlad.)

Bykovs'kyi, Lev

   Z EVROPY DO AMERYKY: PODOROZHNI ZAMITKY, 1946-1948. Naukovo-
   doslidchyi instytut okeanichnoi Ukrainy, no. 20. Denver:
   Mariia Bykovs'ka, 1975. 136 p. (St. Vlad.; U of T)

Chemnyi, Mykhailo

   POTOPTANI MRII. Detroit, 1970. (Minn.)

Chupka, Iuliian

   DE-SHCHO PRO PRAVA I STUDY V SPOLUCHENYKH DERZHAVAKH, A
   OSOBENNO V DERZHAV PENNSIL'VENNIA (sic). Mt. Carmel, Pa.:
   Svoboda, 1898. (Minn.)

Chyz, Yaroslav J.

THE UKRAINIAN IMMIGRANTS IN THE UNITED STATES. Reprinted from
The Almanac of the Ukrainian Workingmen's Association for 1940.
(Minn.)

______, and Lewis Reed

AGENCIES ORGANIZED BY NATIONALITY GROUPS IN THE U.S. Reprinted
from The Annals of the American Academy of Political and
Social Sciences, March 1949. (Minn.)

CONFERENCE ON CARPATHO-RUTHENIAN IMMIGRATION, 1974. Proceedings
of the conference on Carpatho-Ruthenian immigration, June 8,
1974. Transcribed, edited and annotated by Richard Renoff and
Stephen Reynolds. Preface by Oscar Handlin. Sources and
Documents Series. Cambridge, Mass.: Harvard Ukrainian Research
Institute, 1975. 111 p. (Minn.; U of T)

Davis, Jerome Dwight

THE RUSSIANS AND RUTHENIANS IN AMERICA: BOLSHEVIKS OR BROTHERS?
Introd. by Charles Hatch Sears. New York: George H. Doran Co.,
1922. 155 p. (Metro; U of T)

Demydchuk, Semen

NE SKUIE DUSHI ZHYVOI. New York: Holovna ukrains'ka rada
(Office of the delegation from Vienna), 1915. (Minn.)

Derwinski, Edward J.

THE SHEVCHENKO STATUE OF LIBERTY IN THE NATION'S CAPITAL.
Speeches by Edward J. Derwinski et al. in the House and Senate.
Washington, D.C.: U.S. Government Printing Office, 1964.
149 p. (Minn.)

Derzhyruka, Volodymyr

NA TYKHI VODY, NA IASNI ZORI: STSENICHNYI OBRAZ Z ZHYTTIA
NARODU V CHOTYROKH DIIAKH, A ZIMOKII VIDCLONAKH. Narodna
biblioteka, nos. 3-4. Philadelphia: Ameryka, 1918. (Minn.)

Doklia, Teodor

NASHA HROMADA. Yonkers, N.Y., 1969. (Minn.)

Donchuk, Zosym

 LABOUR AND REWARD. Philadelphia: published by the author,
 1973. (Minn.)

Dubovyi, A.

 NA BAT'KIVSHCHYNI I NA CHUZHYNI: Z ISTORII UKRAINS'KYKH
 PIONERIV U NORT DAKOTI. Toronto-Chicago: Doroha pravdy, 1957.
 79 p. (Minn.; UNO)

______.

 "The Power of the Soil." (Minn.: general collection)

Halich, Wasyl

 THE UKRAINIAN AMERICANS: EARLY STRUGGLES, PERSONAL AND
 INSTITUTIONAL, 1865-1918. Paper presented before the annual
 convention of the Ukrainian Academy of Arts and Sciences in
 the U.S., May 24-25, 1969. (Minn.)

______.

 UKRAINIANS IN THE UNITED STATES. Chicago: University of Chicago
 Press, 1937. 174 p. (Minn.; St. Vlad.; UNO; U of T). Reprint.
 New York: Arno Press, 1970. (Metro; U of T)

______.

 UKRAINIANS IN WESTERN PENNSYLVANIA. Reprinted from Western
 Pennsylvania Historical Magazine, June 1935. (Minn.)

IAK STATY HOROZHANYNOM SPOLUCHENYKH DERZHAV. Jersey City, N.J.:
 Svoboda, n.d. (Minn.)

Iarovyi, Petro

 DLIA CHOHO PRYIKHAV DO AMERYKY BANDERIVS'KYI OPERETKOVYI
 "PREMIER," KHLESTAKOV I PROVOKATOR ABN? New York: Ukrains'ka
 vil'na informatsiia, 1952. (Minn.)

Iasinchuk, Lev

 ZA OKEIANOM: OSOBYSTI POMICHENNIA I PEREZHYVANNIA ZA CHAS
 ODNORICHNOHO POBUTU V AMERYTSI. Lviv: Ridna Shkola, 1930.
 255 p. (Minn.; UNO; U of T)

Ievtukh, Volodymyr Borysovych and Vasyl' Tkachenko

   V CHUZHII DALEKII STORONI. Kiev: Ukraina, 1976. 42 p. (U of T)

Ilnytzkyj, Roman

   PRYZNACHENNIA UKRAINTSIV V AMERYTSI. New York: Taras Hunchak,
   1965. 126 p. (Minn.; UNO; U of T)

Isaiv, Vsevolod V.

   SOCIAL STATUS OF RECENT UKRAINIAN IMMIGRANTS IN PHILADELPHIA:
   A STUDY IN ASSIMILATION. Philadelphia, 1955. 68 leaves. (U of T)

_____, ed.

   UKRAINTSI V AMERYKANS'KOMU TA KANADS'KOMU SUSPIL'STVAKH:
   SOTSIOLOHICHNYI ZBIRNYK. Ukrains'kyi sotsiolohichnyi instytut,
   Pratsi (Works of the Ukrainian Sociological Institute), vol. 1.
   Jersey City, N.J.: M.P. Kots', 1976. 360 p. (St. Vlad.; UNO;
   U of T)

Kernyts'kyi, Ivan

   PERELETNI PTAKHY. Literaturna biblioteka IUt, no. 6. New York:
   Iurii Tyshchenko, 1952. 141 p. (Minn.; U of T)

Klodnycky, Vladimir

   THE SOVEREIGN UKRAINIAN STATE AND UKRAINIAN IMMIGRATION ABROAD.
   Newark, N.J.: Ukrainian-American Citizens' League of New
   Jersey, 1945. (Minn.: Klodnycky manuscript collection)

Ko, Vasyl'

   VSE DLIA SEBE, A SHCHO DLIA UKRAINY? New York, 1952. (Minn.)

Koenig, Samuel

   "Ukrainians in the United States." In SLAVONIC ENCYCLOPEDIA,
   pp. 1330-33. Ed. by Joseph S. Roucek. New York, 1949. (Minn.)

Kovalchuk, Pavlo

   CRIMINAL HIRELINGS. Trans. by George Semeniuk. Kiev: Ukraina
   Society, 1975. 32 p. (U of T)

Kuropas, Myron

THE UKRAINIANS IN AMERICA. In America Series. Minneapolis:
Lerner Publications, 1972. (Minn.; St. Vlad.)

Kyrylenko, Orest

UKRAINTSI V AMERYTSI. Vienna: League for the Liberation of
Ukraine, 1916. 40 p. (Minn.)

Kysil', Hnat

SHCHO BUDE V KRAIU PO SKINCHENNIU VIINY. New York: Ukrainian
Publishing Co., n.d. (Minn.)

Marchenko, Iaroslav

V OBORONI UKRAINY. New York: Hlas, 1970. (Minn.)

Margolin, Arnold Davidovich

DERZHAVNYI USTRII SPOLUCHENYKH SHTATIV AMERYKY. New York:
UVAN in the U.S., 1956. 93 p. (Minn.)

Mudry, Vasyl'

"Ukrainian Immigration in the U.S.A." In GUIDE TO UKRAINIAN-
AMERICAN INSTITUTIONS, PROFESSIONALS AND BUSINESS, pp. 5-17.
Ed. by Wasyl Weresh. New York, 1955. (Minn.)

Musiichuk, Stepan

V BOROT'BI ZA VOLIU. Chicago, 1925. (Minn.)

Mykhailovych, Antin

NA INSHYKH KONTYNENTAKH. Feldkirch, Austria: Zahrava, 1946.
(Minn.)

Nastasivs'kyi, M.

SHCHO DAL'SHE ROBYTY: ZAPOMOHOVOHO RUKHU SERED UKRAINS'KOI
EMIHRATSII V SPOLUCHENYKH DERZHAVAKH. New York: Ukrains'ka
robitnycha knyharnia, 1937. (Minn.)

_______.

UKRAINS'KA IMIGRATSIIA V SPOLUCHENYKH DERZHAVAKH. New York:
Soiuz ukrains'kykh robitnychykh orhanizatsii, 1934. 256 p.
(Minn.; UNO; U of T)

Olearchyk, Renata Maria S.

TYPES OF ETHNIC IDENTIFICATION AND GENERATIONAL POSITION: A
STUDY OF THE UKRAINIAN IMMIGRANT GROUP IN THE USA. Offprint.
Liverpool: Association of Ukrainians in Great Britain, 1971.
72 p. (Minn.; St. Vlad.)

Pavlovs'ka, Iryna

NA HROMAD'SKYI SHLIAKH: Z NAHODY 70-LITTIA UKRAINS'KOHO
ZHINOCHOHO RUKHU. Philadelphia: Svitova federatsiia ukrains'kykh
orhanizatsii, 1956. (Minn.)

PIDRUCHNYK HROMADIANSTVA. Biblioteka suspil'noi sluzhby ZUADK,
   no. 2. Philadelphia: United Ukrainian-American Relief Committee,
   1954. (Minn.)

POBUT PREZYDENTA UKRAINS'KOI NATSIONAL'NOI RADY V EKZYLI, D-RA
   S. VYTVYTS'KOHO, V MINNEAPOLISI TA SEINT-POLI, TRAVEN' 1962r.
   Minneapolis, 1962. (Minn.)

Prokhoda, Vasyl'

ZAPYSKY NEPOKIRLYVOHO. Toronto: Proboiem, 1967. 434 p. (Metro;
Minn.; St. Vlad.; UNO)

Prystai, O.

Z TRUSKAVTSIA U SVIT KHMARODERIV. 4 vols. Lviv-New York:
published by the author, 1933, 1935-37. (Minn.; UNO)

REPRESENTATIVE SURVEY OF COMMENT APPEARING IN THE UKRAINIAN PRESS
   IN THE U.S., CANADA AND EUROPE REGARDING THE UKRAINIAN PROGRAM
   OF VOICE OF AMERICA. n.p., n.d. (Minn.)

Rudnyts'kyi, Iaroslav Bohdan

Z PODOROZHI PO AMERYTSI, 1956. Kliub pryiateliv ukrains'koi
knyzhky, vol. 29. Winnipeg: Ivan Tyktor, 1956. 128 p. (St. Vlad.;
UNO; U of T)

Shapoval, Mykyta Iukhymovych

STARA I NOVA UKRAINA: LYSTY V AMERYKU. New York: Ukrains'ka
hromada, 1925. 32 p. (Minn.)

Shtohryn, Dmytro M., ed.

UKRAINIANS IN NORTH AMERICA: A BIBLIOGRAPHICAL DIRECTORY OF
NOTEWORTHY MEN AND WOMEN OF UKRAINIAN ORIGIN IN THE UNITED
STATES AND CANADA. Champaign, Ill.: Association for the
Advancement of Ukrainian Studies, 1975..424 p. (Metro; UNO;
U of T)

Sichyns'kyi, Myroslav

NARODNA SPRAVA V AMERYTSI. New York: Ukrainian Printing and
Publishing Assn., 1919. 23 p. (Minn.; U of T)

Skchar, Hryhorii G.

PO AMERYTSI/ACROSS AMERICA. 2nd ed. Winnipeg: I. Andrusiak,
1940. 224 p. (Minn.; UNO)

Skubova, Mariia

SPOMYNY. Toronto, 1950. (Minn.)

Stakhiv, Matvii

NASHE MYNULE I MAIBUTNIE V AMERYTSI. Scranton, Pa., 1950.
(Minn.)

Stasiuk, Platon

V NOVOMU SVITI: SPOMYNY I DUMKY BYZNESMENA. New York, 1958.
158 p. (Metro; Minn.; St. Vlad.; UNO; U of T)

Stechyshyn, Myroslav

SMERT' ZA 8-HODYNNYI DEN' PRATSI: PODIIA 11 NOVEMBRA 1887r.
Winnipeg: Robochyi narid, 1910. (Minn.)

THE UKRAINIANS IN AMERICA, 1608-1975: A CHRONOLOGY AND FACT BOOK.
Comp. and ed. by Vladimir Wertsman. Ethnic Chronology Series,
no. 25. Dobbs Ferry, N.Y.: Oceana Publications, 1976. 140 p.
(U of T)

TSINNI INFORMATSII DLIA RIL'NYKIV TA ROBITNYKIV RUSYNIV. Del Rio,
    Texas: American government land syndicate, n.d. (Minn.)

Tsymbalistyi, Bohdan
    PROBLEMA IDENTYCHNOSTY: UKRAINA CHY AMERYKA? Chicago: Ukrainian
    Research and Information Institute, 1974. 56 p. (U of T)

Tyshovnyts'kyi, Omelian Mykhailo
    MOI PAM'IATKY. Los Angeles, 1974. 518 p. (Minn.; U of T)

Ukrainian Civic Center, Rochester, N.Y.
    VIL'NI KOZAKY. Rochester: Ukrainian National Home, 1970.
    352 p. (U of T)

UKRAINIANS IN PENNSYLVANIA: A CONTRIBUTION TO THE GROWTH OF THE
    COMMONWEALTH. Philadelphia: Ukrainian Bicentennial Committee,
    1976. 134 p. (St. Vlad.)

United American Ukrainian Organizations Committee of New York
    ZOLOTA IUVILEINA KNYHA, VYDANA Z NAHODY 50-LITTIA ZORHANIZOVANOHO
    UKRAINS'KOHO HROMADS'KOHO ZHYTTIA V NIU IORKU, 1950-1955. Ed.
    by O. Sokolyshyn. New York, 1956. 192 p. (Minn.)

U.S. Congress, House Committee on the Judiciary
    DISPLACED PERSONS ACT: PUBLIC LAW 774, EIGHTIETH CONGRESS,
    JUNE 25, 1948. With amendments of June 16, 1950: Public Law
    555, 81st Congress and Notes of Amendments, June 17, 1950.
    Washington, D.C.: U.S. Government Printing Office, 1950. (Minn.)

V KRAINI VOLI: PIDRUCHNYK DLIA NOVYKH IMIGRANTIV. Jersey City,
    N.J.: Ukrainian National Association, 1949. 31 p. (Minn.; UNO)

Verkhovynets', M.
    IDESH, BRATE MII. Pittsburgh: Beskyd, 1957. 80 p. (Minn.; UNO)

Wichorek, Michael and Martha Wichorek
    UKRAINIANS IN DETROIT. Detroit: published by the authors,
    1968. 192 p. (Minn.; St. Vlad.)

Autobiographies/Biographies

General

DIRECTORY OF UKRAINIAN PROFESSIONALS IN THE UNITED STATES.
n.p.: Ukrainian Professionals Association of the U.S.,
1939. (Minn.)

Individual

Vasyl' Avramenko

Kobers'kyi, Ivan
DVA VECHERI AVRAMENKA. Winnipeg, 1927. 11 p. (UNO)

Lev Bykovs'kyi

______.

U SLUZHBAKH UKRAINS'KII KNYZHTSI. Bio-bibliography. Denver,
1972. 275 p. (Minn.; U of T)

Vasyl' Chaplenko

Ovechko, Ivan, comp.
VASYL' CHAPLENKO: ZBIRNYK Z NAHODY IOHO 75-RICHCHIA. New York,
1975. 203 p. (U of T)

Mykola Chubatyi

Zhdan, Mykhailo
MYKOLA CHUBATYI: Z NAHODY 80-LITTIA. Ukrains'ki vcheni (UVAN
Ukrainian Scholars Series), no. 2. Munich-New York: Ukrainian
Historical Association, 1970. (Minn.)

Volodymyr Galan

______.

   BATERIIA SMERTY. New York: Chervona kalyna, 1970. 239 p.
   (Metro; Minn.; UNO; U of T)

Anatol' Hak

______.

   VID HULIAI-POLIA DO NIU-IORKU: SPOHADY. Philadelphia: Ukrainian
   News, 1973. 326 p. (Metro; St. Vlad.)

Ahapii Honcharenko

______.

   SPOMYNKY. Edmonton: Slavuta Publishing, 1965. 18 p. (Minn.)

Lutsiv, Theodore
   FATHER AGAPIUS HONCHARENKO: FIRST UKRAINIAN PRIEST IN AMERICA.
   Introd. by Walter Dushnyk. New York: Ukrainian Congress
   Committee of America, 1970. 223 p. (Minn.)

______, and Vasyl' Lutsiv
   AHAPIUS HONCHARENKO AND THE ALASKA HERALD. Toronto: Slavia
   Library, 1963. 120 p. (Minn.; UNO; U of T)

John Hundiak

St. Demetrius Ukrainian Church, Carteret, N.J.
   TESTIMONIAL DINNER GIVEN BY THE BOARD OF TRUSTEES AND AFFILIATED
   ORGANIZATIONS OF THE ST. DEMETRIUS UKRAINIAN CHURCH HONORING
   THE VERY REV. FR. JOHN HUNDIAK. Carteret, N.J., 1957. (Minn.)

Ivan Kedryn

______.

   ZHYTTIA-PODII-LIUDY: SPOMYNY I KOMENTARI. New York: Chervona
kalyna, 1976. 724 p. (Metro; UNO; U of T)

Vasyl' Kuziv

Bykovs'kyi, Lev

   VASYL' KUZIV, 1887-1958: IOHO ZHYTTIA I DIIAL'NIST. Toronto-
Detroit, 1966. 103 p. (Minn.)

Bishop Kyr Bohdan

Ukrainian Orthodox Church in America

   SOBOR UKRAINS'KOI PRAVOSLAVNOI TSERKVY V AMERYTSI: I DVADTSIAT'
LITNYI IUVILEI VLADYKY KYR BOHDANA, 1957. Allentown, Pa., 1957.
(Minn.)

Kalenyk Lysiuk

POLITYCHNA, KUL'TURNA TA HROMADS'KA DIIAL'NIST' KALENYKA LYSIUKA,
   1887-1967. Cleveland: Ukrainian Museum-Archives, 1967. 45 p.
(Minn.; U of T)

Peter Mayevsky

St. Vladimir's Ukrainian Orthodox Parish, Los Angeles

   FORTY-FIFTH ANNIVERSARY OF THE REBIRTH OF THE CHURCH IN UKRAINE,
1921-1966. FORTY-FIFTH ANNIVERSARY OF THE PRIESTHOOD OF REV. P.
MAYEVSKY, 1921-1966. TWENTIETH ANNIVERSARY OF THE PARISH OF
ST. VLADIMIR, 1946-1966. Los Angeles, 1966. 240 p. (Minn.;
UNO; U of T)

————.

GOLDEN JUBILEE SOUVENIR: FIFTIETH ANNIVERSARY OF THE HOLY
PRIESTHOOD OF REV. PETER MAYEVSKY. FIFTIETH ANNIVERSARY OF THE
REBIRTH OF THE CHURCH IN UKRAINE. TWENTY-FIFTH ANNIVERSARY OF
THE PARISH OF ST. VLADIMIR. n.p., 1971. (St. Vlad.)

Luke Myshuha

Dragan, Antin

LUKA MYSHUHA: ZBIRNYK. Jersey City, N.J.: Svoboda, 1973. 355 p.
(Metro; Minn.; St. Vlad.; U of T)

Ivan Ovechko

PEROM I SLOVOM: IVAN OVECHKO U DZERKALI 25-RICHNOI DIIAL'NOSTY
   ZA OKEANOM, 1950-1975. Los Angeles: Jubilee Committee, 1975.
   291 p. (U of T)

Michelo (Michael) Panchuk

Panchuk, John

DESCENDANTS OF MICHELO (MICHAEL) PANCHUK OF ONUT, BUKOVINA,
UKRAINE. Battle Creek, Mich., 1975. (Minn.)

Michael Paukiw

Sokolyszyn, Aleksander

UKRAINS'KI VIRSHI MYKHAILA PAN'KOVA. New York: published by
friends of the author, 1958. 16 p. (Minn.)

P.I. Porzhy-Oleksiienko

————.

50-LIT NA EMIHRATSII NA SLUZHBI BAT'KIVSHCHYNI. Denver, 1971.
286 p. (Minn.; UNO)

Oleksa Remez

________.

CHEREZ KORDON: Z DNEVNYKA EMIHRANTA. Scranton, Pa.: Antin
Bohchevsky Publishing Co., 1906. (Minn.)

Roman Smal'-Stocki

Dushnyk, Walter, ed.

PROFESSOR ROMAN SMAL'-STOCKI AND HIS CONTRIBUTIONS TO THE
UKRAINIAN NATION. Ukrainian Studies Series, vol. 17. English
Section, vol. 8. New York: Shevchenko Scientific Society,
1970. 69 p. (Minn.; U of T)

Oleksa Stefanovych

Antonovych-Rudnyts'ka, Maryna

OLEKSA STEFANOVYCH. Literatura series, no. 11. Winnipeg: UVAN,
1970. 20 p. (U of T)

Mykola Sydor-Chartoryis'kyi

________.

MANDRY ZHYTTIA. Vol. 1. New York: Chartoryis'kyi Publishers,
1973. (Metro; U of T)

2nd ed.: 3 vols. 1973-75. (St. Vlad.)

John Basil Turchin

Horodys'kyi, Orest

HENERAL IVAN VASYL'OVYCH TURCHYN: OSOBYSTYI PRYIATEL'
PREZYDENTA LINKOL'NA. New York: Chervona kalyna, 1971. 16 p.
(Minn.)

Joseph Zelechivs'kyi

THIRTIETH ANNIVERSARY, 1919-1949: THE REVEREND FATHER ZELECHIVSKY,
PASTOR OF ST. JOHN'S AND ST. STEPHEN'S UKRAINIAN ORTHODOX
PARISHES. Providence and Manville, R.I., 1949. (Minn.)

FORTIETH ANNIVERSARY OF THE HOLY PRIESTHOOD OF THE VERY REVEREND
    FATHER ZELECHIVSKY, PASTOR OF ST. JOHN'S AND ST. STEPHEN'S
    UKRAINIAN ORTHODOX PARISHES, 1919-1959. Providence and Manville,
    R.I., 1959. (Minn.)

Iaroslav Zubal'

———.

    MYSLYVS'KI SPOHADY. Wallingford, Pa.: published by the author,
    1971. 147 p. (Metro; UNO; U of T)

Economic Life

Halich, Wasyl

ECONOMIC ASPECTS OF UKRAINIAN ACTIVITY IN THE UNITED STATES.
Ph.D. dissertation, University of Iowa, 1934. (Minn.)

______.

"Ukrainian Farmers in the United States." In AGRICULTURAL
HISTORY, 10, no. 1 (January 1963), pp. 25-39. (Minn.)

UKRAINS'KA KOOPERATSIIA DO DOBRA I KRASY. Conference proceedings
of the Verkhovyna co-operatives, 1969. Chicago: Samopomich,
1969. (Minn.)

UKRAINS'KO AMERYKANS'KE KOOPERATYVNE TOVARYSTVO "SAMODOPOMOHA" V
CHIKAGO TA OSELIA V RAVNO-LEIKU. n.p., n.d. (Minn.)

Religious Life

Ukrainian Evangelical-Baptist Church and Others

Pasichnyk, Ivan

UKRAINS'KYI VIDDIL PRY TEOLOHICHNII SEMINARII V BLUMFIL'DI:
SPOMYNY. Ramsey, N.J.-Toronto: Harmony Printing, 1974. 149 p.
(UNO)

PERSHA UKRAINS'KA PRESVYTERS'KA TSERKVA SV. PETRA I PAVLA V
NIUARKU, N. DZH. n.p., n.d. 29 p. (St. Vlad.)

Podvorniak, Mykhailo

NEBESNYI DIM: PAM'IATI TYKH "SHCHO VAM HOVORYLY BULO SLOVO
BOZHE." Doroha pravdy, no. 33. Chicago-Winnipeg: Doroha pravdy,
1965. 240 p. (Minn.)

UKRAINS'KYI IEVANHEL'S'KYI RUKH: Z NAHODY VIDKRYTTIA PAM'IATNYKA
TARASOVI SHEVCHENKOVI DNIA 27 CHERVNIA 1964 ROKU U VASHYNGTONI.
Hartford, Conn.: Nash pryiatel', 1964. (Minn.)

Ukrainian Orthodox Churches*

DIRECTORY OF EASTERN ORTHODOX CHURCHES: UNITED STATES, CANADA AND
MEXICO. Detroit: Council of Eastern Orthodox Youth Leaders of
the Americas,n.d. (Minn.)

Harashchenko, Ivan

1921-1971: MATERIALY DO ISTORII UKRAINS'KOI AVTOKEFAL'NOI
PRAVOSLAVNOI TSERKVY. Chicago: Ukrainian Orthodox Brotherhood
of Metropolitan Vasylii Lypkivs'kyi, 1975. 440 p. (St. Vlad.)

Holy Trinity Ukrainian Orthodox Church, Boston

FACTS ABOUT UKRAINE. Boston, 1939(?) (Minn.)

Hryshchyshyn, Bohdan

TEN YEARS' GROWTH OF THE UKRAINIAN ORTHODOX LEAGUE OF THE U.S.A.
South Bound Brook, N.J., 1958. (Minn.)

---

* Includes the Ukrainian Orthodox Church of the USA (Ukrains'ka
pravoslavna tserkva v SShA) and the Ukrainian Orthodox Church
in America (Ukrains'ka pravoslavna tserkva v Amerytsi/Ameryky/v ZDA).

Hubarzhevs'kyi, Ihor

> ZAKHODY SHCHODO POIEDNANNIA UKRAINS'KYKH PRAVOSLAVNYKH
> IURYSDYKTSII. New York: Nasha bat'kivshchẏna, 1968. 61 p.
> (UNO; U of T)

St. Andrew Ukrainian Orthodox Church, Boston

> PROPAM'IATNA KNYHA. Boston, 1959. (Minn.)

St. John's Ukrainian Orthodox Church, Johnson City, N.Y.

> TWENTY-FIFTH ANNIVERSARY, 1926-1951. n.p., n.d. (Minn.)

St. Mary Protectress Ukrainian Orthodox Church, Philadelphia

> PROPAMIATNA KNYHA, 1950-1960. Philadelphia, 1960. (Minn.)

St. Michael's Ukrainian Orthodox Church, Hammond, Ind.

> SILVER JUBILEE, 1937-1962. Hammond, 1962. (Minn.)

St. Michael's Ukrainian Orthodox Church, Woonsocket, R.I.

> BLESSING AND DEDICATION OF INTERIOR OF ST. MICHAEL'S,
> SEPTEMBER 5, 1954. Woonsocket, 1954. (Minn.)

St. Sophia Ukrainian Orthodox Church, Chicago. Brotherhood of
St. George the Conqueror

> PROPAMIATNA KNYHA: VYDANA Z NAHODY POSVIACHENNIA PRAPORA
> BRATSTVA, 1963r. Chicago, 1963. (Minn.)

St. Vladimir's Ukrainian Orthodox Cathedral, Chicago

> PROPAM'IATNA KNYHA Z NAHODY 50-LITTIA. Chicago: Ukrains'ko-
> amerykans'ka vydavnycha spilka, 1966. 112 p. (St. Vlad.)

St. Vladimir's Ukrainian Orthodox Church, Ambridge, Pa.

> FIFTIETH ANNIVERSARY: JUNE 31, 1975. Ambridge, 1975. (St. Vlad.)

St. Vladimir's Ukrainian Orthodox Church, New York

> PROPAMIATNA KNYHA, 1926-1944. New York, 1944(?) (Minn.)

St. Vladimir's Ukrainian Orthodox Parish, Los Angeles

FORTY-FIFTH ANNIVERSARY OF THE REBIRTH OF THE CHURCH IN
UKRAINE, 1921-1966. FORTY-FIFTH ANNIVERSARY OF THE PRIESTHOOD
OF REV. P. MAYEVSKY, 1921-1966. TWENTIETH ANNIVERSARY OF THE
PARISH OF ST. VLADIMIR, 1946-1966. Los Angeles, 1966. 240 p.
(Minn.; UNO; U of T)

————.

GOLDEN JUBILEE SOUVENIR: FIFTIETH ANNIVERSARY OF THE HOLY
PRIESTHOOD OF REV. PETER MAYEVSKY. FIFTIETH ANNIVERSARY OF
THE REBIRTH OF THE CHURCH IN UKRAINE. TWENTY-FIFTH ANNIVERSARY
OF THE PARISH OF ST. VLADIMIR. n.p., 1971. (St. Vlad.)

THE UKRAINIAN CHURCH AT CALVARY. New York, 196(?). 15 p. (U of T)

Trinity Ukrainian Orthodox Church, Buffalo

P'IAT' ROKIV, SVIATO: TROITS'KOI UKRAINS'KOI PRAVOSLAVNOI
TSERKVY V BOFALO, 1950-1955. n.p., n.d. (Minn.)

Ukrainian Orthodox Church in America

ZVIT PRO PIATYI SOBOR UKRAINS'KOI PRAVOSLAVNOI TSERKVY
ZLUCHENYKH DERZHAV AMERYKY, 7-9 CHERVNIA 1936. New York, 1936.
(Minn.)

Ukrainian Orthodox Church of the USA

KHAI BUDE VIDOMO VSIM.... New York: Jubilee Committee of
Orthodox Ukrainians, 1971. (Minn.)

Ukrainian Catholic (Uniate) Church

THE CATHOLIC DIRECTORY. Philadelphia: Archeparchy of Philadelphia,
Byzantine rite, 1955, 1956, 1959, 1961. (Minn.)

Dragan, A.

OUR UKRAINIAN CARDINAL. Jersey City, N.J.: Ukrainian National
Association and Svoboda, 1966. 88 p. (Minn.)

Dushnyk, Walter

THE UKRAINIAN-RITE CATHOLIC CHURCH AT THE ECUMENICAL COUNCIL,
1962-1965. New York-Paris-Winnipeg: Shevchenko Scientific
Society, 1967. 191 p. (Metro; Minn.)

KATEKHYZM DLIA PARAFIIAL'NYKH SHKIL I VIRNYKH UKRAINS'KOI KATOLYTS'KOI
EKZARKHII V ZLUCHENYKH DERZHAVAKH AMERYKY. Philadelphia, 1954.
(Minn.)

Markus, Vasyl'

KONSTYTUTSIIA POMISNOI UKRAINS'KOI KATOLYTS'KOI TSERKVY:
ANALIZA I KOMENTA. Chicago: Brotherhood of St. Andrii
Pervozvannyi, 1975. 40 p. (U of T)

_______.

SYNOD I POSYNODAL'NA DIISNIST' V UKRAINS'KII KATOLYTS'KII
TSERKVI. Chicago: Brotherhood of St. Andrii Pervozvannyi,
1970. 40 p. (Minn.)

POSLANIIE PASTYRSKE SOTERA ORTYN'SKOHO IEPYSKOPA DLIA HREKO-
KATOLYKOV V SPOLUCHENYKH DERZHAVAKH PIVNOCHNOI AMERYKY DO
VSEHO HREKOKATOLYTSKOHO SVIASHEN'STVA I VSIEKH HREKOKATOLYTSKYKH
VIERNYKH Z NAHODY BULLY. Philadelphia, 1908. (Minn.)

Ruthenian Church in America

UNIIA V AMERYTSI. New York: Narodnyi fond, 1902. 73 p. (U of T)

Smyk, Roman

DRUHA PATRIIARSHA VIZYTATSIIA IKH BLAZHENSTVA IOSYFA I V 1973
ROTSI. Chicago: Brotherhood of St. Andrii Pervozvannyi, 1974.
(Minn.)

_______.

UKRAINS'KA KATOLYTS'KA TSERKVA U VIL'NOMU SVITI. 2nd ed.
Chicago: Brotherhood of St. Andrii Pervozvannyi, 1972. (Minn.)

St. John's Ukrainian Catholic Church, Pittsburgh

DIAMOND JUBILEE. Pittsburgh, 1967. (Minn.)

St. Nicholas Ukrainian Catholic Cathedral, Chicago

FINANCIAL REPORT, 1968. Chicago, 1968. (Minn.)

St. Nicholas Ukrainian Catholic Church of the Byzantine Rite,
Minersville, Pa.
   SIXTIETH JUBILEE, 1896-1956. Minersville, 1956. (Minn.)

St. Vladimir's Ukrainian Catholic Church, Stamford, Conn.
   FIFTIETH ANNIVERSARY, 1916-1966. Stamford, 1966. (Minn.)

Ss. Peter and Paul Catholic Church of the Byzantine Rite, Chisholm,
Minn.
   GOLDEN JUBILEE. Chisholm, n.d. (Minn.)

Ss. Peter and Paul Ukrainian Greek Catholic Church, Carnegie, Pa.
   FIFTY-FIFTH ANNIVERSARY, 1903-1958. Carnegie, 1958. (Minn.)

Ukrainian Catholic Cathedral, Philadelphia
   PROPAMIATNA KNYHA. Philadelphia: Ameryka, 1942. (Minn.)

WOES AND TRIUMPHS OF THE UKRAINIAN CATHOLIC CHURCH. New York:
   Ukrainian Congress Committee of America, 1972. (Minn.)

Cultural and Intellectual Life: Learned Societies,
Academies, Universities, Museums

Archimovych, O.

   PIDSUMKY DIIAL'NOSTY UVAN V 1967-68 AKADEMICHNOMU ROTSI.
   Reprint. New York, 1969. (Minn.)

Boiko, Max

   KUL'TURNA PRATSIA VOLYNIAN U PIVNICHNI AMERYTSI. Pratsi
   Oseredka bibliohrafii Volyni, no. 13. Bloomington, Ind.:
   Society of Volyn in Toronto, 1978. 213 p. (U of T)

Bykovs'kyi, Lev

   DVADTSIAT' LIT NAUKOVO-ORHANIZATSIINYKH ZUSYL' NA ZAKHODI ZSA:
   DENVERS'KA HRUPA UVAN, 1954-1974. Denver-Salt Lake City:
   Ukrains'kyi bibliohichnyi instytut, 1974. 79 p. (Minn.; UNO;
   U of T)

DESIATYLITTIA UVAN U SShA, 1950-1960. Reprint. New York, 1960.
   (Minn.)

Doroshenko, Volodymyr

   OHNYSHCHE UKRAINS'KOI NAUKY. In commemoration of the 75th
   anniversary of the Shevchenko Scientific Society. New York-
   Philadelphia, 1951. 116 p. (Minn.; St. Vlad.; U of T)

______.

   PROSVITA: II ZASNUVANNIA I PRATSIA, 1868-1958. Philadelphia:
   Moloda Prosvita im. Mytr. A. Sheptyts'koho, 1959. 102 p.
   (Minn.; St. Vlad.; UNO)

IAK TVORYT'SIA UKRAINS'KYI KUL'TURNYI TSENTR U STEMFORDI, KONN.
   Stamford, Conn.: Stamford Ukrainian School Buildings
   Renovation Fund, 1937. (Minn.)

Iasinchuk, Lev

   DLIA RIDNOHO KRAIU. Lviv: published by the author, 1933. (Minn.)

IUVILEINE VYDANNIA PRYSVIACHENE DVADTSIATYLITTIU DIIAL'NOSTY UVAN, 1945-1965. New York, 1967. (Minn.)

Kovaliv, P.

VIRA I ZNANNIA: PRATSI NAUKOVO-BOHOSLOVS'KOHO INSTYTUTU UPTs v ZDA. New York: Ukrainian Orthodox Church in America, 1954. 140 p. (Minn.; St. Vlad.)

Kubijovyč, Volodymyr

NAUKOVE TOVARYSTVO IM. SHEVCHENKA U 1939-1952rr. Reprint. n.p., 1973. (Minn.)

Kuryllo, Kost'

RIDNA SHKOLA NA EMIHRATSII. Buffalo: Rev. O. Nyzhankovs'kyi Ukrainian Catholic Society, 1924. (Minn.)

Lesia Ukrainka Ukrainian School, Syracuse, N.Y.

TSVIT UKRAINY. Almanac, 1954-1964. New York: L. Ukrainka School, 1965. (Minn.)

Lev, Vasyl'

A BRIEF HISTORY OF THE SHEVCHENKO SCIENTIFIC SOCIETY. Trans. by Walter Dushnyk. New York: Shevchenko Scientific Society, 1973. (Minn.)

———.

STO ROKIV PRATSI DLIA NAUKY I NATSII: KOROTKA ISTORIIA NAUKOVOHO TOVARYSTVA IM. SHEVCHENKA. New York: Shevchenko Scientific Society, 1972. 55 p. (U of T)

Lutsiv, Vasyl'

SLOVO PEDAHOHA. "Shkil'na biblioteka" Series. State College, Pa.: Zhyttia i shkola, 1971. 173 p. (U of T)

PAMIATKA IZ SVIATA VIDKRYTTIA UKRAINS'KOI KATOLYTS'KOI VYSHCHOI SHKOLY V STEMFORDI, KONN., 4 VERESNIA 1933. Philadelphia: Ameryka, 1933. (Minn.)

Porzhy-Oleksiienko, P.I.

P'IATDESIAT' LIT NA EMIHRATSII NA SLUZHBI BAT'KIVSHCHYNI. Denver, 1971. 286 p. (Minn.; UNO)

Pritsak, Omelian

CHOMU KATEDRY UKRAINOZNAVSTVA V HARVARDI: VYBIR STATTEI NA
TEMY NASHOI KUL'TURNOI POLITYKY, 1967-1973. Cambridge, Mass.:
Harvard University Chair of Ukrainian Studies Fund, 1973. 188 p.
(Metro; Minn.; St. Vlad.; UNO; U of T)

PROS'VITA. Lviv: Prosvita, n.d. (Minn.)

PRYKHYL'NYKY T-VA PROSVITA UKRAINS'KOMU HROMADIANSTVU V AMERYTSI.
Lviv: Friends of Prosvita, 1924. (Minn.)

Shevchenko Scientific Society

CONGRESS OF UKRAINIAN SCHOLARS ON THE CENTENNIAL OF THE SHEVCHENKO
SCIENTIFIC SOCIETY. Program and abstract of papers. New York:
Centennial Celebration Committee, 1973. (Minn.)

________.

ISTORIIA NAUKOVOHO TOVARYSTVA IM. SHEVCHENKA. New York:
Shevchenko Scientific Society, 1949. 51 p. (Minn.; U of T)

________.

ISTORIIA NAUKOVOHO TOVARYSTVO IM. SHEVCHENKA, 1873-1948.
New York-Munich, 1949. (Minn.)

________.

NAUKOVE TOVARYSTVO IM. SHEVCHENKA V ZDA. New York, 1960. 29 p.
(Minn.; St. Vlad.)

________.

STATUT HOLOVNOI RADY NAUKOVOHO TOVARYSTVA IM. SHEVCHENKA.
n.p., 1955. (Minn.)

________.

ZAPYSKY NAUKOVOHO TOVARYSTVA IM. SHEVCHENKA. Vol. 173.
Chicago-Paris, 1962. (Minn.)

Shtohryn, Dmytro M.

SVITLA I TINI UKRAINS'KYKH STUDII U HARVARDI. Chicago: Mykola
Mikhnovs'kyi Ukrainian Students' Society, 1973. 81 p. (U of T)

Solovei, Dmytro

UKRAINS'KA NAUKA V KOLONIIAL'NYKH PUTAKH. Suspil'no-politichna
biblioteka, no. 14. New York, 1963. 276 p. (UNO; U of T)

St. Nicholas Ukrainian Catholic School, Chicago

PROPAMIATNA KNYHA POSV'IACHENNIA UKRAINS'KOI KATOLYTS'KOI
SHKOLY V SHIKAGO. Chicago: St. Nicholas parish, 1954. (Minn.)

Ukrainian Academy of Arts and Sciences (UVAN) in the U.S.

DESIATYLITTIA UKRAINS'KOI VIL'NOI AKADEMII NAUK U SShA, 1950-
1960. Reprint. New York, 1961. (Minn.)

______.

IUVILEINE VYDANNIA, 1945-1965. New York, 1967. 75 p. (Minn.;
St. Vlad.)

______.

VISTI UVAN. nos. 1- . New York, 1970. (Minn.)

Ukrainian Arts Club, Inc., comp.

UKRAINIAN DIRECTORY. Chicago, 1953. (Minn.)

Ukrainian Congress Committee of America

SHKIL'NA RADA: PROHRAMY NAVCHANNIA I VYKHOVANNIA. New York:
Educational Council of the UCCA, 1960. (Minn.)

Ukrainian Engineers Society of America, New York branch

UKRAINS'KYI INZHENER: ZBIRNYK. New York, 1969. 93 p. (UNO)

Ukrainian Institute of America

FIFTEENTH ANNIVERSARY, 1948-1963. New York, 1963. (Minn.)

Ukrainian National Home

GRAND OPENING OF NEW HALL AT THE UKRAINIAN HOME, OCTOBER 30,
1955. New York, 1955. (Minn.)

Ukrainian Professionals Society of North America

SILVER ANNIVERSARY DIRECTORY, 1933-1958. Cleveland, 1958. (Minn.)

UKRAINS'KA VYSOKA POLITEKHNICHNA SHKOLA NA CHUZYNI. *3 vols.*
   New York: Alumni of the Ukrainian Technology Academy,
   Ukrainian Technical University, 1959-72. (Metro; St. Vlad.;
   U of T)

UKRAINS'KI VYSOKI SHKOLY V AMERYTSI: Z NAHODY BLAHOSLOVENNIA NOVOI
   BUDOVY UKRAINS'KOHO KATOLYTS'KOHO SEMYNARIA V STEMFORDI, DNIA
   7-oho VERESNIA 1942r. Philadelphia, 1942. (Minn.)

Weresh, Wasyl, comp.

   GUIDE TO UKRAINIAN-AMERICAN INSTITUTIONS, PROFESSIONALS AND
   BUSINESS. New York: Carpathian Star, 1955. (Minn.)

World Congress of Free Ukrainian Scholarship

   COMMEMORATING THE ONE HUNDREDTH ANNIVERSARY OF THE DEATH OF
   UKRAINE'S POET TARAS SHEVCHENKO. Held in New York, September 9-10,
   1961. New York, 1961. (Minn.)

Zamsha, Ivan, comp.

   CHRONICLE. Conferences and lectures of the Ukrainian Academy
   of Arts and Sciences in the U.S., July 1, 1963-December 3, 1967.
   Reprint. New York, 1968. (Minn.)

Organizations

American Committee for Liberation
from Bolshevism (ACLFB)

______.

SVITOVA DILEMA I VYKHID Z NEI: VYZVOLENNIA NARODIV SOVIETS'KOHO
SOIUZU. New York, n.d. (Minn.)

DVA BOKY MEDALI: DOKAZ NEOBKHIDNOI OB'IEKTYVNOSTY. New York:
ACLFB, n.d. (Minn.)

American Ukrainian Congress/
Kongres amerykans'kykh ukraintsiv (KAU)

______.

DEV'IATYI KONGRES AMERYKANS'KYKH UKRAINTSIV. New York, 1966.
(Minn.)

______.

KONGRES UKRAINTSIV U ZSA, XI. Philadelphia: Ameryka, 1972.
(Minn.)

______.

KONHRES AMERYKANS'KYKH UKRAINTSIV: POLITYCHNA PLAFORMA-
REZOLIUTSII-ZVIT Z NARAD. Washington, D.C., 1940. (Minn.)

THE AMERICAN UKRAINIAN CONGRESS REPRESENTING UKRAINIAN ORGANIZATIONS
IN THE UNITED STATES: WASHINGTON, D.C., MAY 24, 1940. n.p.,
n.d. (Minn.)

Association of Ukrainian Journalists of America/
Spilka ukrains'kykh zhurnalistiv Ameryky (SUZhA)

______.

DVA Z'IZDY. New York, 1965. (Minn.)

Chornomors'ka Sich

IUVILEINYI AL'MANAKH Z NAHODY 50-RICHCHIA DIIAL'NOSTY, 1924-1974. Newark, N.J.: Jubilee Committee, 1974. (Minn.)

IUVILEINYI ZBIRNYK: 60 RICHCHIA ORHANIZATSII SICH V KRAIU, 35-RICHCHIA CHORNOMORS'KOI SICHI, 5-RICHCHIA SPORTOVOHO KLIUBU, 27 LYSTOPADA 1960r. Newark, N.J., 1960. (Minn.)

PROPAM'IATNA KNYHA Z NAHODY 10-RICHCHIA DIIAL'NOSTY, 1956-1966. Newark, N.J.: Jubilee Committee, 1967. (Minn.)

Federation of Ukrainians in the U.S./ Federatsiia Ukraintsiv v Zluchenykh Derzhavakh (FUZD)

STATUT FEDERATSII UKRAINTSIV V ZLUCHENYKH DERZHAVAKH. New York, 1916. (Minn.)

"Haidamaky" Ukrainian Progressive Workers Organization of America

STATUTY UKRAINS'KOI POSTUPOVO-ROBITNYCHOI ORGANIZATSII HAIDAMAKY V AMERYTSI. New York: Haidamaky, 1911. (Minn.)

"Levy" Ukrainian-American Sport Association

ZVIT IZ DIIAL'NOSTY TOVARYSTVA ZA 1965 RIK. Chicago, 1966. (Minn.)

ZVIT IZ DIIAL'NOSTY TOVARYSTVA ZA IUVILEINYI 1969 RIK. Chicago, 1970. (Minn.)

ZVIT IZ DIIAL'NOSTY TOVARYSTVA ZA 1971 RIK. Chicago, 1972. (Minn.)

Ob'iednannia ukrains'kykh lisnykiv i derevnykiv (OBULID)

UKRAINS'KYI LISNYTS'KYI AL'MANAKH V 10-LITTIA OBULID'U: 1946-1956. New York, 1958. (Minn.)

Organization for the Rebirth of Ukraine/
Orhanizatsiia derzhavnoho vidrodzhennia Ukrainy (ODVU)

______.

STATUT I PRAVYL'NYK ODVU, UKRAINS'KOHO ZOLOTOHO KHRESTA ODVU I
MOLODI ODVU. New York, 1940. (Minn.)

Haivas, Iaroslav

NA IASNYKH I TVERDYKH POZYTSIIAKH. Philadelphia, 1969. (Minn.)

Organization of Ukrainian Nationalists (OUN)

______.

DVA ETAPY: MATERIIALY P'IATOHO I SHOSTOHO VELYKYKH ZBORIV
UKRAINS'KYKH NATSIONALISTIV. Paris: OUN, 1966. 171 p. (Minn.)

______.

UKRAINA SPIL'NE DOBRO VSIKH II HROMADIAN: MATERIIALY VII
VELYKOHO ZBORU UKRAINS'KYKH NATSIONALISTIV. Paris-Baltimore:
Smoloskyp, 1971. 130 p. (UNO)

Kvitkovs'kyi, D., comp.

U 40-RICHCHIA OUN. Papers from the conference of Ukrainians
of America and Canada held in Detroit, Mich., September 1-3,
1969. New York-Toronto: Organization for the Rebirth of Ukraine
and the Ukrainian National Federation of Canada, 1970. 98 p.
(UNO)

Orhanizatsiia oborony Ukrainy (OOU)/
Organization for the Defense of Ukraine

ORHANIZATSIIA OBORONY UKRAINY: PROHRAMA I STATUT. New York, 1924.
(Minn.)

Orhanizatsiia "Za voliu Ukrainy"

PROIEKT STATUTU: ORHANIZATSII "ZA VOLIU UKRAINY." New York, 1949.
(Minn.)

Plast

Chekhut, Bohdan

  RIDNYMY PLAIAMY: PLASTOVI OPOVIDANNIA. Omaha, Neb.: Molode
  zhyttia, 1957. 157 p. (St. Vlad.; UNO)

Kedr, Rostyslav

  SKOBYNE HNIZDO: PLASTOVA POEMA. Toronto: Lisovi chorty, 1957.
  (Minn.)

MY DITY SONTSIA I VESNY: ODNODNIVKA. Rochester, N.Y., 1958. (Minn.)

NA BAIDAKAKH. VYPRAVA III. KURENIA "LISOVI CHORTY" NA POLISSIA
  V 1930-MU ROTSI. Detroit: Lisovi chorty, 1957. (Minn.)

NOVYI SOKIL: 10-LITTIA. Buffalo, 1960. (Minn.)

ROZBUDUIMO PLASTOVU OSELIU V IST CHETEM: ODNODNIVKA. New York:
  Uprava plastovoi oseli, 1954. (Minn.)

VEDE NAS DUKH MAZEPY. New York: Plast, 1953. (Minn.)

Soiuz het'mantsiv derzhavnykiv Ameryky i Kanady

————.

  ZA UKRAINU: PODOROZH VEL'MOZHIVOHO PANA HET'MANYCHA DANYLA
  SKOROPADS'KOHO DO ZLUCHENYKH DERZHAV AMERYKY I KANADY. Comp.
  by Ivan Isaiv. Edmonton: Soiuz het'mantsiv derzhavnykiv, 1938.
  318 p. (UNO)

Soiuz trudovoi demokratii v Amerytsi (STDA)

Hryhorijiv, Nikifor

  SOIUZ TRUDOVOI DEMOKRATII V AMERYTSI. Detroit: Ukrains'ka
  hromads'ka pora, 1945. (Minn.)

Soiuz uchasnykiv ukrains'koi vyzvol'noi borot'by (SUUVB)

MATERIIALY PIDHOTOVCHOI KOMISII SUUVB. New York, 1954. 11 p. (Minn.)

<u>Soiuz ukrains'kykh robitnychykh orhanizatsii</u> (SURO)

______.

PROTOKOL Z'IZDU, 1926. New York, 1927. (Minn.)

______.

PROTOKOL CHETVERTOHO Z'IZDU SURO, 1930. New York,, 1936. (Minn.)

______.

PROTOKOL, 1936. New York: Ukrains'ka robitnycha knyharnia,
1936. (Minn.)

<u>Soiuz ukrains'kykh students'kykh tovarystv
Ameryky (SUSTA)/Federation of Ukrainian Student
Organizations of America</u>

Antonovych, Marko

NARYS ISTORII TSENTRAL'NOHO SOIUZU UKRAINS'KOHO STUDENTSTVA,
1921-1945. Monograph Series, no. 4. Munich-New York-Toronto:
Ukrainian Historical Association, 1976. 57 p. (UNO)

UKRAINS'KE STUDENTSTVO V AMERYTSI: PROPAMIATNA KNYHA SUSTA Z
NAHODY DESIATYLITN'OI DIIAL'NOSTY. Baltimore-New York, 1963.
156 p. (Minn.; St. Vlad.; UNO)

<u>Soiuz vyzvolennia Ukrainy</u>

______.

SAMOSTIINA UKRAINA RUP. Reprint. New York: Howerla, 1971.
43 p. (UNO)

<u>Soiuz zemel' sobornoi Ukrainy, selians'koi partii</u> (SZSU)

INTERV'IU LIDERA SOIUZU ZEMEL' SOBORNOI UKRAINY V.A. DOLENKA,
1953. New York: SZSU, n.d. 24 p. (UNO)

<u>Spilka vyzvolennia Ukrainy</u>(SVU)

______.

PROHRAMA SPILKY VYZVOLENNIA UKRAINY. New York: SVU, 1960.
(Minn.)

Ukrainian-American Citizens Association

_____, Philadelphia

SIXTY YEARS OF THE UKRAINIAN COMMUNITY IN PHILADELPHIA.
Published in commemoration of the thirty-fifth anniversary of
the association. Philadelphia, 1944. 216 p. (Minn.)

_____.

ZOLOTYI IUVILEI, 1909-1959. Philadelphia, 1959. (Minn.)

Ukrainian-American Federation of Michigan (UAFM)

_____.

ZVIT Z DIIAL'NOSTY FEDERATSII AMERYKANS'KYKH UKRAINTSIV V
MISHIGEN, 1939-1949. Detroit: UAFM, 1949. (Minn.)

Ukrainian Congress Committee of America (UCCA)

_____.

CONSTITUTION AND BY-LAWS OF THE UCCA. New York, 1953. 45 p.
(Minn.)

_____.

DVA ROKY PRATSI UKKA. New York, 1957. (Minn.)

_____.

KONSTYTUTSIIA I STATUT UKKA. New York, 1953. (Minn.)

_____.

THE STORY OF THE UKRAINIAN CONGRESS COMMITTEE OF AMERICA,
1940-1951. New York, 1951. 64 p. (Minn.; St. Vlad.)

_____.

THE SUMMIT OF FREEDOM: ITS INDIVISIBILITY ON THE JUST CAUSE OF
UKRAINE AND OTHER CAPTIVE NON-RUSSIAN NATIONS IN THE USSR.
Presented to the U.S. president for the Four Power Conference
in Geneva, July 1955. n.p., 1955. 16 p. (Minn.)

______.

TWENTY YEARS OF DEVOTION TO FREEDOM. Survey of purposes and
activities of the UCCA on its twenty-ninth anniversary. New
York: UCCA, 1960. 104 p. (Minn.; UNO)

______.

UKRAINS'KA HROMADA V BOFALO, N.I., KVITEN' 1967. n.p., n.d.
54 p. (UNO)

______.

UKRAINS'KYI KONGRESOVYI KOMITET: Z NAHODY DESIATYLITTIA, 1940-
1950. New York, n.d. (Minn.)

______.

UKRAINS'KYI NARODNYI FOND: 1952-1953. New York: UCCA, 1953.
(Minn.)

Danylovych, V.

NA MARGINESI VII KONGRESU UKKA. Reprint. Detroit, 1959. (Minn.)

Haivas, Iaroslav

NA IASNYKH I TVERDYKH POZYTSIIAKH. Philadelphia, 1969. (Minn.)

Halychyn, Dmytro

NA PERELOMI: ZVIT Z DIIAL'NOSTY UKRAINS'KOHO KONGRESOVOHO
KOMITETU ZA ROKY 1952-1955. n.p., n.d. (Minn.)

Shypyliavyi, Stepan

MY U SVITLI CHYSEL NARODNOHO FONDU UKKA. Buffalo, 1961. (Minn.)

Ukrainian Democratic Youth Association/Ob'iednannia
demokratychnoi ukrains'koi molodi (ODUM)

______, Philadelphia

ZBIRNYK MATERIIALIV Z KONFERENTSII ODUMU V FILIADEL'FII 30-ho
VERESNIA 1967 ROKU. Baltimore-Philadelphia-Toronto: ODUM,
1968. (Minn.)

<u>Ukrainian Federated Socialist Party</u> (UFSP)

______.

KONSTYTUTSIIA UKRAINS'KOI FEDERATSIINOI SOTSIIALISTYCHNOI
PARTII. Cleveland, 1918. (Minn.)

<u>Ukrainian Medical Society/Ukrains'ke likars'ke</u>
<u>tovarystvo v Amerytsi</u> (ULTA)

LIKARS'KYI AL'MANAKH. Chicago: ULTA, 1958. (Minn.)

<u>Ukrainian National Aid Association of America/</u>
<u>Ukrains'ka narodna pomich</u>

______.

FIFTIETH ANNIVERSARY, 1914-1964. Banquet and concert, February 29,
1964. Pittsburgh, 1964. (Minn.)

______.

STATUT UKRAINS'KOI NARODNOI POMICHI V AMERYTSI. Statute adopted
in 1927. Pittsburgh: The National Word, n.d. (Minn.)

______.

ZAHAL'NE REKORDOVE I FINANSOVE SPRAVOZDANIA UKRAINS'KOI
NARODNOI POMOCHI V PITTSBURGH. Pittsburgh: The National Word,
1950. (Minn.)

<u>Ukrainian National Association (UNA)/</u>
<u>Ukrains'kyi narodnyi soiuz</u> (UNS)

______.

DRUHYI DEN' UNS ULADZHENYI ZAKHODAMY VSIKH VIDDILIV UNS V
SHIKAGO I OKOLYTSI. Chicago, 1937. (Minn.)

______.

PROTOKOL Z XX KONVENTSII UNS. Jersey City, N.J.: Svoboda, 1941.
(Minn.)

______.

PROTOKOL XXIII ZVYCHAINOI KONVENTSII UNS. Jersey City, N.J.,
1954. (Minn.)

————.

PROHRAMA XXIII ZVYCHAINOI KONVENTSII UNS. Jersey City, N.J., n.d. (Minn.)

————.

PROTOKOL XXIV ZVYCHAINOI KONVENTSII UNS. Jersey City, N.J.: UNA, 1958. (Minn.)

————.

DVADTSIAT'P'IATA KONVENTSIIA. New York, 1962. (Minn.)

————.

MINUTES OF THE TWENTY-SEVENTH REGULAR CONVENTION OF THE UKRAINIAN NATIONAL ASSOCIATION. Jersey City, N.J.: UNA, 1970. (Minn.)

————.

PROTOKOL Z XVIII KONVENTSII UNS. Jersey City, N.J.: Svoboda, 1933. (Minn.)

————.

STATUT UKRAINS'KOHO NARODNOHO SOIUZA DLIA UPRAVY HOLOVNOHO URIADU, PIDVLADNYKH VIDDILIV I CHLENIV. Statute adopted by the sixteenth convention, 1925. n.p., n.d. (Minn.)

————.

STATUT UKRAINS'KOHO NARODNOHO SOIUZU. Statute adopted by the nineteenth convention, 1937. n.p., n.d. 170 p. (Minn.; St. Vlad.)

————.

STATUT UKRAINS'KOHO NARODNOHO SOIUZU. Statute adopted by the twentieth convention, 1941. n.p., n.d. (Minn.)

————.

STATUT UKRAINS'KOHO NARODNOHO SOIUZU. Statute adopted by the twenty-first convention, 1946. n.p., n.d. (Minn.)

————.

STATUT UKRAINS'KOHO NARODNOHO SOIUZU. Statute adopted by the twenty-second convention, 1950. n.p., n.d. (Minn.)

—————.

STATUT UKRAINS'KOHO NARODNOHO SOIUZU. Statute adopted by the
twenty-third convention, 1954. n.p., n.d. (Minn.)

—————.

ZAHAL'NI POPRAVKY DO STATUTU UKRAINS'KOHO NARODNOHO SOIUZY.
Amendments adopted at the twenty-second convention, 1950.
Jersey City, N.J.: Svoboda, 1950. (Minn.)

—————.

ZVITY HOLOVNOHO URIADU UKRAINS'KOHO NARODNOHO SOIUZU NA XX
ZVYCHAINU KONVENTSIIU UNS. Annual reports to be presented at the
twentieth regular convention, 1941. Jersey City, N.J.:
Svoboda, 1941. (Minn.)

—————.

ZVITY HOLOVNOHO URIADU UKRAINS'KOHO NARODNOHO SOIUZU NA XXII
ZVYCHAINU KONVENTSIIU UNS. Annual reports to be presented at
the twenty-second convention, 1950. Jersey City, N.J.:
Svoboda, 1950. (Minn.)

—————.

ZVIT HOLOVNOHO URIADU UNS ZA CHAS VID 1-ho SICHNIA 1958 DO
31-ho HRUDNIA 1961. Four-year report presented at the twenty-
fifth convention, 1962. Jersey City, N.J.: Svoboda, 1962.
(Minn.)

—————.

ZVIT HOLOVNOHO URIADU UKRAINS'KOHO NARODNOHO SOIUZU ZA CHAS
VID 1-ho SICHNIA 1966 DO 31-ho HRUDNIA 1969. Four-year report
presented at the twenty-seventh convention, 1970. Jersey City,
N.J.: Svoboda, n.d. (Minn.)

—————.

TO OUR YOUTH. Jersey City, N.J., 1939. 46 p. (U of T)

—————.

V SOROKOLITTIA UKRAINS'KOHO NARODNOHO SOIUZA: IUVYLEINYI
POKLYK. Jersey City, N.J.: UNA, 1934.

_____.

VASHE SOTSIIAL'NE ZABEZPECHENNIA. Jersey City, N.J., 1957.
(Minn.)

_____, and Brotherhood of St. Nicholas

P'IATDESIATI ROKOVYNY BRATSTVA SV. O. NYKOLAIA, VIDDIL 5,
1915-1965. Astoria, N.Y., 1965. (Minn.)

_____, Manville, R.I., and Ukrainian Benevolent Society of Mykhailo
Drahomanov

FIFTIETH ANNIVERSARY, 1907-1957. (Minn.)

Dragan, A.

UKRAINS'KYI NARODNYI SOIUZ, 1894-1964. Jersey City, N.J.:
Svoboda, 1964. (Minn.)

Halychyn, Dmytro, comp.

PIDRUCHNYK DLIA VIDDILOVYKH URIADNYKIV TA ORGANIZATORIV
UKRAINS'KOHO NARODNOHO SOIUZU. Jersey City, N.J.: UNA, 1935.
(Minn.)

Myshuha, Luka, ed.

IUVILEINYI AL'MANAKH, 1894-1944. Jersey City, N.J.: UNA, 1944.
320 p. (Minn.; UNO; U of T)

_____, ed.

PROPAMIATNA KNYHA: VYDANA Z NAHODY SOROKOLITN'OHO IUVYLEIU
UKRAINS'KOHO NARODNOHO SOIUZU. Jersey City, N.J.: UNA, 1936.
752 p. (Minn.; UNO; U of T)

_____ and A. Dragan, eds.

UKRAINTSI U VIL'NOMU SVITI: IUVILEINA KNYHA UNS, 1894-1954.
Jersey City, N.J.: UNA, 1954. 383 p. (Minn.; St. Vlad.; UNO;
U of T)

Padokh, Iaroslav

NA PIONERS'KIM SHLIAKHU. Introd. by D. Halychyn. Jersey City,
N.J.: Svoboda, 1964. 96 p. (Minn.)

______.

UKRAINS'KYI NARODNYI SOIUZ U SVITLI CHYSEL. Jersey City, N.J.:
UNA, 1960. (Minn.)

PRAVDA PRO SPRAVU ZLUKY SOIUZIV. Scranton, Pa.: Narodna volia,
1939. (Minn.)

Ukrainian National Rada/Ukrains'ka natsional'na rada (UNR)

______.

UKRAINKA U VIL'NOMU SVITI. New York, 1959. 91 p. (Minn.; UNO)

______.

Z MATERIIALIV CHETVERTOI SESII UKRAINS'KOI NATSIONAL'NOI RADY.
New York: Association of Friends of the Ukrainian National
Republic in America, n.d. (Minn.)

Ukrainian National Women's League of America (UNWLA)/ Soiuz ukrainok Ameryky

______.

IUVILEINA KNYZHKA SOIUZA UKRAINOK AMERYKY, 1925-1940. New
York: UNWLA, 1941. (Minn.; St. Vlad.; UNO)

______.

PAM'IATKOVA KNYZHKA XI KONVENTSII SOIUZU UKRAINOK AMERYKY,
3-5 VERESNIA 1955. Philadelphia, 1955. (Minn.)

______.

P'IATDESIAT LIT, 1925-1975: PAM'IATKOVA KNYZHKA XVII KONVENTSII
SOIUZU UKRAINOK AMERYKY. Clifton, N.J.: UNWLA, 1975. 298 p.
(Minn.; U of T)

______.

SRIBNYI VINOK: IUVILEINYI ZBIRNYK SOIUZU UKRAINOK AMERYKY.
Jubilee almanac, 1925-1950. Philadelphia: UNWLA Jubilee
Committee, 1950. (Minn.)

_______.

STATUT SOIUZU UKRAINOK AMERYKY. n.p., n.d. (Minn.)

_______.

STATUT SOIUZU UKRAINOK AMERYKY. Jersey City, N.J., 1975.
(Minn.)

_______.

STATUT: TSENTRALI-OKRUZHNYKH RAD-VIDDILIV. New York, 1959.
(Minn.)

_______.

ZVITY SOIUZU UKRAINOK AMERYKY, HOLOVNOI UPRAVY, OKRUZHNYKH
RAD VIDDILIV, 1946, 1947, 1948. Philadelphia, 1948. (Minn.)

_______.

WOMAN OF UKRAINE: HER PART ON THE SCENE OF HISTORY, IN
LITERATURE, THE ARTS, AND STRUGGLE FOR FREEDOM. Philadelphia,
1955. 48 p. (Minn.; St. Vlad.; UNO)

WOMEN POLITICAL PRISONERS IN THE USSR. New York: UNWLA and the
Committee in Defense of Soviet Political Prisoners, 1975.
(Minn.)

Ukrainian National Youth Federation of America (UNYFA)/ Molodi ukrains'ki natsionalisty v ZDA

IUVILEINYI AL'MANAKH: 25-LITTIA MUN, 1933-1958. New York: UNYFA,
1958. 65 p. (Minn.; UNO)

Ukrainian Orthodox League of the USA (UOLA)

_______.

CONSTITUTION AND BY-LAWS. Johnson City, N.Y.: St. John's senior
and junior UOLA chapters, n.d. (Minn.)

_______.

CONSTITUTION AND BY-LAWS OF THE UKRAINIAN ORTHODOX LEAGUE OF
THE USA. Adopted June 1948. New York: Trident Press, 1948.
(Minn.)

————.

THIRD ANNUAL CONVENTION OF THE UKRAINIAN ORTHODOX LEAGUE OF
THE USA. Newark, N.J., 1950. (Minn.)

————.

YEARBOOK: ELEVENTH ANNUAL CONVENTION. Johnson City, N.Y.,
1958. (Minn.)

Ukrainian Revolutionary Democratic Party (URDP)/
Ukrains'ka revoliutsiino-demokratychna partiia

————.

PROHRAMA UKRAINS'KOI REVOLIUTSIINO-DEMOKRATYCHNOI PARTII.
Sixth conference, 1970. Chicago: Hartur, 1970. 48 p. (UNO)

————.

TYMCHASOVYI STATUT UKRAINS'KOI REVOLIUTSIINOI PARTII-URDP.
n.p., 1948. (Minn.)

Ukrainian Sich Riflemen (USR)/
Ukrains'ki sichovi stril'tsi (USS)

KORPUS SICHOVYKH STRIL'TSIV: VOIENNO-ISTORYCHNYI NARYS, 1917-1967.
Ed. by Oleksa Babii. Chicago: USR Jubilee committee, 1969.
663 p. (Metro; Minn.; St. Vlad.; UNO; U of T)

Ripets'kyi, Stepan

UKRAINS'KE SICHOVE STRILETSTVO: VYZVOL'NA IDEIA I ZBROINYI
CHYN. New York: Chervona kalyna, 1956. 360 p. (Metro; Minn.;
St. Vlad.; UNO)

Ukrainian Workingmen's Association (UWA)/
Ukrains'kyi robitnychyi soiuz

————.

AMENDMENTS TO THE BY-LAWS OF THE UKRAINIAN WORKINGMEN'S
ASSOCIATION. Adopted at the eleventh convention, Buffalo, N.Y.,
May 13-18, 1946. Scranton, Pa., 1946. 23 p. (Minn.)

______.

CONSTITUTION AND BY-LAWS OF THE UKRAINIAN WORKINGMEN'S
ASSOCIATION. Amended by the tenth convention, Rochester, N.Y.,
May 19-24, 1941. Scranton, Pa.: Narodna volia, 1941. (Minn.)

______.

IUVILEINA KNYHA UKRAINS'KOHO ROBITNYCHOHO SOIUZU, 1910-1960.
Ed. by Matvii Stakhiv. Scranton, Pa.: UWA, 1960. 332 p.
(Metro; Minn.; St. Vlad.; U of T)

______.

KONSTYTUTSIIA I STATUT UKRAINS'KOHO ROBITNYCHOHO SOIUZU.
Fourteenth convention, Scranton, Pa., May 19-24, 1958. Scranton,
Pa.: Narodna volia, n.d. (Minn.)

______.

PROTOKOL RICHNOHO ZASIDANNIA HOLOVNOI RADY UKRAINS'KOHO
ROBITNYCHOHO SOIUZU, 19-24 CHERVNIA 1967. Scranton, Pa.,
n.d. (Minn.)

______.

PROTOKOL RICHNOHO ZASIDANNIA HOLOVNOI RADY UKRAINS'KOHO
ROBITNYCHOHO SOIUZU VID 16 DO 21 CHERVNIA 1969. Scranton, Pa.,
n.d. (Minn.)

______.

VAZHNI INFORMATSII: DLIA ORHANIZATORIV I NOVYKH CHLENIV
UKRAINS'KOHO ROBITNYCHOHO SOIUZU. Scranton, Pa., 1945. (Minn.)

______.

ZVIT HOLOVNOHO URIADU: 1950-1953, 1958-1969. Scranton, Pa.,
1969. (Minn.)

<u>Ukrainian Youth Association in America/
Spilka ukrains'koi molodi Ameryky</u> (SUMA)

NASH SHLIAKH: IUVILEINA ODNODNIVKA, 1950-1970. Buffalo: SUMA,
1970. (Minn.)

PIDRUCHNYK IUNATSTVA SUMA: CHASTYNA 1. New York, 1960. (Minn.)

SPILKA VYZVOLENNIA UKRAINY I SPILKA UKRAINS'KOI MOLODI: SPOHADY,
   DOKUMENTY I MATERIIALY PRO DIIAL'NIST'. Vol. 2. New York-
   Munich: Spilka vyzvolennia Ukrainy, 1964. (Minn.)

Ukrainian Youth League of North America (UYLNA)

UYLNA DIRECTORY, 1966. New York, n.d. (Minn.)

Ukrains'ka zhinocha hromada

_____, New York City
   IUVILEINYI AL'MANAKH UKRAINS'KOI ZHINOCHOI HROMADY V NIU
   IORKU, 1921-1931. New York, 1931. (Minn.)

Ukrains'ke akademichne kozatstvo "Zaporozhe"

Sokolyszyn, Aleksander, comp.
   IUVILEINYI AL'BOM. New York, 1970. (Minn.)

Ukrains'ke zhinotstvo Ditroitu

UKRAINS'KE ZHINOTSTVO DITROITU: IUVILEINE VYDANNIA Z NAHODY
   70-LITTIA UKRAINS'KOHO ZHINOCHOHO RUKHU TA 35-LITTIA HROMADS'KOI
   PRATSI ZHINOTSTVA DITROITU. Detroit: Zlucheni zhinochi
   orhanizatsii Ditroitu, 1955. 247 p. (Minn.)

Ukrains'kyi narodnyi fond

_____.

   I NA TVOIU POMICH CHEKAIE UKRAINA. n.p., 1955. (Minn.)

United Ukrainian-American Relief Committee (UUARC)/
Zluchenyi ukrains'kyi amerykans'kyi dopomohovyi komitet (ZUADK)

_____.

   KOLIADA NA SKYTAL'TSIV. Philadelphia: Ameryka, 1946. (Minn.)

______, Munich

ZVIDOMLENNIA ZLUCHENOHO UKRAINS'KOHO AMERYKANS'KOHO DOPOMOHOVOHO
KOMITETU Z DIIAL'NOSTY V ZAKHIDNII EVROPI ZA 1948 RIK. Munich,
1949. 36 p. (Minn.; UNO)

Gallan, Walter, comp.

REPORT, SEPTEMBER 30TH, 1951, OF THE UNITED UKRAINIAN AMERICAN
RELIEF COMMITTEE, INC. General meeting, October 12-14.
Philadelphia, 1951. (Minn.)

Tarnavs'kyi, Ostap

BRAT-BRATOVI: KNYKH PRO ZUADK. Philadelphia: UUARC, 1971. 262 p.
(Minn.)

World Congress of Free Ukrainians (WCFU)/
Svitovyi kongres vil'nykh ukraintsiv

______.

CAPTIVE UKRAINE: CHALLENGE TO THE WORLD'S CONSCIENCE. New York,
1967. (Minn.)

______.

MEMORANDUM: SUBMITTED TO THE SECRETARY GENERAL OF THE UNITED
NATIONS. New York, 1967. (Minn.)

______.

PERSHYI MANIFEST DO UKRAINS'KOHO NARODU V UKRAINU I POZA II
MEZHAMY V SSSR TA V KRAINAKH MOSKOVS'KOHO BL'OKU, 16-19
LYSTOPADA. New York, 1967. (Minn.)

______.

PERSHYI SVITOVYI KONGRES VIL'NYKH UKRAINTSIV. Winnipeg-New York-
London: WCFU, 1969. 479 p. (Minn.; St. Vlad.; U of T)

______.

REZOLIUTSII: 16-19 LYSTOPADA. New York: WCFU, 1967. (Minn.)

———.

   SVITOVA VYKHOVNO-OSVITNIA SESIIA, 11-12 LYSTOPADA 1967r.
   n.p., 1967. 32 p. (UNO)

———.

   VIOLATION OF HUMAN RIGHTS IN UKRAINE: DOCUMENTS. Winnipeg-New
   York-London: Ukrainian Press and Information Service, 1970.
   (Minn.)

———.

   ZVERNENNIA DO UKRAINTSIV POZA UKRAINOIU SUSHCHYKH, 16-19
   LYSTOPADA. New York, 1967. (Minn.)

Figol', Atanas

   SVITOVYI KONGRES VIL'NYKH UKRAINTSIV. Paris-Rome-Munich,
   1965. (Minn.)

World Congress of Free Ukrainian Scholarship/
Svitovyi kongres ukrains'koi vil'noi nauky

———.

   REZIUME DOPOVIDEI. New York, 1967. (Minn.)

World Congress of Ukrainian Women/
Svitovyi kongres ukrains'koho zhinotstva

———.

   PAMIATKOVA KNYZHKA, 1948. Philadelphia: Ameryka, 1948. (Minn.;
   St. Vlad.)

———.

   UKRAINKA U VIL'NOMU SVITI: ZBIRNYK, VYDANYI U 75-LITTIA
   UKRAINS'KOHO ZHINOCHOHO RUKHU I 10-LITTIA SVITOVOI FEDERATSII
   UKRAINS'KYKH ZHINOCHYKH ORHANIZATSII. New York, 1959. 91 p.
   (Minn.; UNO)

IV. LANGUAGE

General

Bidwell, Charles Everett

    OUTLINE OF UKRAINIAN MORPHOLOGY. International Studies Program.
Pittsburgh: University of Pittsburgh, 1967. 55 p. (Minn.)

    _______.

    OUTLINE OF UKRAINIAN MORPHOLOGY. rev. ed. University Center
for International Studies. Pittsburgh: University of Pittsburgh,
1971. 69 p. (U of T)

Bochkovs'kyi, Ol'gerd Ippolit

    B. BIERNSON-PONEVOLENI NARODY TA UKRAINS'KA SPRAVA. Winnipeg:
Ukrainian Voice, 1939. 51 p. (Minn.; UNO; U of T)

Boorak, W.J.

    THE B.B. ENGLISH PHONETIC ALPHABET: HOW TO PRONOUNCE, HOW TO
WRITE UKRAINIAN AND SLAVIC NAMES AND WORDS. Aberdeen, Sask.:
W.J. Burak, 1971. 71 p. (U of T)

Chaplenko, Vasyl'

    ADYHEIS'KI MOVY: KLIUCH DO TRIEMNYTS' NASHOHO SUBSTRATU. New
York, 1966. 54 p. (Minn.; U of T)

    _______.

    DESHCHO PRO MOVU: ZBIRKA STATEI. New York, 1959. 63 p. (Minn.;
St. Vlad.; UNO; U of T)

    _______.

    ISTORIIA NOVOI UKRAINS'KOI LITERATURNOI MOVY. New York, 1970.
447 p. (U of T)

    _______.

    MOVNA POLITYKA BIL'SHOVYKIV NA UKRAINI V 1950-60 ROKAKH.
Chicago: Ukrainian Research and Information Institute, 1974.
214 p. (Metro; UNO; U of T)

________.

NOVI ZNADOBY DO ETNOHENEZY SLOV'IAN TA INSHYKH NARODIV. Vol. 2.
New York, 1967. 63 p. (U of T)

________.

UKRAINS'KA LITERATURNA MOVA, XVI ST.-1917r. Vol. 1. New York:
Ukrainian Technical Institute, 1955. (Minn.; UNO; U of T)

Depolovych, L.P.

BUKVAR. Toronto: Novi dni, 1961. (Minn.)

Duravetz, George N.

THE IMPORTANCE OF UKRAINIAN LANGUAGE STUDY. Recommendation for
the introduction of Ukrainian language instruction in Ontario
secondary schools. Toronto: Ministry of Community and Social
Services, 1972. 52 p. (UNO)

Ewach, Honore

KLIUCH DO MOVY: KOROTKA HRAMATYKA UKRAINS'KOI MOVY. Winnipeg:
Ukrainian Cultural and Educational Centre, 1943. 48 p. (Minn.;
St. Vlad.; UNO)

Hrushka, Mykhailo

IAK PYSATY DO CHASOPYSIV. Winnipeg: published by the author,
1938. 17 p. (Minn.; St. Vlad.; UNO)

Ilarion, Metropolitan of Winnipeg and All Canada

HRAMATYCHNO-STYLISTYCHNYI SLOVNYK SHEVCHENKOVOI MOVY. Winnipeg:
Volyn', 1961. 256 p. (Minn.; UNO; U of T)

________.

ISTORIIA UKRAINS'KOI LITERATURNOI MOVY. Nasha kul'tura, no. 12.
Winnipeg: Nasha kul'tura, 1949. 381 p. (Minn.; UNO; U of T)

________.

NASHA LITERATURNA MOVA. Winnipeg: Nasha kul'tura, 1958. 424 p.
(Metro; UNO; U of T)

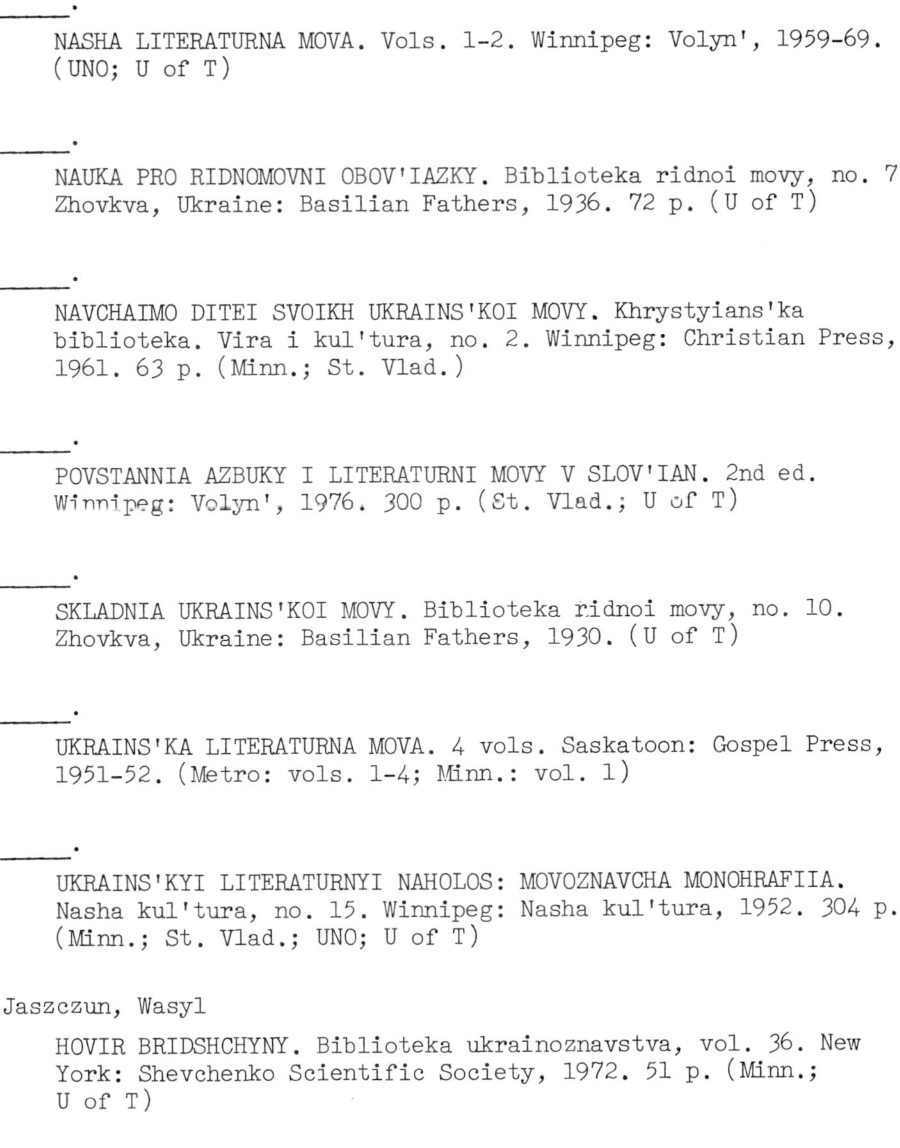

—————.

NASHA LITERATURNA MOVA. Vols. 1-2. Winnipeg: Volyn', 1959-69.
(UNO; U of T)

—————.

NAUKA PRO RIDNOMOVNI OBOV'IAZKY. Biblioteka ridnoi movy, no. 7.
Zhovkva, Ukraine: Basilian Fathers, 1936. 72 p. (U of T)

—————.

NAVCHAIMO DITEI SVOIKH UKRAINS'KOI MOVY. Khrystyians'ka
biblioteka. Vira i kul'tura, no. 2. Winnipeg: Christian Press,
1961. 63 p. (Minn.; St. Vlad.)

—————.

POVSTANNIA AZBUKY I LITERATURNI MOVY V SLOV'IAN. 2nd ed.
Winnipeg: Volyn', 1976. 300 p. (St. Vlad.; U of T)

—————.

SKLADNIA UKRAINS'KOI MOVY. Biblioteka ridnoi movy, no. 10.
Zhovkva, Ukraine: Basilian Fathers, 1930. (U of T)

—————.

UKRAINS'KA LITERATURNA MOVA. 4 vols. Saskatoon: Gospel Press,
1951-52. (Metro: vols. 1-4; Minn.: vol. 1)

—————.

UKRAINS'KYI LITERATURNYI NAHOLOS: MOVOZNAVCHA MONOHRAFIIA.
Nasha kul'tura, no. 15. Winnipeg: Nasha kul'tura, 1952. 304 p.
(Minn.; St. Vlad.; UNO; U of T)

Jaszczun, Wasyl

HOVIR BRIDSHCHYNY. Biblioteka ukrainoznavstva, vol. 36. New
York: Shevchenko Scientific Society, 1972. 51 p. (Minn.;
U of T)

—————.

THE TERM AND NAME "BRODY." Paper read at the thirteenth annual
meeting of the American Name Society in New York, December 30,
1964. UVAN Onomastica Series, no. 29. Winnipeg: UVAN, 1965.
31 p. (Minn.; U of T)

Kirkconnell, Watson

COMMON ENGLISH LOAN WORDS IN EAST EUROPEAN LANGUAGES. UVAN
Slavistica Series, no. 14. Winnipeg: UVAN, 1952. 20 p.
(Minn.; St. Vlad.)

Kotsovs'kyi, V. and I. Ohonovs'kyi

METODYCHNA HRAMATYKA UKRAINS'KOI MOVY. 3rd rev. ed. Winnipeg:
Kanadyiskyi farmer, n.d. (Minn.)

______.

METODYCHNA HRAMATYKA UKRAINS'KOI MOVY. 4th rev. ed. Winnipeg:
Ukrainian Booksellers and Publishers, n.d. (Minn.)

Kovalenko, Liudmila

DO ISTORII ZNUSHCHANNIA NAD UKRAINS'KOIU MOVOIU. South Bound
Brook, N.J.: Ukrainian Orthodox Church of the USA, 1976. 62 p.
(U of T)

Kovaliv, Panteleimon Kindratovych

LEKSYCHNYI FOND LITERATURNOI MOVY KYIVS'KOHO PERIODU X-XIV ST.
2 vols. New York, 1962- . (Minn.: vol. 1; UNO: vols. 1-2;
U of T: vols. 1-2)

______.

OSNOVY FORMUVANNIA UKRAINS'KOI MOVY V PORIVNIANNI Z INSHYMY
SHKIDN'OSLOV'IANS'KYMY MOVAMY. Zapysky NTSh, vol. 168. Zbirnyk
filolohichnoi sektsii, vol. 29. New York: Shevchenko Scientific
Society, 1958. 240 p. (Minn.)

______.

PARTICIPIAL ADJECTIVES IN THE SLAVIC LANGUAGES. UVAN Slavistica
Series, no. 29. Winnipeg: UVAN, 1957. (Minn.)

______.

SLOV'IANSKI FONEMY. New York, 1965. 256 p. (U of T)

______.

UKRAINS'KA MOVA. Biblioteka ukrainoznavstva, no. 19. New York:
Shevchenko Scientific Society, 1966. 218 p. (Metro; UNO; U of T)

______.

UKRAINS'KA MOVA TA II STANOVYSHCHE SERED INSHYKH SLOV'IANS'KYKH
MOV. UVAN Slavistica Series, no. 20. Winnipeg: Ridna shkola im.
M. Shashkevycha, 1954. 46 p. (Minn.; U of T)

______.

UKRAINS'KYI PRAVOPYS. Biblioteka ukrainoznavstva. New York:
Shevchenko Scientific Society, 1976. 96 p. (U of T)

______.

VSTUP DO ISTORII SKHIDN'OSLOV'IANS'KYKH MOV. New York:
Shevchenko Scientific Society, 1970. 159 p. (Minn.; U of T)

Kurylo, Olena Borysivna

UVAHY DO SUCHASNOI UKRAINS'KOI LITERATURNOI MOVY. 5th ed.
Toronto: Novi dni, 1960. 199 p. (Metro; Minn.; UNO; U of T)

Kysilevs'kyi, Kost'

ISTORIIA UKRAINS'KOHO PRAVOPYSNOHO PYTANNIA. New York, 1956.
(U of T)

______.

SLOVO RIDNE. New York: Uchytel's'ka hromada, 1952. (Minn.)

______.

UKRAINOZNAVSTVO V SHKOLI: PROHRAMA I DYDAKTYKA. New York:
Educational Council of the Ukrainian Congress Committee of
America, 1955. (Minn.)

Kyslytsia, Dmytro

HRAMATYKA UKRAINS'KOI MOVY. Vol. 1. Toronto: Novi dni, 1958.
(Metro; U of T)

______.

HRAMATYKA UKRAINS'KOI MOVY. 2nd ed. 2 vols. Toronto: Novi dni,
1963. (Minn.)

Levyts'kyi, Vasyl' Sofroniv

   IDIOMY UKRAINS'KOI MOVY. Litopys UVAN (Chronicles), no. 21.
   Winnipeg: UVAN, 1963. 64 p. (Metro; Minn.; UNO; U of T)

Lomats'kyi, Mykhailo

   UKRAINS'KE VCHYTEL'STVO NA HUTSUL'SHCHYNI. Pedahohichna biblioteka. Toronto: Association of Ukrainian Educators in Canada,
   1958. 72 p. (Minn.; UNO; U of T)

Luchakovs'kyi, Konstantyn

   NACHERK STYLISTYKY, POETYKY I RETORYKY. Winnipeg: Ukrains'ka
   vydavnycha spilka, 1917. 64 p. (Minn.; St. Vlad.; U of T)

Lutsyk, W.M.

   STARO-TSERKOVNO-SLOV'IANS'KA MOVA IAK MOVA RELIGIINOHO KUL'TU.
   UVAN Slavistica Series, no. 17. Winnipeg: UVAN, 1953. 32 p.
   (UNO)

Mackey, Ilonka Schmidt

   THE CYRILLIC ALPHABET. A programmed, self-teaching introduction
   to the reading of Russian, Ukrainian, Serbian and Bulgarian.
   Montreal: M. Didier, 1969. 48 p. (U of T)

Matthews, W.K.

   SOME OBSERVATIONS ON THE UKRAINIAN LANGUAGE. Reprinted from
   The Ukrainian Review, 2, no. 3 (September 1955). (Minn.)

NASHA RIDNA MOVA, GEOGRAFIIA UKRAINY I KHARAKTER UKRAINTSIA,
   POLIAKA, I MOSKALIA. Winnipeg: Ukrains'ka vydavnycha spilka,
   1917. (Minn.)

Novovirsky, Nestor P.

   INTRODUCTION TO THE STUDY OF THE UKRAINIAN LANGUAGE AND CULTURE.
   2 vols. New York, 1949. (Minn.; St. Vlad.)

Olynyk, Roman

   KHIBA HUSY VRIATUIUT' UKRAINS'KU HIDNIST'. Winnipeg: Trident
   Press, 1965. 7 p. (U of T)

Paneiko, Oleksander

   UKRAINS'KA STENOHRAFIIA. New York: Shevchenko Scientific
   Society, 1961. (Minn.)

POMIANYK OF HORODYSHCHE. Ed. by J.B. Rudnyckyj. Readings in
   Slavic Literature, no. 2. Winnipeg: University of Manitoba
   Press, 1962. (U of T)

RIDNA SHKOLA: PROHRAMY NAVCHANNIA I VYKHOVANNIA. Toronto:
   Association of Ukrainian Educators in Canada, 1952. (Minn.)

Royick, Alexander

   LEXICAL BORROWINGS IN ALBERTA UKRAINIAN. M.A. thesis, Department
   of Slavonic Languages and Literatures, University of Alberta,
   1965. (Minn.)

Rubakin, N.

   PRO POKHODZHENIE TA ROZVYTOK MOV (sic). New York: Holos
   pravdy, 1918. 48 p. (Minn.; UNO)

Rudnyts'kyi, Iaroslav Bohdan

   AN ETYMOLOGICAL DICTIONARY OF THE UKRAINIAN LANGUAGE. Winnipeg:
   UVAN, 1962- . (Metro; Minn.; U of T)

   2nd rev. ed.: UVAN, 1966-78. (Metro: vol. 1; U of T: vol. 1,
   pts. 1-10; vol. 2, pts. 1-5)

————.

   "Ґ"--A PROSCRIBED LETTER IN THE SOVIET UNION. UVAN Slavistica
   Series, no. 67-68. Winnipeg: UVAN, 1970. 128 p. (UNO)

————.

   NAROSTKY, -YZHCHE, -YZ'KY, -S'KO. 2nd ed. 2 vols. UVAN
   Slavistica Series, no. 58-59. Winnipeg: UVAN, 1967. (Minn.)

————.

   UKRAINS'KA MOVA TA II HOVORY. 3rd rev. and enl. ed. Winnipeg:
   T-vo plekannia ridnoi movy, 1965. 115 p. (Metro; Minn.;
   St. Vlad.; U of T)

_______.

UKRAINS'KYI PRAVOPYS. 3rd ed. Winnipeg: Ukrainian Canadian
Committee, 1949. 64 p. (Minn.; St. Vlad.; UNO)

Shevchenko Scientific Society

PROCEEDINGS. Philological Section. Vols. 1- . New York, 1952-
(U of T)

_______.

ZAPYSKY NAUKOVOHO T-VA IM. SHEVCHENKA. Vol. 162. Proceedings
of the Philological Section, vol. 25. New York, 1954. (Minn.;
U of T)

_______.

ZAPYSKY NAUKOVOHO TOVARYSTVA IM. SHEVCHENKA. Vol. 165.
Proceedings of the Philological Section, vol. 26. New York,
1956. (Minn.; U of T)

Shevelov, George Y. and Fred Holling, comps.

A READER IN THE HISTORY OF THE EASTERN SLAVIC LANGUAGES:
RUSSIAN, BELORUSSIAN, UKRAINIAN. Columbia Slavic Studies. New
York: Columbia University Press, 1968. 81 p. (U of T)

Shklanka, Elias

UKRAINIAN GRAMMAR. Winnipeg: Promin, 1944- . (Minn.; U of T)

SHKOLA NARODNA: DLIA TRETOI I CHETVERTOI KLIASY. Winnipeg:
Kanadyiskyi farmer, n.d. (Minn.)

Simovych, Vasyl'

NAZVONAVCHI STATTI. 2nd ed. UVAN Seriia Nazvoznavstvo
(Onomastica Series), no. 34. Winnipeg: UVAN, 1967. 24 p.
(U of T)

Simpson, George W.

WHY LEARN UKRAINIAN? Edmonton: Gateway Publishers, 1960. 12 p.
(St. Vlad.)

Slavutych, Iar

    AN INTRODUCTION TO UKRAINIAN. Edmonton: Slavuta Publishing,
1962. 22 p. (Minn.; St. Vlad.)

_____.

    ROZMOVNYI METOD NAVCHANNIA UKRAINS'KOI MOVY. Toronto:
Association of Ukrainian Educators in Canada, 1961. 10 p. (UNO)

_____.

    UKRAINS'KA MOVA ZA ZOROVO-SLUKHOVOIU METODOIU. Montreal:
Didier, 1968. (U of T)

Smal'-Stocki, Roman

    UKRAINS'KA MOVA V SOVIETS'KII UKRAINI. 2nd enl. ed. Biblioteka
ukrainoznavstva, no. 28. New York: Shevchenko Scientific
Society, 1969. 318 p. (Metro; Minn.; U of T)

_____, and Fedir Gartner, comps.

    RUSKA PRAVOPYS' ZI SLOVARTSEM. 3rd ed. Winnipeg: Rus'ka knyharnia,
1918. 152 p. (Minn.; U of T)

_____.

    UKRAINS'KA HRAMATYKA. Winnipeg: Rus'ka knyharnia, 1919. 242 p.
(Minn.; St. Vlad.; UNO; U of T)

Sydor-Chartoryis'kyi, Mykola

    DITY I SHKOLA: OSNOVNI PYTANNIA. New York: Chartoryis'kyi Publishers,
1975. 70 p. (U of T)

Syniavs'kyi, Oleksa

    NORMY UKRAINS'KOI LITERATURNOI MOVY. 3rd ed. State College, Pa.:
Zhyttia i shkola, 1967. 363 p. (Metro; Minn.; UNO; U of T)

Tymchenko, Ievhen

    KURS ISTORII UKRAINS'KOHO IAZYKA: VSTUP I FONETYKA. Shkil'na
biblioteka. State College, Pa.: Zhyttia i shkola, 1972. 170 p.
(Metro; UNO; U of T)

Ukrainian Canadian Committee

BRIEF TO THE ROYAL COMMISSION ON EDUCATION IN MANITOBA. Request
for introducing Ukrainian as an elective subject in grades 9-12
in Manitoba. Winnipeg, 1957. 6 p. (U of T)

Vahylevych, Kost'

UKRAINS'KYI BUKVAR. Illus. by Edward Kozak. New York: published
by the author, 1957. 64 p. (Minn.)

Veryha, Vasyl'

COMMUNICATION MEDIA AND SOVIET NATIONALITY POLICY. Report on
the status of national languages in Soviet television broadcasting.
New York: Ukrainian Congress Committee of America, 1972. 57 p.
(Minn.; St. Vlad.; UNO; U of T)

Zaharychuk, Andrew

THE UKRAINIAN ALPHABET. Winnipeg, 1961. 32 p. (Minn.; U of T)

Zilyns'kyi, Ivan, comp.

UKRAINS'KYI SHKIL'NYI PRAVOPYS. 5th ed. New York-Toronto:
Educational Council of the Ukrainian Congress Committee of
America, 1964. (Minn.)

Dictionaries

Andrusyshen, Constantine Henry and J.N. Krett

UKRAINS'KO-ANHLIIS'KYI SLOVNYK. UKRAINIAN-ENGLISH DICTIONARY.
Saskatoon: University of Saskatchewan, 1955. 1163 p. (Metro;
U of T)

Derkach, Pylyp Maksymovich

KOROTKI SLOVNYK SYNONIMIV UKRAINS'KOI MOVY. 2nd rev. and enl.
ed. Biblioteka terminolohichnych slovnykiv i monohrafii. New
York: Naukovo-doslidche tovarystvo ukr. terminolohii, 1975.
213 p. (St. Vlad.; U of T)

Gauk, Roma

UKRAINIAN CHRISTIAN NAMES: A DICTIONARY. Ed. by Iar Slavutych.
Edmonton: Orma, 1961. 31 p. (Minn.)

Gregorovich, Andrew S.

A LIST OF DICTIONARIES, 1918-1933. Toronto, 1957. (Minn.)

Holoskevych, Hryhorii

PRAVOPYSNYI SLOVNYK. 8th ed. New York: A. Bilous, 1952. 451 p.
(Metro; UNO; U of T)

9th ed.: New York, 1962. 451 p. (Metro; U of T)

Kozlovsky, Evhen

A POCKET DICTIONARY OF THE ENGLISH AND UKRAINIAN LANGUAGES.
3rd rev. ed. 2 pts. in 1 vol. Winnipeg: Ruthenian Booksellers
and Publishers, 1917. (Minn.)

————.

KYSHENKOVYI SLOVAR ANGLIIS'KOI I UKRAINS'KOI MOVY. 2nd rev. ed.
2 pts. in 1 vol. Winnipeg: Ruthenian Booksellers and Publishers,
1917. (U of T)

Kozlovs'kyi, Iakiv

   MII BUKVAR. 3 pts. Toronto: published by the author, 1974-76.
(Metro)

Krett, James Nicholas

   A POCKET DICTIONARY OF THE ENGLISH AND UKRAINIAN LANGUAGES.
Winnipeg: Ukrainian Booksellers and Publishers, 1931. (Metro)

   ————.

   KYSHENKOVYI SLOVAR ANGLIIS'KOI I UKRAINS'KOI MOVY Z PODANNIAM
VYMOVY. Winnipeg: Ukrainian Booksellers and Publishers, 1931.
(Minn.)

   ————.

   TOVARYSH: PRAKTYCHNYI PIDRUCHNYK DO NAUKY ANGLIIS'KOI MOVY.
Winnipeg: Ukrainian Booksellers and Publishers, 1931. (Minn.)

Lisovyi, Iurii

   Z NAUKY I TEKHNIKY: POPULIARNI VIDOMOSTI. Samoosvitnia biblioteka.
Winnipeg: Novyi shliakh, 1954. 154 p. (St. Vlad.; UNO)

   ————.

   Z PRYRODY I TEKHNIKY: POPULIARNI VIDOMOSTI. Samoosvitnia
biblioteka, nos. 2-4. Winnipeg: Ukrains'ka natsional'na
vydavnycha spilka v Kanadi, 1953. 95 p. (UNO)

Paliiv, Kekyliia, comp.

   MII PERSHYI SLOVNYK. Toronto: Association of Ukrainian
Educators in Canada, 1975. 104 p. (Metro)

Pliatsko, H.

   NOVYI PRAKTYCHNYI UKRAINS'KO-ANGLIIS'KYI I ANGLIIS'KO-
UKRAINS'KYI SLOVAR. Winnipeg: Ukrainian Booksellers and
Publishers, 1929. 134 p. (Metro; Minn.)

Romanenchuk, Bohdan

   AZBUKOVNYK: ENTSYKLOPEDIIA UKRAINS'KOI LITERATURY. Philadelphia:
Kyiv Publishing, 1966- . (Metro: 1969; Minn.: 1966, 1967, 1969;
U of T: 1966-74)

Rozhin, Ivan

>   LATYNS'KO-UKRAINS'KYI SLOVNYK VETERYNARNOI MEDYTSYNY. Vol. 1.
>   Chicago, 1954. (U of T)

Salastin, John, comp.

>   ENGLISH-UKRAINIAN DICTIONARY. Richmond Hill, N.Y., 1956. 893 p.
>   (U of T)

Shtepa, Pavlo

>   SLOVNYK CHUZHOSLIV: ZNADIBKY. Shevchenko Scientific Society.
>   Toronto: Ivan Hladun and sons, 1976. 37 p. (UNO)

______.

>   SLOVNYK CHUZHOSLIV: ZNADIBKY. Toronto: Ivan Hladun and sons,
>   1977. 452 p. (Metro; UNO; U of T)

______.

>   ZNADIBKY DO SLOVNYKA CHUZHOSLIV. Toronto: Semen Stasyshyn,
>   1967. 165 p. (Minn.; UNO)

Stepankowsky, Vladimir J., comp.

>   AMERICAN-UKRAINIAN NAUTICAL DICTIONARY. New York, 1953. (Minn.)

Textbooks

Andrusyshen, Constantine Henry

READINGS IN UKRAINIAN AUTHORS. Winnipeg: Ukrainian Canadian
Committee, 1949. 240 p. (Metro; Minn.; U of T)

Bilash, Borislaw N.

UKRAINIAN WITH EASE. Pt. 1. Preface by Paul Yuzyk. Winnipeg:
Hignell Printing, 1974. (St. Vlad.)

Bilets'kyi, Leonid

RIDNE SLOVO: CHYTANKA DLIA CHETVERTOHO ROKU TA POZASHKIL'NOHO
NAVCHANNIA. Winnipeg: Rada ukrains'koi shkoly, 1956. (Minn.)

Bodnarchuk, Ivan

CHYTANKA 2: ROMASHKA. Toronto, 1974. (Minn.)

______.

ZBIRNYK DYKTATIV Z UKRAINS'KOI MOVY DLIA SHKIL I SAMONAVCHANNIA.
Toronto: published by the author, 1974. (Minn.)

Carlton, T.R.

THE DECLENSION OF NOUNS IN UKRAINIAN. Department of Slavic
Languages. Edmonton: University of Alberta, 1971. 96 p.
(U of T)

Chernorizets, Khrabur

MONK CHRABR ON SLAVIC WRITINGS: THE OLDEST CYRILLIC VERSION OF
1348. Ed. by Metropolitan Ilarion. With notes and commentaries
in Ukrainian. Readings in Slavic literature, no. 4. Winnipeg:
University of Manitoba Press, 1964. (Minn.)

Chornii, Stepan

HRAMATYKA UKRAINS'KOI MOVY. CHASTYNA I: FONETYKA I MORFOLOHIIA.
Brockport, N.Y., 1970. 117 p. (St. Vlad.; UNO; U of T)

_____.

    HRAMATYKA UKRAINS'KOI MOVY. CHASTYNA II: SYNTAKSA. Brockport,
N.Y., 1969. 119 p. (St. Vlad.; UNO; U of T)

Deiko, Mariia

    BUKVAR IZ MOVNYMY VPRAVAMY I SLOVNYKOM. Toronto: Association of
Ukrainian Educators in Canada, 1970. 80 p. (Metro; Minn.)

Duravets, George Nicholas

    UKRAINIAN, CONVERSATIONAL AND GRAMMATICAL: LEVEL I. Toronto:
Ukrainian Teachers' Committee, Ontario Modern Language Teachers'
Association, 1973. 312 p. (U of T)

    2nd rev. ed.: 1977. 311 p. (Metro)

_____.

    UKRAINIAN, CONVERSATIONAL AND GRAMMATICAL: LEVEL II. Toronto:
Ukrainian Teachers' Committee, Ontario Modern Language Teachers'
Association, 1976. 435 p. (Metro)

Ewach, Honore

    UKRAINIAN SELF-EDUCATOR FOR THE BEGINNER: UKRAINIAN GRAMMAR
SIMPLIFIED. Winnipeg: Ukrainian Cultural and Educational Centre,
1946. 91 p. (Minn.)

    2nd ed.: Winnipeg, Kalyna Ukrainian Cooperative, 1953. 96 p.
(St. Vlad.)

_____, and Paul Yuzyk, comp.

    UKRAINIAN READER. With vocabulary and notes. Winnipeg:
Ukrainian Canadian Committee, 1960. 240 p. (UNO)

    3rd ed.: 1966. (Minn.; St. Vlad.)

Foty, G., comp.

    READINGS IN UKRAINIAN LITERATURE. Department of Slavic Studies.
Saskatoon: University of Saskatchewan, 1966. 104 p. (St. Vlad.;
U of T)

Koryts'kyi, I.

MOVA RIDNA!: BUKVAR-CHYTANKA Z POSIBNYKOM DLIA UCHNIV ANHLOMOVNYKH
SHKIL. New York, 1951. (Minn.)

4th ed.: Jersey City, N.J., Mykhailo Borets'kyi, 1967. 127 p.
(Metro)

Kovaliv, P.

NAHOLOS V UKRAINS'KII LITERATURNII MOVI. New York, 1952. 31 p.
(UNO; U of T)

Kozlovsky, Eugene

UKRAINIAN SELF-TAUGHT WITH PHONETIC PRONUNCIATIONS. Winnipeg:
Ukrainian Booksellers and Publishers, n.d. 120 p. (Metro; Minn.)

Kuz'menko, Svitlana

IVASYK I IOHO ABETKA. Toronto-New York: Ob'iednannia pratsivnykiv
literatury dlia ditei i molodi, 1974. 48 p. (Metro; Minn.)

Kyriiak, Illia

MARUSIA: UKRAINS'KA CHYTANKA. 2nd ed. Winnipeg: Rada ukrains'koi
shkoly kanady, 1959. 91 p. (Metro)

Kysilevs'kyi, Kost'

HRAMATYKA UKRAINS'KOI MOVY DLIA SHKOLY I SAMONAVCHANNIA. 4th
rev. ed. New York: Educational Council, UCCA, 1955. 52 p. (Minn.;
UNO)

______.

KHRYSTOMATIIA Z UKRAINS'KOI LITERATURY: DLIA SHKIL I KURSIV
UKRAINOZNAVSTVA. 2nd rev. ed. New York: Educational Council,
UCCA, 1962. 268 p. (Minn.)

______.

PRAVOPYSNI LYSTKY DLIA PEREPYSUVANNIA V SHKOLI TA VDOMA. Pt. 1.
New York, 1962. (Minn.)

______.

UKRAINS'KA CHYTANKA DLIA 5 ROKU. New York: Educational Council,
UCCA, 1962. (Minn.)

________.

   UKRAINS'KA CHYTANKA DLIA 6 ROKU. New York: Educational Council,
   UCCA, 1958. (Minn.)

________.

   VYVCHAIMO UKRAINS'KU MOVU! Pt. 1. New York: Educational Council,
   UCCA, 1962. 87 p. (Minn.; St. Vlad.)

Labiuk, N.

   INTRODUCTORY UKRAINIAN FOR HIGH SCHOOLS. Saskatoon, 1962. 79 p.
   (St. Vlad.)

Luckyj, George S.N.

   ENGLISH FOR UKRAINIANS. Toronto: Thomas Allen, n.d. 262 p. (Metro)

________.

   PIDRUCHNYK ANHLIIS'KOI MOVY. New York: published by the author,
   1949. 258 p. (Minn.)

________, and Iaroslav Bohdan Rudnyts'kyi

   A MODERN UKRAINIAN GRAMMAR. Minneapolis: University of Minnesota
   Press, 1949. 186 p. (Metro; St. Vlad.; U of T)

   1961: Winnipeg, UVAN (Metro; U of T)

Matviichuk, Mykola

   DRUHA KNYZHECHKA DLIA DRUHOHO ROKU NAUKY. 2nd ed. Winnipeg:
   Narodna drukarnia, 1941. 123 p. (Minn.; U of T)

________.

   PERSHA KNYZHECHKA: UKRAINS'KYI POVISTKOVYI BUKVAR. Rev. ed.
   Winnipeg: A. Homik, 1927. (Minn.)

________.

   TRETIA KNYZHECHKA DLIA TRET'OI KLIASY. Winnipeg: A. Homik, n.d.
   (Minn.)

Myroliubnyi, Panas

    UKRAINS'KA MOVA (PYS'MO). Syracuse, N.Y.: Ridna shkola, 1954.
(Minn.)

NEW UKRAINIAN-ENGLISH INTERPRETER. 2nd rev. ed. Winnipeg: Ukrains'ka
knyharnia, 1926. 226 p. (St. Vlad.)

    3rd rev. ed.: 1948. 426 p. (Metro)

NOVYI BUKVAR I PERSHA CHYTANKA. New York: Educational Council,
UCCA, 1962. (Minn.)

Odarchenko, Petro

    ZOLOTI VOROTA: CHYTANKA DLIA UKRAINS'KOI MOLODI. Comp. by Mariia
Ovcharenko. Chicago-Toronto: Basilian Press, 1955. 263 p. (Minn.)

———.

    ZOLOTI VOROTA: CHYTANKA DLIA VII I VIII ROKU NAVCHANNIA
UKRAINS'KOI MOVY. 3rd rev. ed. Comp. by Mariia Ovcharenko. New
York: Educational Council, UCCA, 1962. 256 p. (Minn.)

Pelens'kyi, E. Iu.

    UKRAINS'KA CHYTANKA DLIA III ROKU NAVCHANNIA UKRAINS'KOI MOVY.
New York: Educational Council, UCCA, 1962. (Minn.)

———.

    UKRAINS'KA CHYTANKA DLIA IV ROKU NAVCHANNIA UKRAINS'KOI MOVY.
New York: Educational Council, UCCA, 1962. (Minn.)

PIDRUCHNYK ARYTMETYKY DLIA PERSHOI KLIASY POCHATKOVOI SHKOLY.
Pt. 1. New York: Howerla, 1959. 63 p. (Minn.; UNO)

Radzykevych, Volodymyr

    ISTORIIA UKRAINS'KOI LITERATURY. New York: Educational Council,
UCCA, 1964. 159 p. (Minn.)

———, and K. Kysilevs'kyi

    PROMENI: CHYTANKA Z UKRAINOZNAVSTVA. New York: Educational
Council, UCCA, 1955. (Minn.)

RAKHUNKOVA KNYZHKA: DLIA UZHYTKU SHKIL'NOI MOLODIZHY. Pt. 1.
   Winnipeg: Rus'ka knyharnia, 1919. (Minn.)

RAKHUNKOVA KNYZHOCHKA: DLIA UZHYTKU AMERYKANS'KYKH UKRAINTSIV Z
   DODATKOM DEIAKYKH TSIKAVYKII VIDOMOSTYI. Jcrscy City, N.J.:
   Svoboda, 1926. (Minn.)

Romanenchuk, Bohdan
   UKRAINS'KA CHYTANKA DLIA II ROKU. New York: Educational Council,
   UCCA, 1956. (Minn.)
   2nd rev. and enl. ed.: 1960. 179 p. (Minn.)

_______.

   UKRAINS'KA CHYTANKA: DLIA III ROKU NAVCHANNIA UKRAINS'KOI
   MOVY. New York, 1955. (Minn.)

_______.

   UKRAINS'KA CHYTANKA: DLIA IV ROKU NAVCHANNIA UKRAINS'KOI MOVY.
   New York: Educational Council,UCCA, 1956. 151 p. (Minn.)

_______.

   UKRAINS'KA MOVA: HRAMATYCHNI I PRAVOPYSNI VPRAVY DLIA DRUHOHO
   ROKU NAVCHANNIA UKRAINS'KOI MOVY. 2 vols. Philadelphia: UCCA,
   1953. (Metro: 2 vols.; Minn.: 2 vols.; UNO: 2 vols; U of T:
   vol. 1)
   2nd rev. ed.: Philadelphia, Kyiv Publishing, 1965. (Minn.)

Rudnyts'kyi, Iaroslav Bohdan, ed.
   A THIRTEENTH CENTURY CYRILLIC GOSPEL FRAGMENT. Readings in
   Slavic Literature, no. 5. Winnipeg: University of Manitoba Press,
   n.d. (Minn.; U of T)

_______, ed.
   READINGS IN SLAVIC LITERATURE. Winnipeg, 1963- . (Minn.)

Sawchuk, William
   LET US LEARN UKRAINIAN. Rev. ed. Edmonton: published by the
   author, 1977. 101 p. (St. Vlad.)

Shklanka, Elias

    UKRAINIAN PRIMER. 7th rev. ed. Illus. by Margaret Messer.
New York: Knyho-spilka, 1969. 125 p. (Metro)

Slavutych, Iar

    CONVERSATIONAL UKRAINIAN. 2 vols. Edmonton: Gateway Publishers,
1959-60. (St. Vlad.; U of T)

    2nd rev. ed.: 1961. 608 p. (Metro; UNO; U of T). 3rd enl. ed.:
1969 (U of T). 4th ed.: 1973 (St. Vlad.)

————.

    UKRAINIAN FOR BEGINNERS. 4th rev. ed. Edmonton: Slavuta
Publishing, 1968. 60 p. (U of T)

    5th rev. ed.: 1975 (St. Vlad.)

————.

    UKRAINIAN FOR CHILDREN. Edmonton: Slavuta Publishing, 1962.
(Minn.)

————.

    UKRAINIAN IN PICTURES. Edmonton: Gateway Publishers, 1965.
90 p. (St. Vlad.)

Solovei, Dmytro

    TSIKAVA HRAMATYKA. Toronto: Ob'iednannia pratsivnykiv dytiachoi
literatury, 1968. 79 p. (Metro)

Stechyshyn, Iuliian

    UKRAINIAN GRAMMAR. Winnipeg: Ukrainian Canadian Committee, 1951.
(Minn.)

————.

    UKRAINIAN GRAMMAR. Reprint. Winnipeg: Trident Press, 1958.
502 p. (Metro). 1963: St. Vlad.; 1966: U of T.

TRETIA CHYTANKA DLIA UKRAINS'KYKH SHKIL V AMERYTSI. Philadelphia:
   Syrits'kyi dim, 1933. (Minn.)

Trukh, O.A.

UKRAINS'KA MOVA, HRAMATYKA UKRAINS'KOI LITERATURNOI MOVY.
Monder, Alta.: Basilian Fathers, 1947. 127 p. (U of T)

UCHIT'SIA PO ANGLIIS'KY!/LEARN ENGLISH: UKRAINS'KO-ANGLIIS'KI
ROZMOVY DLIA EMIGRANTIV/URKAINIAN-ENGLISH CONVERSATIONS FOR
EMIGRANTS. Lviv: Tovarystvo opiky nad ukrains'kymy emigrantamy
u L'vovi, 1927. (UNO)

U.S. Army Language School, Monterey, Calif.

UKRAINIAN. Background Reader, vol. 22. Monterey, 1956. 95 p.
(U of T)

Volyniak, Petro

BARVINOK: CHYTANKA DLIA II KLIASY TA POZASHKIL'NOHO CHYTANNIA.
4th ed. Toronto: Novi dni, 1959. (Minn.)

______.

DNIPRO: CHYTANKA DLIA V KLIASY. Toronto: Novi dni, 1953. (Minn.)

______.

DNIPRO: LITERATURNA CHYTANKA TA ISTORIIA UKRAINS'KOI LITERATURY.
Pt. 1. Toronto: Novi dni, 1958. (Minn.)

______.

LANY: CHYTANKA DLIA 4-OI KLIASY TA POZASHKIL'NOHO CHYTANNIA.
Toronto: Novi dni, 1952. (Minn.)

2nd rev. and enl. ed.: 1957 (Minn.). 3rd ed.: 1962 (Minn.)

Onomastics

Andrusiak, Mykola

NAZVA "UKRAINA." Chicago: Samostiina Ukraina, 1951. 40 p.
(St. Vlad.; UNO)

Barvins'kyi, Bohdan

NAZVA "UKRAINA" NA ZAKARPATTI. UVAN Seriia Nazvoznavstvo
(Onomastica Series), no. 4. Winnipeg: Carpathian Sich
Brotherhood, 1952. 16 p. (Minn.; St. Vlad.; UNO)

Bohdan, F.

DICTIONARY OF UKRAINIAN SURNAMES IN CANADA. UVAN Onomastica
Series, no. 47. Winnipeg: Onomastic Commission of UVAN and
Canadian Institute of Onomastic Sciences, 1974. 354 p. (Metro;
St. Vlad.; UNO; U of T)

Borovs'kyi, Mykhailo Leontiievych

UKRAINS'KE MISTSEVE I OSOBOVE NAZVONYTSTVO V INTERNATSIONAL'NII
BOTANICHNII TERMINOLOHII. UVAN Seriia Nazvoznavstvo (Onomastica
Series), no. 9. Winnipeg: UVAN, 1955. 62 p. (Metro; Minn.;
St. Vlad.; U of T)

Borshchak, Il'ko

LES NOMS DE FAMILLE UKRAINIENS. UVAN Onomastica Series, no. 18.
Winnipeg: UVAN, 1959. (Metro; Minn.)

Dawson, R.M.

PLACE NAMES IN NOVA SCOTIA. Paper read before the Linguistic
Circle of Manitoba and North Dakota, May 16, 1959. UVAN
Onomastica Series, no. 19. Winnipeg: UVAN, 1960. 16 p. (Metro;
Minn.; U of T)

Gerus-Tarnavets'ka, Iraida

ANTHROPONYMY IN THE POMIANYK OF HORODYŠČE OF 1484. 2nd rev. ed.
UVAN Onomastica Series, no. 30. Winnipeg: UVAN, 1965. 80 p.
(Minn.; U of T)

_____, ed.

ONOMASTICA CANADIANA 1970. UVAN Onomastica Series, no. 42.
Winnipeg: Canadian Institute of Onomastic Sciences and UVAN,
1971. 32 p. (UNO)

Hordyns'kyi, Sviatoslav

NAZVY "RUSYCHI" I "RUSOVYCHI." UVAN Seriia Nazvoznavstvo
(Onomastica Series), no. 25. Winnipeg: UVAN, 1963. 13 p.
(Metro; Minn.; U of T)

Hrabets', Vasyl'

NAZVOZNAVCHI MATERIIALY Z HALYCHYNY. UVAN Seriia Nazvoznavstvo
(Onomastica Series), no. 27. Winnipeg: UVAN, 1964. 16 p.
(U of T)

Jones, Cyril Meredith

INDIAN AND PSEUDO-INDIAN PLACE NAMES IN THE CANADIAN WEST.
UVAN Onomastica Series, no. 12. Winnipeg: UVAN, 1956. 19 p.
(Metro)

Kirkconnell, Watson

CANADIAN TOPONYMY AND THE CULTURAL STRATIFICATION OF CANADA.
UVAN Onomastica Series, no. 7. Winnipeg: UVAN, 1954. 16 p.
(Metro; Minn.)

Klymasz, Robert Bogdan

A CLASSIFIED DICTIONARY OF SLAVIC SURNAME CHANGES IN CANADA.
UVAN Onomastica Series, no. 22. Winnipeg: UVAN, 1961. 64 p.
(Metro; UNO; U of T)

Kupranets', Orest

TOPONOMASTYKA GVANINUSA Z 1611r. UVAN Seriia Nazvoznavstvo
(Onomastica Series), no. 8. Winnipeg: UVAN, 1954. 31 p.
(Metro; Minn.)

Mardon, Ernest G.

THE HISTORY OF PLACE NAMES IN SOUTHERN ALBERTA. UVAN Onomastica
Series, no. 43. Lethbridge, Alta.: Canadian Institute of
Onomastic Sciences and UVAN, 1972. 23 p. (Metro)

Mulyk-Lutsyk, Iurii

   DO METODOLOHII NAZVOZNAVSTVA: TOPO I KHORONIMY TA IKHNE
   POKHODZHENNIA. UVAN Seriia Nazvoznavstvo (Onomastica Series),
   no. 6. Winnipeg: UVAN, 1953. 22 p. (Metro; Minn.; UNO)

Nemeth, J.

   LA PROVENANCE DU NOM BULGAR. UVAN Onomastica Series, no. 28.
   Winnipeg: UVAN, 1964. 15 p. (Minn.; U of T)

Okhrym, O.

   NAZVOZNAVCHI MATERIIALY Z ZAKHIDNOI UKRAINY. UVAN Onomastica
   Series, no. 20. Winnipeg: UVAN, 1960. 24 p. (St. Vlad.; U of T)

Rudnyts'kyi, Iaroslav Bohdan

   ETYMOLOGICAL FORMULA IN ONOMASTICS. 2nd rev. ed. UVAN
   Onomastica Series, no. 33. Winnipeg: UVAN, 1967. 24 p. (U of T)

______.

   GEOGRAFICHNI NAZVY BOIKIVSHCHYNY. UVAN Seriia Nazvoznavstvo
   (Onomastica Series), no. 23-24. Winnipeg: UVAN, 1962. 264 p.
   (Metro; U of T)

______.

   KANADIIS'KI MISTSEVI NAZVY UKRAINS'KOHO POKHODZHENNIA. 2nd ed.
   UVAN Seriia Nazvoznavstvo (Onomastica Series), no. 2. Winnipeg:
   Ukrainian National Home, 1951. 88 p. (Metro; Minn.; UNO; U of T)

   3rd ed.: 1957. 96 p. (Metro)

______, comp.

   MANITOBA, MOSAIC OF PLACE NAMES. Introd. by Watson Kirkconnell.
   Winnipeg: Canadian Institute of Onomastic Sciences, 1970. 221 p.
   (UNO; U of T)

______.

   MOSAIC OF WINNIPEG STREET NAMES. Winnipeg: Canadian Institute
   of Onomastic Sciences, 1974. 333 p. (Metro; U of T)

______.

NAZVY "HALYCHYNA" I "VOLYN'." UVAN Seriia Nazvoznavstvo
(Onomastica Series), no. 3. Winnipeg: Ukrainian National
Home, 1952. 32 p. (Metro; Minn.; St. Vlad.; UNO; U of T)

______.

SLOVO I NAZVA "UKRAINA." UVAN Seriia Nazvoznavstvo (Onomastica
Series), no. 1. Winnipeg: Ukrainian Bookstore, 1951. 131 p.
(Metro; Minn.; St. Vlad.; UNO; U of T)

______.

STUDII Z NAZVOZNAVSTVA. UVAN Seriia Nazvoznavstvo (Onomastica
Series), no. 11. Winnipeg: UVAN, 1956- . (Metro)

______.

STUDIES IN ONOMASTICS II: TOPONYMY. UVAN Onomastica Series,
no. 15. Winnipeg: UVAN, 1958. 64 p. (Metro; UNO)

______.

THE ORIGIN OF THE NAME "SLAV." Presidential address delivered
at the 8th annual meeting of the American Name Society, in
Chicago, December 27, 1959. 2nd rev. ed. UVAN Onomastica Series,
no. 21. Winnipeg: UVAN, 1961. 24 p. (Metro; U of T)

Scargill, Matthew Harry

TEN YEARS OF "ONOMASTICA", 1951-1961. Winnipeg: UVAN, 1961.
8 p. (Metro)

Simpson, George W.

THE NAMES "RUS'," "RUSSIA," "UKRAINE" AND THEIR HISTORICAL
BACKGROUND. UVAN Slavistica Series, no. 10. Winnipeg: UVAN
and Ukrainian National Association in America, 1951. 24 p.
(Minn.; St. Vlad.; UNO; U of T)

Skok, Petar

SUR QUELQUES NOMS DE LIEU D'ORIGINE UKRAINIENNE EN ROUMANIE.
UVAN Onomastica Series, no. 13. Winnipeg: UVAN, 1957. 16 p.
(Metro; Minn.; U of T)

Skorobohata, Ie.

VLASNI IMENA I ZAHAL'NI NAZVY HRETS'KOHO POKHODZHENNIA V
"METAMORFOZAKH" OVIDIIA. 2nd ed. UVAN Seriia Nazvoznavstvo
(Onomastica Series), no. 32. Winnipeg: UVAN, 1966. 16 p.
(Minn.; U of T)

Smal'-Stocki, Roman

PRAVDYVE ZNACHENNIA SOVIETS'KOHO TERMINU "UKRAINA." New York:
Spilka vyzvolennia Ukrainy, 1968. 48 p. (Minn.)

_______.

SLAVS AND TEUTONS: THE OLDEST GERMANIC-SLAVIC RELATIONS.
Preface by Alfred Senn. Milwaukee: Bruce, 1950. 108 p. (Minn.)

_______.

THE ORIGIN OF THE WORD "RUS." UVAN Slavistica Series, no. 6.
Winnipeg: Prosvita, 1949. 24 p. (St. Vlad.)

Sotiroff, G.

SLAVONIC NAMES IN GREEK AND ROMAN ANTIQUITIES. UVAN Onomastica
Series, no. 37. Winnipeg: Canadian Institute of Onomastic
Sciences and UVAN, 1969. 23 p. (St. Vlad.)

Tibon, Gutierre

MEXICO-THE NAME. Trans. by J. Rahtz. UVAN Onomastica Series,
no. 17. Winnipeg: UVAN, 1959. 32 p. (Minn.)

Tsehel's'kyi, Lonhyn

ZVIDKY VZIALYSIA I SHCHO ZNACHAT' NAZVY "RUS'" I "UKRAINA."
Winnipeg: Ukrains'ka vydavnycha spilka, 1917. (Minn.)

Tsurkovs'kyi, Antin

PRO POCHATKY PYS'MA I AZBUKY. Philadelphia: Ameryka, 1953.
(Minn.)

Unbegaun, Boris

L'ORIGINE DU NOM DES RUTHENES. UVAN Onomastica Series, no. 5.
Winnipeg: UVAN, 1953. 12 p. (Metro; Minn.; UNO)

Velyhors'kyi, Ivan

SLOVO I NAZVA "KANADA." UVAN Seriia Nazvoznavstvo (Onomastica
Series), no. 10. Winnipeg: UVAN, 1955. 30 p. (Metro; Minn.;
UNO)

Zhenets'kyi, Stepan

NASHA NATSIONAL'NA NAZVA. Biblioteka Lemkivs'kykh vistei, no. 2.
New York: Organization for the Defense of the Lemkian Region,
1962. 77 p. (Minn.; UNO)

V. UKRAINIAN EMIGRE LITERATURE IN NORTH AMERICA

History and Criticism; Anthologies

Andrusyshen, Constantine Henry and Watson Kirkconnell, eds. and trans.

THE UKRAINIAN POETS, 1189-1962. Toronto: University of Toronto
Press, 1963. 500 p. (Metro; Minn.; St. Vlad.; U of T)

Bida, Konstantyn, ed.

POEZIIA SUCHASNOHO KVEBEKU. Introd. by C.C. Voitsekhovs'ka.
University of Ottawa Slavic Studies Series, no. 2. Montreal:
Librarie Déom, 1968. 195 p. (Metro; St. Vlad.; UNO; U of T)

Bratun', Rostyslav Andriiovych

KANADS'KA KNYHA. Kiev: Khudozhna literatura, 1963. 132 p.
(U of T)

Canadian-Ukrainian Educational Association

ANTOL'OGIIA UKRAINS'KOHO PYS'MENSTVA V KANADI. Vol. 1.
Winnipeg, 1941. (Metro; Minn.; UNO; U of T)

Dontsov, Dmytro

DVI LITERATURY NASHOI DOBY. 2nd ed. Biblioteka vydavnytstva
Homin Ukrainy, no. 8. Toronto: Homin Ukrainy, 1958. 295 p.
(Metro; Minn.; UNO; U of T)

————.

IAKOIU MAIE BUTY LITERATURA? Toronto, 1949. 12 p. (Minn.; UNO)

Ewach, Honore, ed. and trans.

UKRAINIAN SONGS AND LYRICS: A SHORT ANTHOLOGY OF UKRAINIAN
POETRY. Winnipeg: Ukrainian Publishing Co., 1933. 77 p. (Metro)

KONTRASTY: ZBIRKA MOLODECHOI TVORCHOSTY. Ed. by Larysa Zales'ka
Onyshkevych. Biblioteka plastovoho zhurnala Iunak, no. 1. New
York: Plast, 1970. 150 p. (UNO; U of T)

Krawchuk, Peter

    UKRAINS'KA LITERATURA V KANADI. Kiev: Dnipro, 1964. 152 p.
    (Minn.; U of T)

_______, comp.

    UKRAINS'KI KANADS'KI PYS'MENNYKY. Lviv: Kameniar, 1971. 102 p.
    (U of T)

LITERATURNO-NAUKOVYI ZBIRNYK. New York: UVAN, 1952- . (Minn.;
    U of T)

Luchkovich, Michael, ed.

    THEIR LAND: AN ANTHOLOGY OF UKRAINIAN SHORT STORIES. Preface
    by Clarence A. Manning. Introd. by Luke Luciw. Biographical
    sketches by Bohdan Krawciw. Jersey City, N.J.: Svoboda, 1964.
    325 p. (Minn.; St. Vlad.; UNO; U of T)

Mandryka, Mykyta Ivanovych

    HISTORY OF UKRAINIAN LITERATURE IN CANADA. Winnipeg: UVAN,
    1968. 247 p. (Minn.)

NASH TEATR: KNYHA DIIACHIV UKRAINS'KOHO TEATRAL'NOHO MYSTETSVA,
    1915-1975. Vol. 1. New York-Toronto: Shevchenko Scientific
    Society, 1975. 847 p. (St. Vlad.)

OKRUHLI KVADRATY/THE ROUND SQUARES: A COLLECTION OF HUMOROUS
    POEMS AND STORIES. Ed. by Teofil' T. Starukh. New York: Plemia
    Siromantsi, 1975. 132 p. (Metro)

Olynyk, Roman

    NA P'IATDESIATII PARALELI: STATTI I KOMENTARI, 1959-1969.
    Winnipeg: Trident Press, 1969. 266 p. (Minn.)

POEZIIA KVEBEK: VID SEN-DENI-GARNO DO NASHYKH DNIV. Comp. by
    Vol'fram Burhardt. Trans. by V. Burhardt, I. Kostets'kyi,
    B. Oleksandriv, V. Vovk. New York: New York Group, 1972.
    345 p. (Metro)

Poltava, Leonid, ed.

SLOVO I ZBROIA: ANTOLOHIIA UKRAINS'KOI POEZII PRYSVIACHENOI
UPA I REVOLIUTSIINO-VYZVOL'NII BOROT'BI, 1942-1967. Shevchenko
Scientific Society, Biblioteka ukrainoznavstva, vol. 29.
Toronto: Tovarystvo kanadiis'kykh voiakiv UPA im. R. Shukhevycha,
1968. 415 p. (Metro; Minn.; UNO; U of T)

Rusov, Iurii

POEZIIA VYZVOL'NYKH ZMAHAN'. Toronto: Na varti, 1954. 110 p.
(Minn.; St. Vlad.; UNO; U of T)

Sherekh, Iurii

NE DLIA DITEI: LITERATURNO-KRYTYCHNI STATTI I ESEI. New York:
Prolog, 1964. 414 p. (Metro; Minn.; UNO; U of T)

Slavutych, Iar, comp.

ANTOLOHIIA UKRAINS'KOI POEZII V KANADI, 1898-1973. Edmonton:
Slovo, 1975. 159 p. (Metro)

————.

MODERNA UKRAINS'KA POEZIIA, 1900-1950. Philadelphia: Ameryka,
1950. 71 p. (Metro; Minn.; U of T)

————.

THE CONQUERORS OF PRAIRIES: UKRAINIAN POEMS. Edmonton: Slavuta
Publishing, 1968. 48 p. (Metro)

————.

UKRAINIAN LITERATURE IN CANADA. Edmonton: Slavuta Publishing,
1966. 15 p. (U of T)

————.

UKRAINIAN POETRY IN CANADA: A HISTORICAL ACCOUNT. Reprint.
Edmonton: Ukrainian Pioneers' Association of Alberta, n.d.
(UNO)

————.

UKRAINS'KA POEZIIA V KANADI. Edmonton: Slavuta Publishing,
1976. 103 p. (U of T)

———.

ZAVOIOVNYKY PRERII: S'OMA ZBIRKA POEZII. Edmonton: Slavuta
Publishing, 1968. 48 p. (U of T)

2nd rev. ed.: With an English translation. 1974. 112 p. (Metro)

SLOVO PLAMENEM VZIALOS': MYSTETSTVO ZHYVOHO UKRAINS'KOHO SLOVO.
Shevchenko Scientific Society, Biblioteka ukrainoznavstva,
no. 30. Toronto: Ievshan-Zillia, 1972. 224 p. (Metro; St. Vlad.;
U of T)

VOLOSOZHAR: ANTOLOHIIA UKRAINS'KOI POEZII. Toronto: St. Vladimir
Orthodox Brotherhood, 1962. 64 p. (Minn.; U of T)

Yourinyak, Anatol

KAYTYCHNYM PEROM. Los Angeles, 1974. 318 p. (Minn.)

———.

TVORCHI KOMPONENTY LITERATURNOHO TVORU. Chicago: Ukrainian-
American Publishing and Printing, 1964. 67 p. (Minn.; UNO)

The Experience of Ukrainian Immigrants Portrayed in
Fiction, Drama and Poetry

Chaplenko, Vasyl'

SUMNA DOLIA DOBRODIIA BEZORUD'KA: N'IU-IORKS'KA POVIST'.
New York: published by the author, 1974. 243 p. (Metro;
U of T)

Cherin', Hanna

ID'MO ZI MNOIU!: REPORTAZHI. Buenos Aires: Julian Serediak,
1965. 235 p. (Minn.; U of T)

Coleman, Marion Moore, trans.

MAZEPPA: POLISH AND AMERICAN. A translation of Juliusz
Slowacki's Mazeppa, with a discussion of American literature
on Mazeppa. Cheshire, Conn.: Cherry Hill Books, 1966. 73 p.
(St. Vlad.; UNO)

Donchuk, Zosym

KUDY VEDE KAZKA: ROMAN. Philadelphia: published by the author,
1971. 384 p. (Minn.; U of T)

Dzobko, Iosafat, comp.

"CHYIE TO POLECHKO NE ZORANE?" I INSHE NARODNI PISNI.
Biblioteka pionera, no. 1. Winnipeg, 1956. 126 p. (Metro;
UNO; U of T)

———.

MY SONGS: A SELECTION OF UKRAINIAN FOLKSONGS IN ENGLISH
TRANSLATION. Ukrainian Canadian Pioneers' Library, no. 2.
Winnipeg, 1958. 102 p. (Metro; U of T)

Ewach, Honore

HOLOS ZEMLI: KOROTKA POVIST' Z ZHYTTIA V KANADI. Winnipeg:
Ukrainian Publishing Co., 1937. 92 p. (St. Vlad.; UNO)

2nd ed.: Winnipeg, Trident Press, 1973. 122 p. (Metro)

_____.

TSIKAVI OPOVIDANNIA Z DAVN'OI ISTORII KANADY. Winnipeg:
Ukrainian Cultural and Educational Centre, 1944. (Minn.)

Fedyk, Teodor

PISNI IMIGRANTIV PRO STARYI I NOVYI KRAI. Winnipeg, 1927.
(Minn.)

_____.

PISNI PRO KANADU I AVSTRIIU Z DODATKOM PISNI TA DUMKY PRO
MYROSLAVA SICHYN'S'KOHO. Winnipeg: Rus'ka knyharnia, 1914.
(Minn.)

Forman, Joan

WESTWARD TO CANAAN. Toronto-Montreal: Holt, Rinehart &
Winston, 1972. 40 p. (Metro; UNO; U of T)

Horishnyi, Mykola

NA UKRAINS'KII FARMI: DITOCHA STSENICHNA KARTYNA. Jersey
City, N.J.: Dnipro, 1956. (Minn.)

Humeniuk, Peter

MY QUOTATIONS AND COMMENTS. Winnipeg: published by the
author, 1975. 30 p. (St. Vlad.)

Humenna, Dokiia

VICHNI VOHNI AL'BERTY. Edmonton: Petro A. Paush, 1959.
(Metro; Minn.)

Hun'kevych, Dmytro

KLIUB SUFRAZHYSTOK: KOMEDIIA V 5-TY DIIAKH Z AMERYKANS'KOHO
ZHYTTIA. Lviv-Winnipeg: Rozvaha, 1925. 46 p. (UNO)

_____.

ZHERTVY TEMNOTY: DRAMA NA 5 DII ZI SPIVAMY I TANTSIAMY Z
ZHYTTIA UKRAINS'KYKH PERESELENTSIV V KANADI. Lviv-Winnipeg:
Rusalka, 1923. 43 p. (UNO)

Iaroslavs'ka, Dariia

   II NIU IORK: SKOROCHENA POVIST'. n.p.: Ukrainian National
   Women's League of America, 1959. 156 p. (UNO; U of T)

Ichnians'kyi, Myroslav

   LIRA EMIGRANTA: LIRYKA. Winnipeg: Ukrains'ka knyharnia, 1936.
   138 p. (Minn.; UNO; U of T)

Irchan, Myroslav

   KARPATS'KA NICH: OPOVIDANNIA. Winnipeg: Robitnycho-farmers'ke
   vydavnyche tovarystvo, 1924. 178 p. (Minn.; St. Vlad.)

Kalynets', Syl'vester

   VUIKO Z AMERYKY: KOMEDIIA NA I DIIU. Lviv: I. Fridman, n.d.
   (Minn.)

Kazanivs'kyi, V.

   "ADAMOVI SL'OZY," ABO, PIANA KOROVA: Z ZHYTTIA NASHYKH
   PERESELENTSIV V KANADI. Teatral'na biblioteka. Lviv-Detroit:
   Rusalka, 1926. (Minn.)

Khomliak, Petro

   NA ROZDORIZHZHI: KOMEDIIA V TROKH DIIAKH Z KANADIIS'KO-
   UKRAINS'KOHO ZHYTTIA. Winnipeg: Ukrainian Cultural and
   Educational Centre, 1946. 29 p. (UNO)

Klym, Pan'ko

   DOBRI DITY: OBRAZ Z ZHYTTIA AMERYKANS'KYKH SHKOLIARIV. A
   comedy in three acts. New York: T. Shevchenko Ukrainian
   Bookstore, 1926. 16 p. (Minn.; UNO)

Kobzar, Havryil

   DVOIE: DRAMATYCHNYI MALIUNOK NA ODNU DIIU. New York:
   Ukrains'ka knyharnia, 1918. (Minn.)

Kotyk, S.

   NAD OZEROM: OPOVIDANNIA Z AMERYKANS'KOHO ZHYTTIA. Winnipeg:
   published by the author, 1946. 109 p. (Metro; Minn.; St. Vlad.;
   UNO)

Kovbel', S.

SVIATYI MYKOLAI V KANADI: DITOCHA KARTYNA DLIA UKRAINS'KYKH
RIDNYKH SHKIL V KANADI. Winnipeg: Narodne vydavnytstvo, n.d.
31 p. (UNO)

______.

VIRNA SESTRA, TO ZOLOTO: KOMEDIIA NA ODNU DIIU. Winnipeg:
Narodne vydavnytstvo, n.d. 20 p. (UNO)

Kyriiak, Illia

SONS OF THE SOIL. Toronto: Ryerson Press, 1959. 303 p.
(St. Vlad.; U of T)

______.

SYNY ZEMLI: POVIST' Z UKRAINS'KOHO ZHYTTIA V KANADI. Edmonton,
1939. 3 vols. (UNO)

2nd ed.: Winnipeg, Trident Press, 1973. 3 vols. (Metro; Minn.;
St. Vlad.; UNO; U of T)

Lavrivs'ka, Iryna

PERSHYI KOZAK V AMERYTSI. Homin Ukrainy, no. 46. Toronto:
Homin Ukrainy, 1975. 220 p. (Metro; U of T)

Luhovyi, Oleksander

BEZ VYNY KARANI: DRAMA Z SUCHASNOHO KANADS'KOHO ZHYTTIA V
4-OKH DIIAKH. Winnipeg: Ukrains'ka knyharnia, 1938. 66 p.
(UNO)

______.

BEZKHATNYI (DITY STEPU): POVIST' Z ZHYTTIA UKRAINTSIV V
KANADI U DVOKH CHASTYNAKH. Edmonton: Alberta Printing, 1946.
301 p. (Metro; Minn.; St. Vlad.)

______.

OL'HA BASARABOVA: DRAMA V 5-OKH DIIAKH. Saskatoon: Ukrainian
Women's Organization of Canada, 1936. 46 p. (Minn.; UNO)

Lutsyk, Ieronym

V NEVOLI TEMNOTY: KOMEDIIA Z ZHYTIA NASHYKH VYSELENTSIV V
AMERYTSI (sic). Scranton, Pa.: Vasyl' Hryshko, 1919. 32 p.
(UNO)

Lysak, Lesia

ZAMOK NA VULYTSI MEIN: OPOVIDANNIA. Homin Ukrainy, no. 47.
Toronto: Homin Ukrainy, 1976. 186 p. (Metro; St. Vlad.;
U of T)

Lysenko, Vera

YELLOW BOOTS. Toronto: Ryerson Press, 1954. 314 p. (Metro;
U of T)

Marchenko, Iaroslav

VLASNA KHATA. Jersey City, N.J.: Svoboda, 1917. 15 p. (Minn.;
UNO)

Murovych, Larysa

PIONERY SVIATOI ZEMLI. 3rd ed. Toronto: Svitannia, 1969. 64 p.
(Metro; Minn.; UNO; U of T)

Okhrimenko, Vasyl'

EMIHRANT: VYBRANI TVORY. New York: Bezsmertnist' Ukrainy,
1963. 168 p. (Minn.; UNO)

Oleksandriv, Borys

SVYRYD LOMACHKA V KANADI: FEILETONY. Toronto: V. Usatiuk,
1951. 101 p. (UNO)

Oliinyk, Hryhorii

EMIHRATS'KI VIRSHI HALYTS'KOHO SELIANYNA HRYHORIIA OLIINYKA.
Comp. and introd. by Orest Zilyns'kyi. Toronto: Kobzar,
1972. 64 p. (St. Vlad.)

Paush, Stefaniia

NAUCHKA: NARYSY Z PIONERS'KOHO ZHYTTIA. Edmonton, 1967. 72 p.
(U of T)

Petrivs'kyi, Mykhailo

KANADYIS'KYI ZHENYKH. Winnipeg: Ukrains'ka knyharnia, 1922.
51 p. (Minn.; UNO)

______.

MAGICHNE MISTO: NOVELIA Z ZHYTTIA UKRAINS'KYKH PERESELENTSIV
V AMERYTSI. Illus. by A.T. Moroz. Winnipeg: Ukrainian Voice,
1929. 152 p. (Metro; Minn.; St. Vlad.; UNO)

______.

OI, KANADA, KANADON'KO: OPOVIDANNIA Z POBUTOVOHO ZHYTIIA
UKRAINS'KYKH POSELENTSIV V KANADI. Winnipeg: published by the
author, 1974. 168 p. (Metro; U of T)

POETY KANADY: VIRSHI UKRAINS'KYKH ROBITNYCHO-FARMERS'KYKH POETIV.
Comp. by Petro Krawchuk. Kiev: Radians'kyi pys'mennyk, 1958.
212 p. (Metro; U of T)

Popovych, Pavlo

UKRAINS'KA PISNIA V TUNDRI KANADY. Ed. and introd. by Mykola
Chachkovs'kyi. Toronto: Kobzar, 1975. 394 p. (U of T)

Pylypenko, P.

SVYSHCHEMO NA KRIZU: KOMEDIIA NA ODNU DIIU. Edmonton:
Ukrains'ka knyharnia, n.d. 32 p. (UNO)

Rus, Mstyslav

AMERYKANETS': VESELYI OBRAZ Z ZHYTIA NARODA ZI SPIVAMY.
2nd ed. Scranton, Pa.: Ukrains'ka knyharnia, 1915. (Minn.)

Rybakova, Anastaziia

SYROTY: DRAMA V DVOKH DIIAKH Z ZHYTTIA UKRAINTSIV NA
AMERYKANS'KII ZEMLI. Jersey City, N.J.: Svoboda, n.d. (Minn.)

Samchuk, Ulas

NA TVERDII ZEMLI: ROMAN. Toronto: Ukrainian Credit Union,
1967. 390 p. (Metro; Minn.; St. Vlad.; U of T)

Selians'kyi, Liubomir

HOSTYNETS' Z AMERYKY: ABO, NAUKA PRO TSE, IAK ZHYTY V S'VITI.
Lviv: Shevchenko Scientific Society, 1906. (Minn.)

Shopins'kyi, V.

"BRED LAIN": P'IESA NA 4 DNII. New York: Ukrainian Daily News,
1929. (Minn.)

Sklepovych, Vasyl' T.

HORY KLYCHUT': OPOVIDANNIA: PAM'IATNYK UKRAINS'KYM PIONERAM.
Winnipeg, 1975. 294 p. (Metro; St. Vlad.; U of T)

Slavutych, Iar

THE CONQUERORS OF THE PRAIRIES. Trans. by R.H. Morrison.
Edmonton: Slavuta Publishing, 1974. 112 p. (Minn.; St. Vlad.)

Stepanyk, Olena Mariia

PISNI I DUMKY Z OHAIO. Edmonton: Alberta Printing, 1950.
109 p. (Minn.)

Strutyns'ka, Mariia

AMERYKANKA: P'IESA DLIA MOLODI U TR'OKH AKTAKH, Z EPILOHOM.
Philadelphia: published by the author, 1973. 30 p. (Metro;
UNO; U of T)

SVEKRUKHA LEVDOKHA: OBRAZOK STSENICHNYI V 3-OKH DIIAKH.
Olyphant, Pa.: Nove zhytia, 1919. (Minn.)

Svii

KARA ZA HRIKH: SUMNYI OBRAZ Z ZHYTTIA AMERYKANS'KOHO NARODA
V 3-OKH AKTAKH. Jersey City, N.J.: Svoboda, 1920. 40 p.
(Minn.; UNO)

Tarnovs'kyi, Mykola

DO SVITLOI METY: VYBRANI POEZII. New York: League of American
Ukrainians, 1951. 319 p. (Minn.; U of T)

________.

EMIHRANTY. Kiev: Radians'kyi pys'mennyk, 1958. 197 p.
(St. Vlad.; U of T)

rev. ed.: Kiev, Dnipro, 1970. 206 p. (Minn.; U of T)

Vassyian, Iuliian

ODYNYTSIA I SUSPIL'NIST': SUSPIL'NO-FILOSOFICHNI NARYSY.
Toronto: Zoloti Vorota, 1957. 91 p. (Metro; St. Vlad.; UNO)

______.

SUSPIL'NO-FILOSOFICHNI NARYSY. Biblioteka Samostiinoi Ukrainy,
no. 5. Chicago, 1958. 92 p. (UNO)

______.

TVORY. 2 vols. Toronto: Ievshan-Zillia, 1972-74. (Metro:
vol. 1; St. Vlad.: vol. 1; UNO: vols. 1-2; U of T: vols. 1-2)

Vusatyi, Stepan

EMIHRATSIIA V POKHODI: HUMORESKY. Buenos Aires: Julian
Serediak, 1958. 191 p. (Minn.)

Yanda, Doris Elizabeth

CANADIAN TAPESTRY: POEMS. Winnipeg: Trident Press, 1970.
199 p. (Minn.; St. Vlad.; U of T)

Yrshchenyi, Ivan

SVATANNIA V ... SKACHEVANI: KOMEDIIA NA CHOTYRY DII. Winnipeg:
Kanadiis'kyi Ranok, 1926. 61 p. (St. Vlad.; UNO)

Other Emigré Works

Fiction

Babii, Oleksa

DVI SESTRY: POVIST' ZI ZAPYSOK STARSHYNY. Chicago, 1971. 147 p. (Metro; U of T)

Babiienko, V.V.

I. VARIIAT Z 1906 ROKU: OPOVIDANIE. II. VIRSH. III. MIZH BURLYVYMY FYLIAMY: DRAMA NA 4 DII I 5 ODMIN. Winnipeg: Ukrainian Voice, 1918. 80 p. (Minn.; UNO)

Barka, Vasyl'

RAI: ROMAN. Jersey City, N.J.: Svoboda, 1953. 308 p. (Metro; Minn.; St. Vlad.; U of T)

———.

VERSHNYK NEBA: ESEI. New York: Nasha bat'kivshchyna, 1965. 113 p. (Minn.; U of T)

———.

ZHAIVORONKOVI DZHERELA: ESEI. New York: Association of Ukrainian Writers "Slovo," 1956. 24 p. (Minn.)

———.

ZHOVTYI KNIAZ': POVIST'. 2nd ed. New York: Ukrainian National Women's League of America, 1968. 211 p. (Metro; UNO; U of T)

Bodnarchuk, Ivan

DALEKI OBRII. Toronto, 1968. (Metro; Minn.)

———.

DRUZI MOIKH DNIV: NOVELI. Winnipeg: published by the author, 1967. 96 p. (Metro; St. Vlad.)

———.

NA PEREKHRESNYKH SHLIAKHAKH. Winnipeg: Novyi shliakh, 1954. 69 p. (St. Vlad.; U of T)

———.

POKOLINNIA ZIIDUT'SIA. Edmonton-Winnipeg-Toronto: Association
of Ukrainian Writers in Canada "Slovo," 1974. 151 p. (Metro;
Minn.; St. Vlad.; UNO; U of T)

———.

ZNAIOMI OBLYCHCHIA: OPOVIDANNIA. Winnipeg-Toronto, 1961. 109 p.
(Metro; St. Vlad.; U of T)

Bradovych, M.

NA MOSKVU: POVIST'. Philadelphia: Ámeryka, 1951. 110 p.
(Minn.; St. Vlad.; UNO)

Buriakivets', Iurii

LASTIV'IANOIU TRASOIU: ROMAN. New York: Vasyl' Pustovit,
1977. 320 p. (UNO; U of T)

———.

NEZDOLANNI: ROMAN. 2 vols. Trenton, N.J., 1958-60. (Metro:
vols. 1-2; Minn.: vols. 1-2; St. Vlad.: vol. 1; UNO: vols.
1-2)

———.

PASHPORT NA UKRAINU: ROMAN. New York: Vasyl' Pustovit, 1970.
287 p. (Minn.; U of T)

———.

PRAVO NA VELYKU DOROHU: ROMAN. New York: Ridnyi krai, 1972.
316 p. (Metro; St. Vlad.; U of T)

Buzhenko, Volodymyr

IVAN SULYMA: ISTORYCHNA POVIST' IZ KOZATS'KYKH CHASIV.
Biblioteka istorychnykh povistei, no. 17. Toronto: Dobra
knyzhka, 1961. 216 p. (Minn.; UNO)

Bychyns'kyi, Zh. and Ivan Franchuk

ZHOVNIR. OFERMA. 2 works in 1 vol. Jersey City, N.J.:
Svoboda, 1915. (Minn.)

Bytyns'kyi, Mykola

SUZIR'IA LYTSARIV: ZIBRANI TVORY. Toronto: Nadia Bytyns'ka, 1975. 190 p. (Metro; U of T)

Chaplenko, Vasyl'

CHORNOMORTSI ABO KOSHOVYI KHARKO Z USIM TOVARYSTVOM: ISTORYCHNYI ROMAN. New York, 1957. 336 p. (Metro; St. Vlad.; U of T)

———.

IOHO TRIEMNYTSIA: POVIST' IZ SPOHADAMY. New York, 1976. 126 p. (Metro; U of T)

———.

LIUDY V TENETAKH: SATYRYCHNA POVIST'. Kliub pryiateliv ukrains'koi knyzhky, nos. 3-4. Winnipeg: Ivan Tyktor, 1951. (Metro; St. Vlad.; UNO; U of T)

———.

PISNIA PRO CHAIKU-NEBOHU: TA INSHI TVORY. New York, 1977. 136 p. (Metro; U of T)

———.

PIVTORA LIUDS'KOHO: POVIST'. New York: Svoboda, 1952. 163 p. (Metro; Minn.; UNO; U of T)

———.

PYVORIZ: ISTORYCHNO-POBUTOVA POVIST'. 2nd rev. ed. New York, 1965. 168 p. (Metro; Minn.)

———.

SPRAHA BEZSMERTIA: OPOVIDANNIA I P'IESKY. New York: Nasha bat'kivshchyna, 1969. 192 p. (Metro; U of T)

———..

U NETRIAKH KOPET-DAHU: POVIST'. Toronto: Novi dni, 1951. 124 p. (Minn.; St. Vlad.; UNO; U of T)

_______.

"UKRAINTSI": POVIST'. New York: All Slavic Publishing House,
1960. 176 p. (Metro; Minn.; St. Vlad.; UNO; U of T)

_______.

ZAHYBIL' PEREMIT'KA: POVIST'. New York, 1961. 175 p. (Metro;
Minn.; UNO; U of T)

_______.

ZOIK TA INSHI OPOVIDANNIA. New York-Buenos Aires: Peremoha,
1957. 165 p. (Metro; Minn.; St. Vlad.; U of T)

Cherin', Hanna

KHYTRA MAKITRA: ZBIRKA HUMORESOK. Winnipeg: Ukrainian Gold
Cross, 1973. 319 p. (Metro; Minn.; U of T)

Dibrova, Hnat O. (pseud.)

PODOROZH U SVIT: GRONOK DUMOK. New York, 1955. 78 p. (Minn.;
St. Vlad.; U of T)

Domashovets', Hryhorii

NOVYMY SHLIAKHAMY: OPOVIDANNIA. 2 vols. in 1. Saskatoon,
1957-63. (Minn.)

_______.

PRAVDA I VOLIA: STATTI, POEZII, OPOVIDANNIA I POVIST'.
Cyrillo-Methodian Brotherhood Editions, no. 7. Irvington,
N.Y.: Cyrillo-Methodian Brotherhood, 1970. 207 p. (U of T)

_______.

Z PIT'MY DO SVITLA: POVIST'. Hartford, Conn.: Dmytro Kolishko
and Anastasiia Domashovets', 1963. 143 p. (Minn.)

Donchuk, Zosym

BUDYNOK TYSIACHA TRYSTA TRYNADTSIATYI. Philadelphia: published
by the author, 1964. 295 p. (Minn.; UNO; U of T)

———.

CHORNI DNI: OPOVIDANNIA. Buenos Aires-Philadelphia: Peremoha, 1952. 140 p. (UNO)

———.

DESIATA: ZBIRKA OPOVIDAN'. Philadelphia: published by the author, 1968. 222 p. (Metro; Minn.; U of T)

———.

I BACHYV IA: ROMAN. Philadelphia: published by the author, 1967. 324 p. (Minn.; U of T)

———.

IASNOVYDETS' HERI: SATYRYCHNA POVIST'. Philadelphia: published by the author, 1965. 262 p. (Minn.)

———.

KUDY VEDE KAZKA: ROMAN. Philadelphia: published by the author, 1971. 384 p. (Metro; Minn.; U of T)

———.

MORE PO KOLINA: SATYRYCHNA POVIST'. Philadelphia: published by the author, 1961. 295 p. (Metro; Minn.; UNO; U of T)

———.

PERSHA LIUBOV: ROMAN. Philadelphia: published by the author, 1962. 260 p. (Minn.; UNO; U of T)

———.

PRIRVA: ROMAN. Chicago: Mykola Denysiuk, 1959. 560 p. (St. Vlad.)

———.

SHALOM, MESIIE: SATYRA, ABO VYHADANE V DIISNOMU. Philadelphia: Vlasna khata, 1974. 376 p. (Metro; U of T)

———.

UTRACHENYI RANOK: ROMAN. Philadelphia: published by the author, 1969. 520 p. (Minn.; U of T)

———.

V OBLOZI: ROMAN. Philadelphia: Vlasna khata, 1973. 352 p.
(Metro; Minn.; U of T)

———.

V POSHUKAKH SHCHASTIA: ROMAN. Philadelphia: published by the
author, 1970. 374 p. (Metro; Minn.; U of T)

Dontsov, Dmytro

PRAVDA PRADIDIV VELYKYKH. Philadelphia: Organization for the
Defense of Four Freedoms of Ukraine, 1952. 95 p. (Minn.;
St. Vlad.; UNO)

Fodchuk, Stefan

DYVNI PRYHODY SHTIFA TABACHNIUKA. Vancouver: published by the
author, 1958. 64 p. (Minn.)

Gerus, Iaroslav

PRYHODA SNAIPERA: OPOVIDANNIA. New York: Nasha bat'kivshchyna,
1968. 135 p. (U of T)

Granovsky, Alexander Alekseievych

HYMNY SONTSIU: POEZII. Vol. 5. Chicago-New York: Zhyttia i
mystetstvo, 1958. 143 p. (UNO)

Hai-Holovko, Oleksa

ODCHAIDUSHNI: OPOVIDANNIA. Winnipeg: Muza, 1959. 195 p.
(Minn.; St. Vlad.; UNO; U of T)

———.

POIEDYNOK Z DYIAVOLOM: FIL'MY NASHYKH DNIV. 2 vols. in 1.
Kliub pryiateliv ukrains'koi knyzhky, nos. 1-2. Winnipeg:
Ivan Tyktor, 1950. (Metro; Minn.; St. Vlad.; UNO; U of T)

Hak, Anatol'

NA DVOKH TRYBUNAKH: OPOVIDANNIA TA FEILETONY. Philadelphia:
Ukraina, 1966. 318 p. (UNO; U of T)

Halań, Anatol'

CHARIVNA DRUZHYNA: NOVELI. Buenos Aires-New York: published by the author, 1957. 42 p. (UNO; U of T)

______.

MIRKUVANNIA SERIOZNI, NE DUZHE SERIOZNI I TAK SOBI. Philadelphia, 1971. 178 p. (Minn.; U of T)

______.

MIZH DVOMA SMERTIAMY: POVIST'. New York: Nasha bat'kivshchyna, 1966. 144 p. (U of T)

______.

PRYHODY RUBENSA: POVIST'. Winnipeg: Trident Press, 1968. 118 p. (Metro; Minn.; U of T)

______.

ROZMOVA Z MYNULYM. Buenos Aires: Julian Serediak, 1971. 196 p. (Minn.; U of T)

Humenna, Dokiia

BAHATO NEBA: ZBIRKA NARYSIV. New York: Association of Ukrainian Writers "Slovo," 1954. 236 p. (Metro; Minn.)

______.

BLAHOSLOVY, MATY!: KAZKA-ESEI. New York: Association of Ukrainian Writers "Slovo," 1966. 265 p. (Metro; Minn.; St. Vlad.; UNO; U of T)

______.

CHOTYRY SONTSIA: OPOVIDANNIA I NOVELI. New York: Association of Ukrainian Writers "Slovo," 1969. 246 p. (Metro; Minn.; U of T)

______.

EPIZOD IZ ZHYTTIA EVROPY KRYTS'KOI. New York, 1957. 141 p. (Metro; Minn.; St. Vlad.; U of T)

————.

KHRESHCHATYI IAR. New York: Association of Ukrainian Writers
"Slovo," 1956. 487 p. (Metro; Minn.; St. Vlad.; UNO; U of T)

————.

MANA: POVIST'. New York: Ukrainian-American Publishers,
1952. 97 p. (Metro; Minn.; St. Vlad.)

————.

MYNULE PLYVE V PRYIDESHNIE: ROZPOVID' PRO TRYPILLIA. New York:
UVAN in the U.S.A., 1978. 384 p. (UNO)

————.

OPOVIDANNIA I NOVELI. New York: Association of Ukrainian
Writers "Slovo," 1969. (Minn.)

————.

RODYNNYI AL'BOM. New York: Association of Ukrainian Writers
"Slovo," 1969. 347 p. (UNO)

2nd ed.: 1971. (Metro; Minn.; U of T)

————.

SERED KHMAROSIAHIV: N'IU-IORKS'KA MOZAIKA. New York:
Association of Ukrainian Writers "Slovo," 1962. 178 p.
(Metro; Minn.; U of T)

————.

SKARHA MAIBUTN'OMU: ROMAN. New York: Association of Ukrainian
Writers "Slovo," 1964. 325 p. (Metro; Minn.)

————.

VELYKE TSABE: POVIST'. New York, 1952. 155 p. (Metro; Minn.;
St. Vlad.)

————.

ZHADOBA. New York: Association of Ukrainian Writers "Slovo,"
1959. 217 p. (Metro; Minn.; St. Vlad.; U of T)

———.

ZOLOTYI PLUH: ROMAN. New York: Association of Ukrainian
Writers "Slovo," 1968. 291 p. (Metro; Minn.; UNO; U of T)

Iaroslavs'ka, Dariia

PAPOROT' NE TSVITE: POVIST'. n.p., 1976. 243 p. (Metro; U of T)

———.

PID CHUZHI ZORI: ROMAN. Toronto: Dobra knyzhka, 1971. 258 p.
(Metro)

———.

POMIZH BEREHAMY: POVIST'. Philadelphia: Kyiv Publishing, 1953.
188 p. (Metro; Minn.; St. Vlad.; UNO; U of T)

———.

POVIN': ROMAN. 3 vols. Toronto: Dobra knyzhka, 1964-71.
(U of T)

Ilarion, Metropolitan of Winnipeg and All Canada

TVORY. 3 vols. Winnipeg: Trident Press, 1957-62. (St. Vlad.;
UNO: vol. 1)

Irchan, Myroslav (pseud.)

FIL'MY REVOLIUTSII: NARYSY I NOVELI. Berlin-New York: Kul'tura,
1923. (Minn.)

———.

KARPATS'KA NICH: OPOVIDANNIA. Winnipeg: Robitnycho-farmers'ke
vydavnyche tovarystvo, 1924. 178 p. (Minn.; St. Vlad.)

———.

PROTY SMERTY: OPOVIDANNIA. Montreal: Ivan Hnyda, 1927. 160 p.
(St. Vlad.)

Ivanchuk, Roman

MAL'VY: ISTORYCHNYI ROMAN. New York: Nasha bat'kivshchyna,
1968. 138 p. (UNO; U of T)

2nd ed.: 1970. (Minn.)

Karpenko-Krynytsia, Petro

INDIIANS'KI BALADY. New York, 1968. 95 p. (Metro; St. Vlad.)

Kernyts'kyi, Ivan

BUDNI I NEDILIA: NOVELI, HUMORESKY, FEILETONY. New York:
Association of Ukrainian Writers "Slovo," 1973. 174 p.
(Metro; U of T)

______.

HEROI PEREDMISTIA: POVIST'. Illus. by Liuboslav Hutsaliuk.
New York: Knyhospilka, 1958. 198 p. (Minn.; UNO)

______.

PERELETNI PTAKHY. Literaturna biblioteka "IUt," no. 6. New
York: Iürii Tyshchenko, 1952. 141 p. (Minn.; UNO; U of T)

Khraplyva, Lesia

U TEMRIAVI: NARYSY. Chicago: M. Denysiuk, 1959. 96 p. (Metro;
UNO)

Kmeta-Ichnians'kyi, Ivan

ZAHRAVY VECHIRNI. Mansfield, Conn.: Slovo, 1976. 75 p. (U of T)

Knysh, Zynovii

ZA CHUZHU SPRAVU. Foreword by A. Vysochenko. 2nd ed.
Toronto: Sribna surma, 1961. 364 p. (Metro; St. Vlad.)

Kohus'ka, Natalia Levenets'

V POLETI DO VOLI: ISTORYCHNA POVIST'. Winnipeg: published by
the author, 1938. 102 p. (St. Vlad.; UNO)

Kolasky, John, comp.

LOOK COMRADE-THE PEOPLE ARE LAUGHING: UNDERGROUND WIT, SATIRE
AND HUMOUR FROM BEHIND THE IRON CURTAIN. Toronto: Peter Martin
Associates, 1972. 135 p. (Metro; St. Vlad.; UNO; U of T)

Kolens'ka, Liubov

PAVLIV TRIIUMF. New York, 1971. 205 p. (Metro; UNO; U of T)

______.

SAMOTNIST'. New York, 1966. 116 p. (Metro; UNO; U of T)

Kolisnyk, Dmytro

MOE SELO: OPOVIDANNIA. 3 vols. in 1. Saskatoon: published by
the author, 1950-55. (Metro: vols. 2-3; UNO; U of T)

Kosach, Iurii

ENEI I ZHYTTIA INSHYKH: POVIST'. n.p.: Prometheus, 1947. 92 p.
(St. Vlad.; U of T)

Kozak, Edward

HRYTS' ZOZULIA. Detroit: Lys Mykyta, 1973. 221 p. (Metro; UNO;
U of T)

Krat, Pavlo

KOLY ZIISHLO SONTSE: OPOVIDANIE Z 2000 ROKU. Toronto: Robitnyche
slovo, 1918. 72 p. (Minn.; St. Vlad.; U of T)

______.

POSLIDNE KHOZHDENIIE BOHA PO ZEMLI, ABO, BOH NA REVOLIUTSII:
HUMORESTYCHNA POVIST'. Vol. 1. Winnipeg: Robochyi narod,
1915. (Minn.)

Kravtsiv, Melaniia

DOROHA: ROMAN. Biblioteka Homin Ukrainy, no. 2. Toronto:
Homin Ukrainy, 1955. 244 p. (Minn.; St. Vlad.; UNO)

Krett, James Nicholas

TAIEMNYI ZLOCHYN, ABO INDIIANS'KYI SHERL'OK HOL'MS: KRYMINAL'NE
OPOVIDANNIA. Edmonton: Nash postup, 1926. 96 p. (Minn.; UNO)

Krokhmaliuk, Iurii

   K-SIM: FANTASTYCHNE OPOVIDANNIA. Biblioteka Homin Ukrainy,
   no. 25. Toronto: Homin Ukrainy, 1964. 207 p. (Minn.; UNO;
   U of T)

   ______.

   KONOTOP: OPOVIDANNIA. Biblioteka Homin Ukrainy. Toronto: Homin
   Ukrainy, 1959. 172 p. (St. Vlad.; UNO)

   ______.

   MARKIZA: ISTORYCHNI OPOVIDANNIA. Kliub pryiateliv ukrains'koi
   knyzhky, vol. 19. Winnipeg: Ivan Tyktor, 1954. 127 p. (Minn.;
   UNO)

   ______.

   NA SVITANKU: BIOHRAFICHNA POVIST' Z ZHYTTIA MARKA VOVCHKA.
   Chicago: M. Denysiuk, 1961. 403 p. (UNO; U of T)

   ______.

   SHLIAKHAMY VIKIV: OPOVIDANNIA. Kliub pryiateliv ukrains'koi
   knyzhky, vol. 6. Winnipeg, 1951. 126 p. (Minn.; UNO; U of T)

Krylach, Sava

   SAMOSTIINYK: POVIST'. 3 vols. Kliub pryiateliv ukrains'koi
   knyzhky, vols. 23-24. Winnipeg: Ivan Tyktor, 1955. (Metro;
   St. Vlad.; UNO; U of T)

Kudryk, Vasyl'

   KVITKY PRY DOROZI: OPOVIDANNIA I NARYSY. Niagara Falls, Ont.:
   Committee for the publication of Rev. V. Kudryk's works, 1975.
   208 p. (Metro)

Kupchyns'kyi, Roman

   MYSLYVS'KI OPOVIDANNIA. Toronto: Novyi shliakh, 1964. 207 p.
   (Metro; Minn.)

Kurdydyk, Iaroslav

   ETIUDY: MINIIATURY. Toronto: Nasha slava, 1955. 85 p. (Metro;
   St. Vlad.; UNO; U of T)

Kuz'menko, Svitlana

NOVOTALALAIVS'KI REFLEKSII: OPOVIDANNIA. Edmonton-Toronto: Association of Ukrainian Writers in Canada "Slovo," 1976. 109 p. (Metro; UNO; U of T)

Kuz'movych-Holovins'ka, Mariia

LISOVYI HOLUB: OPOVIDANNIA. Selected Works, vol. 2. Toronto: Dobra knyzhka, 1970. 280 p. (Metro; UNO; U of T)

______.

SEFTA I INSHI OPOVIDANNIA Z BOIKIVS'KOHO ZHYTTIA. Philadelphia: Ameryka, 1952. 199 p. (UNO; U of T)

Lavrenko, Mykhailo

DVA KOLOSKY: ZBIRKA OPOVIDAN' IZ ROKIV VELYKOI TRAHEDII UKRAINS'KOHO NARODU, 1932-33. New York: Ridnyi krai, 1973. 303 p. (UNO; U of T)

______.

DYVNII DILA TVOI, HOSPODY!: ZBIRKA OPOVIDAN' Z TAIEMNOZNAVSTVA. New York: Saphrograph, 1975. 299 p. (UNO)

Levyts'kyi, Vasyl' Sofroniv

LYPNEVA OTRUTA. Toronto: Novyi shliakh, 1972. 236 p. (Minn.; UNO)

Liaturyns'ka, Oksana

IAHILKA. Comp. by Oksana Solovei. Winnipeg: Association of Ukrainian Writers in Canada "Slovo," 1971. 52 p. (U of T)

Loboda, Ivan

VONY PRYISHLY ZNOVU: ROMAN Z FINLIANDS'KO-BOL'SHEVYTS'KOI VIINY. Kliub pryiateliv ukrains'koi knyzhky, vol. 16. Winnipeg, 1953. 132 p. (Minn.; UNO; U of T)

Lopushans'kyi, Volodymyr

PEREMOHA: POVIST' Z VYZVOL'NOI VIINY. 2 vols. Kliub pryiateliv ukrains'koi knyzhky, vols. 20-21. Winnipeg: Ivan Tyktor, 1954. (Minn.; U of T)

Luhovyi, Oleksander

CHORNI KHMARY IZZA PRYPIATY: ISTORYCHNA POVIST' Z CHASIV
KHMEL'NYCHCHYNY. Edmonton: Alberta Printing Co., 1945. 163 p.
(Metro; Minn.; St. Vlad.; UNO; U of T)

_______.

V KIHTIAKH DVOHOLOVOHO ORLA: ISTORYCHNA POVIST'. Edmonton:
published by the author, 1955. 349 p. (Metro; St. Vlad.; UNO;
U of T)

_______.

ZA VOLIU UKRAINY (VIRA BABENKO). Winnipeg: Ukrainian Voice,
1939. 211 p. (St. Vlad.; UNO; U of T)

_______.

ZALIZOM I KROVIU: TRYLOGIIA. 3 vols. Edmonton: Alberta Printing
Co., 1955. (Minn.: vol. 1)

Lutsiv, Vasyl'

MANDRIVKA U VIKY. Shkil'na biblioteka. State College, Pa.:
Zhyttia i shkola, 1970. (Minn.)

Lysak, Lesia

SRIBNA MADONNA: ESEI, NARYSY, OPOVIDANNIA. Biblioteka Homin
Ukrainy, no. 41. Toronto: Homin Ukrainy, 1973. 237 p. (Metro;
UNO; U of T)

_______.

TERPKI PAKHOSHCHI. New York: Svoboda, 1969. 344 p. (Metro; Minn.;
U of T)

Lysenko, Vera

WESTERLY WILD. Toronto: Ryerson Press, 1956. 284 p. (Metro;
U of T)

Lysiak, Oleh

LIUDY TAKI, IAK MY: POVIST'. Biblioteka Homin Ukrainy, no. 15.
Toronto: Homin Ukrainy, 1960. 345 p. (St. Vlad.; UNO; U of T)

Lysniak, Roman

    OSTANNII POLK: SATYRA. New York: Ukrainian Language
Publications, 1960. 20 p. (Minn.; U of T)

Maidanyk, Ia.

    VUIKO SH. TABACHNIUK I YNSHI, KOROTKI OPOVIDANNIA. Illus. by
the author. Winnipeg, 1959. 134 p. (Minn.; UNO)

Mak, Ol'ha

    CHUDASII: POVIST'. Biblioteka Homin Ukrainy, no. 3. Toronto:
Homin Ukrainy, 1956. 213 p. (Minn.; UNO)

————.

    KAMINNIA PID KOSOIU: POVIST'. Biblioteka Homin Ukrainy, no. 44.
Toronto: Homin Ukrainy, 1973. 158 p. (Metro; U of T)

————.

    KUDY ISHLA STEZHKA: OPOVIDANNIA. New York: Bulava, 1961. 156 p.
(UNO)

————.

    PROTY PEREKONAN': ROMAN. Biblioteka Homin Ukrainy, no. 12.
Toronto: Homin Ukrainy, 1959. 368 p. (UNO; U of T)

————, comp.

    PRYZABUTI KAZKY: UKRAINS'KI NARODNI KAZKY PRYDNIPRIANSHCHYNY.
Cover design and illus. by Mykhailo Mykhalevych. Toronto: Nashym
ditiam, 1977. 70 p. (Metro)

————.

    ZHAIRA: ISTORYCHNYI ROMAN Z BRAZILIIS'KOHO ZHYTTIA. 2 vols.
Biblioteka Homin Ukrainy, no. 9. Toronto: Homin Ukrainy,
1957-58. (UNO; U of T)

Makohon, Dmytro

    SHKIL'NI OBRAZKY. Winnipeg: Ukrainian Publishing Co., 1917.
(Minn.)

Malaniuk, Ievhen

MALOROSIISTVO. New York: Organization for the Defense of Four
Freedoms of Ukraine, 1959. 31 p. (Minn.; St. Vlad.; UNO)

Maliar, Pavlo

KHLIB: POVIST'. Detroit: Prometheus, 1954. 215 p. (St. Vlad.;
UNO)

______.

ZOLOTYI DOSHCH: ROMAN. 3 vols. Toronto: Novi dni, 1965-75.
(Minn.; U of T)

Marchenko, Petro

AROMA KVITU: SPIRAL'. Biblioteka Ukrains'koho hromads'koho
slova, no. 5. New York: Ukrains'ka hromada im. M. Shapovala,
1956. 25 p. (St. Vlad.; U of T)

______.

EVENTUALIIA TA INSHI NARYSY. Biblioteka Ukrains'koho
hromads'koho slova, no. 6. New York: Ukrains'ka hromada im.
M. Shapovala, 1958. 43 p. (Minn.; U of T)

______.

V OBORONI UKRAINY. New York: Hlas, 1970. (Minn.)

Mazepa, Bohdan

POLUM'IANI AKORDY: LIRYKA. Edmonton: Association of Ukrainian
Writers in Canada "Slovo," 1976. 62 p. (U of T)

Mudryk-Mryts, Nina

LEGENDY. Toronto: Association of Ukrainian Writers in Canada
"Slovo," 1973. 30 p. (Metro)

Nyzhankivs'kyi-Babai, Bohdan

SVIATO NA OSELI: POVIST'. Illus. by Edward Kozak. New York:
Slovo, 1975. 143 p. (Metro; U of T)

Oleksandriv, Borys

LIUBOV DO BLYZHN'OHO: FEILETONY. New York-Toronto: Moloda
Ukrainy, 1961. 122 p. (Metro; Minn.; UNO)

Olynyk, Roman

CHERVONYI SMIKH NAD KYIEVOM: SATYRYCHNI NARYSY. Montreal-Paris:
Petro Plevak, 1971. 59 p. (UNO)

______.

Z CHOHO SMIIUT'SIA KOLHOSPNI KURY? Reprinted from the Ukrainian
Voice, no. 42. Winnipeg: Trident Press, 1966. 8 p. (St. Vlad.)

Onats'kyi, Ievhen

PORTRETY V PROFIL'. Chicago: Ukrainian-American Publishers,
1965. 300 p. (Metro; Minn.; UNO; U of T)

______.

Z CHUZHOHO POLIA. Chicago: Ukrainian-American Publishers, 1965.
145 p. (Metro; Minn.; UNO; U of T)

Onufriichuk, Fedir

OPOVIDANNIA. Yorkton, Sask.: published by the author, 1964.
16 p. (St. Vlad.; U of T)

Orlyhora, Lev T.

HEROI NASHOHO CHASU: NOVELY. Yorkton, Sask.: Redeemer's Voice,
1959. 154 p. (Metro; UNO)

Os'machka, Teodosii Stepanovych

PLAN DO DVORU: POVIST'. Toronto: Ukrainian Legion, 1951.
184 p. (Minn.; St. Vlad.; UNO; U of T)

______.

ROTONDA DUSHOHUBTSIV: OPOVIDANNIA. Toronto, 1956. 365 p.
(St. Vlad.; U of T)

______.

STARSHYI BOIARYN. Biblioteka novitn'oi literatury. Detroit:
Prometheus, 1946. 116 p. (St. Vlad.)

Ostruk, Iaroslava

PROVALLIA: POVIST'. Chicago: M. Denysiuk, 1961. 191 p.
(Minn.; UNO; U of T)

Ovechko, Ivan

VYBRANE: POEZII, NARYSY, OPOVIDANNIA, STATTI, RETSENZII.
Greeley, Colo.: friends of the author, 1970. (Minn.)

Palii, Lida

MANDRIVKY V CHASI I PROSTORI. Toronto: Association of Ukrainian
Writers in Canada "Slovo," 1973. 48 p. (Metro; UNO; U of T)

Parfanovych, Sofiia

CHARIVNA DIBROVA: OPOVIDANNIA I NARYSY. Chicago: published by
the author, 1964. 202 p. (Metro; Minn.; UNO; U of T)

______.

KARUS' I MY: AVTOBIOHRAFIIA. Chicago: published by the author,
1966. 324 p. (Metro; Minn.; U of T)

______.

LIUBLIU DIBROVU. Detroit: published by the author, 1959.
128 p. (Metro; Minn.; U of T)

______.

LIUDY I TVARYNY: OPOVIDANNIA I NARYSY. Ukrains'ka literaturna
biblioteka, vol. 11. New York: Shevchenko Scientific Society,
1969. 244 p. (Metro)

______.

NA SKHRESHCHENYKH DOROHAKH. Chicago: published by the author,
1963. 417 p. (Metro; Minn.; UNO; U of T)

_______.

POPID KYCHERAMY TA NAD POTOKOM (Z RODYNNOI KHRONIKY): POVIST'.
Shevchenko Scientific Society, Ukrains'ka literaturna biblioteka,
vol. 14. New York: Petro Yamniak, 1974. 240 p. (Metro; U of T)

_______.

U LISNYCHIVTSI. 2nd ed. Detroit: published by the author,
1966. 183 p. (Metro; Minn.)

Pavlychenko, T.K.

DUKH NATSII. Saskatoon: UNO, 1940. 48 p. (Minn.; St. Vlad.;
UNO)

Podvorniak, Mykhailo

BOZHYI SPOKII: OPOVIDANNIA. Doroha pravdy, no. 35. Chicago-
Winnipeg: Doroha pravdy, 1966. (Minn.)

_______.

NEDOSPIVANA PISNIA: POVIST'. Doroha pravdy, no. 37. Chicago-
Winnipeg: Doroha pravdy, 1967. 347 p. (Minn.; U of T)

_______.

ZAPASHNIST' POLIA: OPOVIDANNIA. Doroha pravdy, no. 45. Chicago-
Winnipeg: Doroha pravdy, 1971. 198 p. (Minn.; UNO; U of T)

_______.

ZELENYI HAI: OPOVIDANNIA. Chicago-Toronto: Doroha pravdy,
1959. 198 p. (Minn.; UNO)

_______.

ZOLOTA OSIN': OPOVIDANNIA. Doroha pravdy, no. 54. Toronto-
Winnipeg: Doroha pravdy, 1974. 144 p. (Metro; U of T)

Polianych, B.

HENERAL W: SHPYHUNS'KA POVIST'. 8 vols. in 6. Popular Library
Series. Philadelphia: Kyiv Publishing, 1951. (Minn.; St. Vlad.)

———.

O-313: SHPYHUNS'KA POVIST'. Philadelphia: Ameryka, 1950.
180 p. (Minn.; St. Vlad.)

———.

SIM ZOLOTYKH CHASH: ISTORYCHNA POVIST' Z CHASIV MAZEPYNS'KOI
EMIGRATSII 1720 ROKIV. Toronto: Basilian Press, 1969. 224 p.
(UNO; U of T)

———.

STRIL UNOCHI: SENSATSIINA POVIST'. 3rd rev. ed. Philadelphia:
Konotop, 1974. 107 p. (UNO; U of T)

———.

ZAMOK IANHOLA SMERTY: SENSATSIINA POVIST' Z CHASIV HET'MANA
KYRYLA ROZUMOVS'KOHO I HRYHORA HRAFA ORLYKA. Dobra knyzhka,
no. 178. Toronto: Dobra knyzhka, 1963. 200 p. (Metro; Minn.;
UNO; U of T)

Ponedilok, Mykola

DYVO V RESHETI: OPOVIDANNIA, NARYSY, PROMOVY. Ed. by Iurii
Klynovyi. Illus. by Halyna Mazepa. Edmonton: Association of
Ukrainian Writers in Canada "Slovo," 1977. 352 p. (Metro)

———.

HOVORYT' LYSHE POLE: NOVELI, NARYSY, OPOVIDANNIA. Biblioteka
Homin Ukrainy, no. 19. Toronto: Homin Ukrainy, 1962. 317 p.
(Metro; Minn.; St. Vlad.; UNO; U of T)

———.

RIATUITE MOIU DUSHU: POVIST'. Ed. and introd. by Iurii
Klynovyi. Illus. by Edward Kozak. Jersey City, N.J.: Svoboda,
1973. 502 p. (Metro; St. Vlad.; UNO; U of T)

———.

SMISHNI SL'OZYNY. Jersey City, N.J.: Svoboda, 1966. 272 p.
(Metro; St. Vlad.; UNO; U of T)

———.

ZOREPAD. Toronto: Homin Ukrainy, 1969. 471 p. (Metro; Minn.;
St. Vlad.; UNO; U of T)

Prychodko, Nicholas

DALEKYMY DOROHAMY: POVIST' DLIA DOROSLYKH. 2 vols. Biblioteka
Vil'ne Slovo, no. 2. Toronto: Vil'ne slovo, 1961. (Metro;
Minn.; St. Vlad.; UNO; U of T)

______.

GOOD-BYE SIBERIA. Markham, Ont.: Simon and Schuster, 1976.
345 p. (Metro; St. Vlad.; UNO; U of T)

______.

STORMY ROAD TO FREEDOM. Foreword by Igor Gouzenko. New York:
Vantage Press, 1968. 356 p. (Metro; Minn.; U of T)

Pylypenko, Lev

TINI MYNULOHO: ZBIRKA OPOVIDAN', NOVEL' TA NARYSIV. Philadelphia,
1965. 196 p. (Metro; Minn.; UNO)

Radzykevych, Iuliian

POLKOVNYK DANYLO NECHAI: ISTORYCHNA POVIST'. 2 vols. Winnipeg:
Novyi shliakh, 1961. (Minn.; St. Vlad.; UNO; U of T)

Ripets'kyi, Nestor

KHVYLI SHUKAIUT' BEREHIV. Vol. 1. Toronto: Slovo, 1954.
(UNO; U of T)

______.

R-33: OPOVIDANNIA. Biblioteka Homin Ukrainy, no. 32. Toronto:
Homin Ukrainy, 1967. 223 p. (UNO; U of T)

______.

SONTSE SKHODYT' IZ ZAKHODU. Toronto: Arka, 1954- . (St. Vlad.;
UNO; U of T)

Roienko, Petro

HOMIN VOLI. Toronto: Liubystok, 1975. 128 p. (Metro; U of T)

______.

VELYKA LIUDYNA TA INSHI TVORY. Toronto: Liubystok, 1973.
144 p. (Metro; UNO; U of T)

———.

ZNAVISNILI DNI. Toronto: published by the author, 1973. 80 p. (Metro; U of T)

Samchuk, Ulas

CHOHO NE HOIT' OHON': ROMAN. New York: Visnyk, 1959. 287 p. (Metro; Minn.; UNO; U of T)

———.

HORY HOVORIAT': ROMAN U 2-OKH CHASTYNAKH. Winnipeg: Novyi shliakh, 1944. 194 p. (Minn.; St. Vlad.; UNO; U of T)

———.

IUNIST' VASYLIA SHEREMETY: ROMAN. 2 vols. in 1. Detroit: Prometheus, 1946. (St. Vlad.; U of T)

———.

TEMNOTA: ROMAN U 2-OKH CHASTYNAKH. New York: UVAN in the U.S., 1957. 493 p. (Metro; Minn.; St. Vlad.; UNO; U of T)

———.

VOLYN': ROMAN-KHRONIKA U 3-OKH CHASTYNAKH. Vol. 1. Toronto: published by the author, 1952. (Metro; Minn.; St. Vlad.; UNO; U of T)

3rd ed.: Toronto, 1965-69. 3 vols. (UNO; U of T)

Savyts'ka, Ivanna

Z PTASHYNOHO LETU: OBRAZKY SUCHASNOHO, DRUZHNI ZAPYSKY, REPORTAZHI. New York: Chervona kalyna, 1974. 138 p. (Metro; UNO; U of T)

Sharyk, Mykhailo

DITY VIINY: SPOHADY. 3 vols. Kliub pryiateliv ukrains'koi knyzhky, vols. 26-28. Winnipeg, 1955-56. (Metro: 3 vols; Minn.: 3 vols.; St. Vlad.: vol. 1; UNO: 3 vols; U of T: vols. 1, 3)

Shchypavka, Hryts'

   KHRUNIIADA I NOVOMODNI PISNI. Montreal: Zahal'na knyharnia,
   1913. 16 p. (U of T)

Shpak, Oleksandra

   Z KHYHY ZHYTTIA: OPOVIDANNIA. Buenos Aires-Toronto: published
   by the author, 1968. 290 p. (UNO; U of T)

Skorups'kyi, Volodymyr

   SPOKONVICHNI LUNY: LEHENDY I MITY. New York-Toronto:
   Association of Ukrainian Writers "Slovo," 1977. 70 p. (U of T)

Slonivs'kyi, Ievhen

   NA RUINAKH MYNULOHO: ROMAN. Vol. 1. Buenos Aires-Toronto:
   Peremoha, 1956. (Minn.; St. Vlad.; UNO; U of T)

Smolii, Ivan

   KORDONY PADUT': POVIST'. Kliub pryiateliv ukrains'koi
   knyzhky, vol. 5. Winnipeg: Ivan Tyktor, 1951. 159 p. (Minn.;
   St. Vlad.; UNO)

   ______.

   U ZELENOMU PIDHIRI: POVIST'. Jersey City, N.J.: Svoboda, 1960.
   191 p. (Minn.; St. Vlad.; UNO)

Smotrych, Oleksander

   BUTTIA: 16 NIKOMU NEPOTRIBNYKH OPOVIDAN'. Toronto: Novi dni,
   1973. 123 p. (Metro; UNO; U of T)

   ______.

   VYBRANE. Toronto, 1952. 89 p. (U of T)

Solianych, Dmytro

   KHTO VYNUVATYI, TA INSHI OPOVIDANNIA Z ZHYTTIA SELIANSTVA NA
   POKUTTIU. Edmonton: Ivan Solianych, 1932. 161 p. (UNO)

Stavnychka, Vasyl'

   CHUDO PROFESOR. Winnipeg: published by the author, 1946. (Minn.)

_____.

ZAVZIATYI IURKO: ABO, POSHANA DO RODYCHIV. 2nd ed. Winnipeg:
Promin', n.d. 140 p. (Metro; Minn.; UNO)

Stechyshyn, Mykhailo

BAIKY. Vol. 1. Foreword by Iurii Mulyk-Lutsyk. Winnipeg, 1959.
(Metro; Minn.)

Stefanovych, Oleksa

ZIBRANI TVORY. Ed. by Bohdan Boichuk. Introd. by Ivan Fizer.
Toronto: Iévshan-zillia, 1975. 304 p. (Metro; U of T)

Step, Pavlo

BRATY: KAZKA. Toronto: Nasha bat'kivshchyna, 1960. 38 p.
(St. Vlad.)

Storozhenko, Serhii

VULKAN VOLI: ROZDUMY I SENTENTSII. Toronto: Kiev Printers,
1961. 30 p. (Minn.; St. Vlad.)

Tarnavs'kyi, Iurii O.

MENINGITIS: A WORK OF FICTION. New York: Fiction Collective,
1978. 158 p. (U of T)

Tarnavs'kyi, Ostap

TUHA ZA MITOM: ESEI. New York: Kliuchi, 1966. 159 p. (Minn.;
UNO; U of T)

Tarnavs'kyi, Zenon

DOROHA NA VYSOKYI ZAMOK: NOVELI, OPOVIDANNIA, NARYSY.
Biblioteka Homin Ukrainy, no. 24. Toronto: Homin Ukrainy
and Institute of Ukrainian Culture in America, 1964. 254 p.
(St. Vlad.; UNO; U of T)

Tarnovych, Iuliian

NA RIKAKH VAVYLONS'KYKH. Toronto, 1952. 95 p. (Minn.; St. Vlad.;
UNO)

Ulahai-Krasovs'kyi, L. and M. Dubovs'kyi

   OBZOLOTYLYS'. Winnipeg: Turfdim, 1927. 76 p. (U of T)

Viter, Danko

   DALEKI MANDRY: POVIST' MOLODI. Toronto: M. Maryniak, 1973.
   303 p. (UNO; U of T)

Volkov, Vitalii

   DOVBUSH: ROMAN. Winnipeg: Trident Press, 1963. 304 p. (Minn.;
   St. Vlad.; UNO; U of T)

______.

   ZAHADKOVYI PERSTEN': ZBIRKA OPOVIDAN'. Philadelphia: Ameryka,
   1951. 106 p. (Minn.; St. Vlad.; UNO)

Volyniak, Petro

   POHOVORYMO VIDVERTO: VYBRANI STATTI I OPOVIDANNIA. Introd. by
   V. Svaroh. Toronto: Novi dni, 1975. 662 p. (Metro; St. Vlad.;
   U of T)

Vynnyts'ka, Iryna

   KAM'IANA SOKYRA. 2nd rev. ed. Biblioteka Samopomochi dlia
   molodi, no. 1. New York: Samopomich, 1967. 71 p. (Minn.)

Yourinyak, Anatol

   KAMIKADZE PADAIE SAM: OPOVIDANNIA I FEILETONY. Los Angeles:
   Association of Ukrainian Writers "Slovo," 1973. 184 p. (Metro;
   Minn.; U of T)

______.

   NA DALEKYKH SHLIAKAKH. Detroit: Ukraina, 1955. 56 p. (U of T)

Zahachevs'kyi, Ievstakhii

   L'VIVS'KA BRATIIA: POVIST' PEREZHYTOHO. Toronto: Brotherhood
   of Former Soldiers of the First Ukrainian Division of the UNA,
   1962. 200 p. (Metro; UNO; U of T)

Zhurba, Halyna (pseud.)

    TODIR SOKIR: NA TLI ISTORII: ROMAN. Vol. 1. New York: Nasha bat'kivshchyna, 1967- . (Minn.; UNO; U of T)

Zvychaina, Olena

    MYRHORODS'KYI IARMOROK. Winnipeg: Trident Press, 1953. (Minn.)

———.

    SELIANS'KA SANATORIIA: POVIST'. Winnipeg: Trident Press, 1952. 218 p. (Minn.; St. Vlad.)

———.

    ZOLOTYI POTICHOK Z HOLODNOHO KHARKOVA: POVIST' Z CHASIV NIMETS'KOI OKUPATSII UKRAINY. Winnipeg: Ukrainian Women's Organization of Canada, 1947. 93 p. (Minn.; St. Vlad.)

<u>Drama</u>

Babiienko, V.V.

    I. VARIIAT Z 1906 ROKU: OPOVIDANIE. II. VIRSH. III. MIZH BURLYVYMY FYLIAMY: DRAMA NA 4 DII I 5 ODMIN. Winnipeg: Ukrainian Voice, 1918. 80 p. (Minn.; UNO)

Boichuk, Bohdan

    DIV DRAMY. New York: New York Group, 1968. 70 p. (Metro; St. Vlad.; U of T)

Chaikivs'kyi, P.V.

    HORNIATKO KAVY: ABO, "BL'ONDYNKA DYTYNKA." Winnipeg: Promin', 1932. (Minn.)

Chaplenko, Vasyl'

    DRAMATYCHNI TVORY. New York, 1964. 307 p. (Metro; Minn.; U of T)

———.

    SPRAHA BEZSMERTIA: OPOVIDANNIA I P'IESKY. New York: Nasha bat'kivshchyna, 1969. 192 p. (Metro; U of T)

Darkovych, M.

KOSTEVI ZBYTKY: DITOCHA KOMEDIIKA V ODNIM AKTI. Winnipeg:
Promin', 1928. 32 p. (UNO)

Hun'kevych, Dmytro

ROZHDESTVENS'KA NICH. Winnipeg: Mars, 1924. 60 p. (UNO)

______.

SERED HRADU KUL': ABO, NEUSTRASHYMA HEROINIA. Winnipeg:
Ukrains'ka knyharnia, n.d. 135 p. (Minn.; UNO)

______.

V HALYTS'KII NEVOLI: DRAMA V 5 DIIAKH, ZI SPIVAMY I TANTSIAMY.
Winnipeg: Ukrains'ka knyharnia, 1921. 95 p. (Minn.; UNO)

______.

VYTAI, VESNO!: DITOCHA KARTYNA V ODNIM AKTI. Kanadyis'ka
biblioteka, no. 9. Winnipeg: Promin', 1927. 26 p. (UNO)

Ilarion, Metropolitan of Winnipeg and All Canada

NARODZHENNIA LIUDYNY: FILOSOFS'KA MISTERIA V P'IATY DIIAKH.
Winnipeg: Nasha kul'tura, 1948. 122 p. (Minn.; UNO)

______.

ROZP'IATYI MAZEPA: ISTORYCHNA DRAMA NA P'IAT' DII. Winnipeg:
Nasha kul'tura, 1961. 88 p. (Metro; Minn.; St. Vlad.; U of T)

Irchan, Myroslav

BUNTAR', SYN REVOLIUTSII: DRAMA V 3-OKH DIIAKH Z ZHYTTIA
HALYTS'KOHO PROLIETARIIATU. Lviv-New York: Kul'tura, 1922.
(Minn.)

______.

DVANAITSIAT' (sic): DRAMA V 5-OKH DIIAKH Z ZHYTTIA POVSTANCHOI
VATAHY V SKHIDNII HALYCHYNI V MISIATSI ZHOVTNI-LYSTOPADI 1922
ROKU. Winnipeg: Ukrains'ki robitnychi visti, 1923. 112 p.
(UNO)

______.

RODYNA SHCHITKARIV: DRAMA NA 4 DII. 2nd rev. ed. Teatral'na
biblioteka, no. 2. Winnipeg: Robitnycho-farmers'ke vydavnyche
tovarystvo, 1925. 79 p. (St. Vlad.)

Kazanivs'kyi, V.

PIMSTVA ZA KRYVDU: MYKOLA DZHERIA. Winnipeg: Ukrains'kyi
bazar, 1930. (Minn.)

Kivshenko, P.

BEZBATCHENKO: DRAMA NA 4 DII. Winnipeg: Ukrains'kyi bazar,
1927. 87 p. (Minn.; UNO)

Kovbel', Semen

DIVOCHI MRII: TRAGI-KOMEDIIA V 6-OKH VIDMINAKH, ZI SPIVAMY
I TANTSIAMY. Winnipeg: A. Ionkers, 1918. 125 p. (Minn.;
UNO; U of T)

______.

PARUBOCHI MRII: ZAKLIATA HORA. FANTAZIIA-DRAMA V 4-OKH
DIIAKH. Winnipeg, 1942. 61 p. (UNO)

______.

UKRAINIZATSIIA: KOMEDIIA NA ODNU DIIU Z CHASIV HOLOSNOI
UKRAINIZATSII UKRAINY MOSKALIAMY. n.p., n.d. 32 p. (UNO;
U of T)

Krypiakevych, Mykhailo

IAK KUM KUMA LICHYV: ZHART NA ODNY DIIU. Winnipeg: Populiarne
vydavnytstvo, 1936. 19 p. (UNO)

Lavrenko, Mykhailo

ARSENAL: LYTSEDIISTVO NA 4 DII IZ 6-MA VIDMINAMY. New York:
Ridnyi krai, 1976. 139 p. (UNO)

______.

PARKHYMOVI LASOSHCHI ABO BACHYLY OCHI, SHCHO KUPUVALY-IZHTE,
KHOCH POVYLAZ'TE. New York: Ridnyi krai, 1970. 99 p. (UNO)

Levyts'kyi, Vasyl' Sofroniv

IUNYI SKOMOROKH: P'IESY DLIA DITEI I MOLODI. Teatral'na
biblioteka, no. 1. Toronto, 1972. 303 p. (Minn.; UNO)

_______.

PID VESELYM OBOROHOM: P'IESY DLIA TEATRIV MALYKH FORM.
Teatral'na biblioteka, no. 3. Toronto: Komitet "Za amators'kyi
teatr," 1974. 208 p. (UNO)

Luhovyi, Oleksander

BRAT NA BRATA: DRAMA Z CHASIV REVOLIUTSII NA SHKIDNII UKRAINI
U 4-OKH DIIAKH. Saskatoon: published by the author, 1934.
31 p. (UNO)

_______.

"DALA DIVCHYNA KHUSTYNU": DRAMA Z CHASIV VYZVOL'NOI VIINY
NA VELYKII UKRAINI, 5 DII. Winnipeg: Ukrainian Voice, 1933.
54 p. (Minn.; St. Vlad.; UNO)

_______.

SVATANNIA PO POSHTI: KOMEDIIA U 3 DIIAKH. n.p.: St,sena, n.d.
20 p. (UNO)

_______.

SYRITS'KI SL'OZY: DRAMA Z CHASIV VIINY I REVOLIUTSII NA
SHKIDNII UKRAINI. Saskatoon: Novyi shliakh, 1934. ·27 p.
(Minn.; UNO)

_______.

V LYSTOPADOVU NICH: STSENICHNA FANTAZIIA U TR'OKH VIDSLONAKH.
V DNIAKH SLAVY: DRAMA Z CHASIV REVOLIUTSII I VIINY U SHKIDNII
UKRAINI: U 5-OKH VIDSLONAKH, 4-OKH DIIAKH. Toronto: published
by the author, 1938. 59 p. (Minn.; St. Vlad.; UNO)

_______.

ZA NARID SVII: TRAGEDIIA V 5 DIIAKH, 7 VIDSLONAKH. Stead, Man.:
Ia. Havryliuk, 1932. 50 p. (Minn.; St. Vlad.; UNO)

_____, and T. Pavlychenko

    VIRA BABENKO: DRAMA V 5-OKH DIIAKH. Saskatoon: Ukrainian
Women's Organization of Canada, 1936. 46 p. (UNO)

Maidanyk, Ia.

    MANIGRULA: KOMEDIIA V ODNII DII ZI SPIVAMY I TANTSIAMY.
Winnipeg: Ukrains'ka knyharnia, 1926. (Minn.)

Marchenko, Petro

    VESNA-VESNIANOCHKA: VESNIANKOVA FEIERIIA NA ODNU DIIU. New
York: published by the author, 1965. 15 p. (U of T)

Mirchuk, Petro

    ZI SVIATYM MYKOLAIEM U RIDNOMU KRAIU: STSENICHNA KARTYNA NA
2 VIDSLONY. Philadelphia-Winnipeg: Mii pryiatel', 1955. 15 p.
(UNO)

Romen, Levko

    ZHOVTOSYL: DRAMATYCHNA P'IESA IZ DII UPA. Edmonton: Slavuta
Publishing, 1965. 35 p. (Metro; Minn.)

Sofroniv-Levyts'kyi, Vasyl' et al.

    P'IESY DLIA MOLODI. Edmonton: Ukrainian Women's Association
of Canada, 1973. (Metro)

Tulevitriv, V.

    SHCHASLYVE I VESELE ZHYTTIA: KOMEDIIA V 4-OKH DIIAKH.
Winnipeg: Promin', 1944. 59 p. (UNO)

Yourinyak, Anatol

    NA DALEKYKH SHLIAKHAKH: P'IESA V 5 DIIAKH Z ZHYTTIA UKRAINS'KYKH
SKYTAL'TSIV. Detroit: Ukraina, 1955. (Minn.)

Poetry

Andiievs'ka, Emma

    DZHALAPITA. New York: New York Group, 1962. 16 p. (U of T)

————.

KUTY OPOSTIN': POEZII. New York: New York Group, 1962. 68 p.
(Minn.; U of T)

————.

NARODZHENNIA IDOLA: POEZII. New York: Slovo, 1958. 41 p.
(Minn.; U of T)

————.

RYBA I ROZMIR. New York: New York Group, 1961. 104 p. (Minn.;
U of T)

————.

TYHRY. New York: New York Group, 1962. 48 p. (U of T)

Andriichuk, Mykhailo Mykolaiovych

VYBRANI TVORY. New York: League of American Ukrainians,
1954. 367 p. (U of T)

Babii, Oleksa

POVSTANTSI: POEMA. Chicago: Literaturne vydavnytstvo, 1956.
179 p. (Minn.; St. Vlad.; UNO; U of T)

————.

SVIT I LIUDYNA: POEMY. Chicago: published by the author, 1969.
48 p. (UNO; U of T)

————.

VYBRANE Z TVORIV. Chicago: published by the author, 1969.
112 p. (Minn.; UNO; U of T)

Babiienko, V.V.

I. VARIIAT Z 1906 ROKU: OPOVIDANIE. II. VIRSH. III. MIZH
BURLYVYMY FYLIAMY: DRAMA NA 4 DII I 5 ODMIN. Winnipeg:
Ukrainian Voice, 1918. 80 p. (Minn.; UNO)

Barka, Vasyl'

LIRNYK: VYBRANI POEZII. New York: New York Group, 1968.
301 p. (U of T)

————.

    OKEAN. New York: Slovo, 1959. 239 p. (U of T)

————.

    PSALOM HOLUBYNOHO POLIA: POEZII. New York: Slovo, 1958.
(Minn.)

Beskyd, Iuliian

    SVIATA RIDNA ZEMLIA. Illus. by M. Levyts'kyi. Biblioteka
Lemkivshchyny, no. 1. Toronto: Organization for the Defense
of the Lemkian Region, 1966. 88 p. (Metro)

Boichuk, Bohdan

    CHAS BOLIU: POEZII. New York: Slovo, 1957. 64 p. (Minn.;
U of T)

————.

    MANDRIVKA TIL: POEZII. Graphics by Iaroslav Geruliak. New
York: New York Group, 1967. 78 p. (Metro; U of T)

————.

    PODOROZH Z UCHYTELEM: POEMA. Illus. by Liuboslav Hutsaliuk.
New York: New York Group, 1976. 93 p. (Metro; U of T)

————.

    SPOMYNY LIUBOVY: POEZII. New York: New York Group, 1963.
94 p. (U of T)

————.

    ZEMLIA BULA PUSTOSHNIA: POEMA. New York: Ukrains'ka students'ka
hromada, 1959. 88 p. (U of T)

Buriakivets', Iurii

    LYSTKY SONIASHNYKA: POEZII. New York: Vasyl' Pustovit, 1971.
288 p. (U of T)

————.

    ZIRNYTSI: POEZII. New York: Augsburg, 1950. (Minn.)

Chaplenko, Vasyl'

IS'KO GAVA: VIRSHOVANA BUVAL'SHCHYNA. n.p., 1965. 36 p.
(Minn.)

Chartoryis'kyi, Mykola Sydor

INTER ARMA: POEZII. New York, 1949. 40 p. (St. Vlad.)

Cherin', Hanna

CHORNOZEM. Chicago: Ukrainian-American Publishing and Printing,
1962. 162 p. (Minn.; UNO; U of T)

______.

NEBESNI VIRSHI. Buenos Aires: Julian Serediak, 1973. 107 p.
(Metro; Minn.; U of T)

______.

PRYHODY UKRAINS'KOI KNYZHKY. Chicago: Ukrainian-American
Publishing and Printing, 1972. 11 p. (Metro)

______.

TRAVNEVI MRII. Chicago, 1970. 144 p. (Minn.; UNO; U of T)

______.

VAHONETKY. Chicago-New York: A. Orel, 1969. 70 p. (Minn.;
U of T)

Chernenko, Oleksandra

LIUDYNA: POEMA NA 18 PISEN'. Philadelphia: Kyiv Publishing,
1960. 62 p. (UNO)

Danyl'chuk, Ivan

SVYTAIE DEN': POEZII. Kanadiis'ka biblioteka, no. 46.
Winnipeg: published by the author, 1929. 56 p. (Minn.;
St. Vlad.)

Darkovych, Mykhailo T.

KYIV I RYM: IANYCHARY CHORT. Kanadyis'ka biblioteka, no. 54.
Winnipeg: T. Zolotukha, 1929. 80 p. (Minn.; St. Vlad.)

Dibrova, Hnat O. (pseud.)

HAMY DALECHYN: LIRYCHNI TA INSHI POEZII. New York: Volosozhar, 1957. 68 p. (Minn.; U of T)

______.

KLADKA VYDIN': POEZII. New York, 1953. 64 p. (Minn.; St. Vlad.; U of T)

______.

MISTERIIA ZEMLI: POEZII. Bk. 5. New York: A. Orel, 1968. 46 p. (Minn.; U of T)

______.

RUKH I HARMONIIA: POEZII. New York: A. Orel, 1963. 64 p. (Minn.)

______.

TERNY I TROIANDY: POEZII. ZBIRKA SHOSTA. Clifton, N.J.: P. Yamniak, 1973. 52 p. (U of T)

Dima

TRETII BEREH. New York, 1963. 48 p. (Minn.; U of T)

______.

ZUSTRICH ROKIV: POEZII. New York, 1973. 48 p. (U of T)

Domashovets', Hryhorii

PRAVDA I VOLIA: STATTI, POEZII, OPOVIDANNIA I POVIST'. Cyrillo-Methodian Brotherhood Editions, no. 7. Irvington, N.Y.: Cyrillo-Methodian Brotherhood, 1970. 207 p. (U of T)

______.

VYBRANI TVORY. Hartford, Conn., 1960. (Minn.)

Ewach, Honore

UKRAINS'KYI MUDRETS': POEMA PRO SLAVNOHO UKRAINS'KOHO FILOSOFA-MISTYKA, HRYHORIIA SKOVORODU. Winnipeg: Ukrainian Cultural and Educational Centre, 1945. 16 p. (Minn.; St. Vlad.)

Granovsky, Alexander A.

ISKRY VIRY: POEZII. Vol. 5. New York: Zhyttia i mystetstvo, 1953. 144 p. (Minn.; UNO)

______.

OSINNI UZORY. Vol. 6. 2nd rev. ed. Chicago-New York: Zhyttia i mystetstvo, 1957. 143 p. (Minn.; UNO)

______.

POEZII. 3 vols. New York: Zhyttia i mystetstvo, 1964. (Minn.)

______.

SNY ZRUINOVANOHO ZAMKU: POEZII. Vol. 7. Chicago: Zhyttia i mystetstvo, 1964. 144 p. (Minn.; UNO)

Hai-Holovko, Oleksa

POETYCHNI TVORY. Vol. 1. Toronto: Novi dni, 1970. (Metro; St. Vlad.; U of T)

Halan, Anatol'

PRO RADIST' I BIL': POEZII. Philadelphia: Vlasna khata, 1970. 92 p. (Minn.)

Harmash, Mira

MARIIA LIUIZA: POEMA. Philadelphia: Dunrite Press, 1972. 63 p. (Minn.; U of T)

______.

RAIDUHA V PIT'MI: DRUHA ZBIRKA POEZII. Chicago-Philadelphia, 1972. 60 p. (Minn.; U of T)

______.

VIDNAIDENI ROKY: POEZII. Toronto: Homin Ukrainy, 1968. 62 p. (Minn.; U of T)

Havryliuk, Volodymyr

TIN' I MANDRIVNYK. New York: Organization for the Defense of Four Freedoms of Ukraine, 1969. 105 p. (Minn.; UNO; U of T)

Holovats'kyi, Vasyl' K.

 VINETS' ZHYTTIA. Chicago: published by the author, 1945.
 (Minn.)

Horishnyi, Mykola

 IUNI SNY: VIRSHI. Jersey City, N.J.: Dnipro, 1956. 53 p.
 (Minn.; UNO)

 ______.

 SHLIAKHOM PISEN': VIRSHI. Jersey City, N.J.: Dnipro, 1956.
 38 p. (UNO)

Ilarion, Metropolitan of Winnipeg and All Canada

 PROMETEI: SMERK HRETS'KYKH BOHIV: POEMA. Nasha kul'tura,
 no. 9. Winnipeg: Nasha kul'tura, 1948. 68 p. (Minn.; St. Vlad.;
 U of T)

 ______.

 ZHERTVA VECHIRNIAIA: ISUS I VARAVVA: POEMA. 3rd ed. Biblioteka
 "Slova istyny," no. 2. Winnipeg: Metropolitan Synod, 1949.
 48 p. (Minn.; St. Vlad.)

Kairez, Mykola

 MECH I SERTSE: POEZII. Toronto: Ukrains'kyi robitnyk, 1949.
 128 p. (Minn.; St. Vlad.)

Karpenko-Krynytsia, Petro

 POEMY. Detroit: Prometheus, 1954. 46 p. (St. Vlad.; U of T)

 ______.

 SOLDATY MOHO LEGIONU, 1945-46. Chicago: Orlyk, 1951. 48 p.
 (Minn.; UNO; U of T)

Kedr, Rostyslav

 SKOBYNE HNIZDO: PLASTOVA POEMA. Toronto: Lisovi chorty, 1957.
 (Minn.)

Khmil', Ivan

   HOMIN POLISSIA: POEZII. Biblioteka litopysu Volyni, no. 5.
   Winnipeg, 1960. 243 p. (Minn.; UNO; U of T)

   _____.

   IDU Z KOBZOIU: POEZII. Chicago: published by the author, 1962.
   244 p. (Metro; UNO)

Khraplyva, Lesia

   DALEKYM I BLYZ'KYM: VIRSHI. New York: Hartur, 1972. 123 p.
   (Metro; UNO; U of T)

Kmeta-Ichnians'kyi, Ivan

   CHASHA ZOLOTA: VYBRANE, LIRYKA. Philadelphia: Doroha pravdy,
   1964. (Minn.)

   _____.

   KRYLA NAD MOREM: POEZII. Philadelphia: Slovo, 1970. 111 p.
   (Minn.; U of T)

Kolisnyk, Petro

   MISIIA KYIEVA. Toronto: Kyiv, 1975. 247 p. (U of T)

Kosach, Iurii

   ZOLOTI VOROTA: POEZII. New York: Novi obrii, 1966. 47 p.
   (Minn.; U of T)

Krat, Pavlo

   ZA ZEMLIU I VOLIU! n.p., n.d. (Minn.)

Kravtsiv, Bohdan

   ZYMOZELEN': SONETY I OLEKSANDRYNY. Philadelphia: Ameryka,
   1951. 29 p. (Minn.; UNO; U of T)

Kumka, Mykhailo, comp.

   SNIP: UKRAINS'KYI DEKLIAMATOR. 2 vols. in 5. Winnipeg:
   Ukrainian Voice, 1937, 1939-40. (Minn.; St. Vlad.; UNO: 1937, 1939)

Kupchyns'kyi, Roman

SKOROPAD: POEMA. New York: Chervona kalyna, 1965. 127 p.
(Metro; UNO; U of T)

Kurdydyk, Iaroslav

SERTSE I ZBROIA: ZBIRKA VOIATS'KOI POEZII. Toronto: Brotherhood
of Former Soldiers of the First Ukrainian Division of the UNA,
1976. 76 p. (St. Vlad.; UNO; U of T)

Kylyna, Patrytsiia

LEGENDY I SNY: POEZII. New York: New York Group, 1964. 60 p.
(U of T)

————.

TRAGEDIIA DZHMELIV: POEZII. New York: New York Group, 1960.
31 p. (U of T)

Lavrenko, Mykhailo

BRAMA ZOLOTA: POEZII. New York: Ridnyi krai, 1970. 100 p.
(UNO)

————.

PERSHA KOPA: ZBIRKA PERSHA. New York: Ridnyi krai, 1970. 98 p.
(UNO)

Lesych, Vadym

KREIDIANE KOLO: POEZII: ZOSHYT S'OMYI. Seriia "Dlia amatoriv."
New York: Na hori, 1960. 101 p. (Minn.)

————.

LIRYCHNYI ZOSHYT: POEZII. New York: Pryiateli poezii, 1953.
47 p. (Minn.)

————.

POEZII. New York: Obnova, 1954. 32 p. (Minn.; U of T)

————.

PREDMETNIST' NIZVIDKIL': POEZII. New York: New York Group,
1972. 47 p. (Metro; U of T)

Liaturyns'ka, Oksana

    KNIAZHA EMAL': POEZII. New York: Slovo, 1955. 196 p. (Minn.;
St. Vlad.; UNO; U of T)

Malaniuk, Ievhen

    OSTANNIA VESNA: POEZII. New York: Visnyk, 1959. 100 p.
(Minn.; UNO; U of T)

______.

    PIATA SYMFONIIA: POEMA. Philadelphia: Kyiv Publishing, 1954.
16 p. (Minn.; St. Vlad.)

______.

    POEZII. New York: Shevchenko Scientific Society, 1954. 307 p.
(Minn.; UNO; U of T)

______.

    SERPEN'. New York: New York Group, 1964. 72 p. (Minn.; U of T)

______.

    VLADA. Knyhy Poezii, bk. 6. Philadelphia: Kyiv Publishing, 1951.
75 p. (Minn.; St. Vlad.; UNO; U of T)

Maliar, Pavlo

    POEMA PRO ULIANKU. Zolotyi doshch, bk. 3. Toronto: Novi dni,
1976. 118 p. (Metro)

Mandryka, Mykyta I.

    MAZEPA: POEMA. Preface by Iaroslav Rudnyts'kyi. Winnipeg:
Trident Press, 1960. 87 p. (Metro; Minn.; U of T)

______.

    MII SAD: POEZII. Vol. 2. Winnipeg, 1941. (Minn.)

______.

    RADIST': POEZII. Winnipeg: Trident Press, 1959. 143 p.
(Minn.; St. Vlad.: UNO; U of T)

————.

SONTSETSVIT: POEZII. Vol. 4. Winnipeg: Trident Press, 1965.
128 p. (Metro; Minn.; UNO; U of T)

————.

SYMFONIIA VIKIV: POEMY I LIRYKA. Winnipeg: Trident Press,
1961. 215 p. (Metro)

————.

VIK PETLIURY: POEMA. Winnipeg: Trident Press, 1966. 47 p.
(St. Vlad.; UNO; U of T)

————.

VYNO ZHYTTIA: VYBRANE DLIA VYBRANYKH Z POEZII ZA 1965-69 ROKY.
Vol. 5. Author's original manuscripts. Winnipeg: Ars, 1970.
176 p. (Metro; U of T)

————.

ZAVERSHENNIA LITA: POEZII, 1970-74. Vol. 6. Winnipeg: Ars,
1975. (U of T)

————.

ZOLOTA OSIN': POEZII, 1905-57. Winnipeg: Trident Press,
1958. 175 p. (Minn.; UNO; U of T)

Matiiv-Mel'nyk, Mykola
    HORYT' MII SVIT, 1944-47. Philadelphia: Ameryka, 1951. (Minn.)

Matviienko, T.
    SONETY. Toronto: Kyiv, 1961. (Minn.)

Mel'nychenko, Oleksa
    VID SHCHYROHO SERTSIA: POEZII. New York: Sad, 1973. 94 p.
    (U of T)

Metel's'kyi, Roman
    DESIAT' VINKIV SONETIV. Clifton, N.J.: Petro Yamniak, 1971.
    184 p. (Metro)

______.

MII RIDNYI KRAI: POEMA. Passaic, N.J.: published by the author, 1969. 128 p. (Metro; UNO)

______.

PRAVDA KRIZ' PIT'MU: POEZII. Passaic, N.J.: published by the author, 1964. 128 p. (Metro; UNO; U of T)

Michael, Archbishop of Toronto and Eastern Canada

SVITOVA EPOPEIA: TRYLOHIIA. 3 vols. Winnipeg: Trident Press, 1953-56. (Metro; Minn.; St. Vlad.: vols. 1, 3; UNO: vol. 1)

Mahylianka, Dariia

DUMKY LETIAT' NA UKRAINU: NARODNI VIRSHI. Edmonton: Alberta Printing Co., 1962. 119 p. (St. Vlad.)

______.

PISNI MOHO SERTSIA: DRUHA ZBIRKA POEZII. Edmonton: Alberta Printing Co., 1964. 126 p. (St. Vlad.)

Muliarchuk, Ivan

PROMIN' ZHYTTIA: POEZII. Detroit, 1937. 15 p. (St. Vlad.)

______.

ZHNYVA DOS'PILY: POEZII (sic). Winnipeg, 1917. (Minn.)

Mur, Dan

SKRYZHALI TUHY: POEZII. Edmonton: Vasyl and Natalka Dukhnii, 1973. 118 p. (Minn.; U of T)

______.

ZHAL' I HNIV: POEZII. Edmonton: Vasyl and Natalka Dukhnii, 1966. 93 p. (Minn.; U of T)

Murovych, Larysa

IEVSHAN: POEZII TA POEMY. Toronto: Svitannia, 1971. 64 p. (Metro; Minn.; U of T)

————.

ZHAR-PTAKHA: VYBRANI POEZII. Toronto: Svitannia, 1971. 47 p.
(Metro; Minn.; U of T)

Nepryts'kyi-Hranovs'kyi, Ol.

ISKRY VIRY. Vol. 5. New York: Zhyttia i mystetstvo, 1953.
144 p. (U of T)

————.

OSINNI UZORY. Vol. 6. New York: Zhyttia i mystetstvo, 1957.
(U of T)

Nyzhankivs'kyi, Bohdan

VAHOTA: POEZII. Detroit: Literaturne bratstvo, 1953. 31 p.
(St. Vlad.; UNO)

Oleksandriv, Borys

TUHA ZA SONTSEM: POEZII, 1945-65. New York: Slovo, n.d.
120 p. (Metro; UNO; U of T)

Orlyhora, Lev T.

LIUBLIU: LIRYKA. Edmonton: Alberta Printing Co., 1958. (Minn.)

Os'machka, Teodosii Stepanovych

IZ-PID SVITU: POETYCHNI TVORY. Ed. by Iu. Sherekh-Shevelov.
New York: UVAN in the U.S., 1954. 317 p. (Minn.; St. Vlad.;
UNO; U of T)

————.

PLAN DO DVORU: POVIST'. Toronto: Ukrainian Legion, 1951. 184 p.
(Minn.; St. Vlad.; U of T)

————.

POET: POEMA NA 23 PISNI. n.p.: Ukrains'ke Slovo, n.d. 153 p.
(St. Vlad.)

Ovechko, Ivan

NE PLACH, UKRAINO!: VYBRANI POEZII. Los Angeles, 1965. 45 p.
(Metro; Minn.; UNO)

______.

VYBRANE: POEZII, NARYSY, OPOVIDANNIA, STATTI, RETSENZII.
Greeley, Colo.: friends of the author, 1970. (Minn.)

Pylypenko, Lev

DRUZI ZHYTTIA: CHETVERTA ZBIRKA VIRSHIV. Philadelphia, 1978.
205 p. (UNO)

______.

NA ZAKHODI SONTSIA: DRUHA ZBIRKA VIRSHIV. Toronto: published
by the author, 1971. 103 p. (Minn.; UNO; U of T)

______.

PID SHEPIT SERTSIA: TRETIA ZBIRKA VIRSHIV. Philadelphia:
Vlasna khata, 1973. 128 p. (Minn.; UNO; U of T)

______.

RIDNI DALI: PERSHA ZBIRKA VIRSHIV. Philadelphia, 1969. 118 p.
(Minn.; UNO; U of T)

Romen, Levko

PEREDHRIM'IA: POEZII. Philadelphia, 1953. (Minn.)

______.

POEMY. Toronto: Ievshan-zillia, 1956. 72 p. (Metro; Minn.;
St. Vlad.; UNO)

Rubchak, Bohdan

DIVCHYNI BEZ KRAINY: TRETIA ZBIRKA POEZII. New York: New York
Group, 1963. 48 p. (U of T)

______.

KAMINNYI SAD: POEZII. New York: Slovo, 1956. 64 p. (Metro;
Minn.; U of T)

———.

OSOBYSTA KLIO: CHETVERTA ZBIRKA POEZII. New York: New York Group, 1967. 45 p. (U of T)

———.

PROMENYSTA ZRADA. New York, 1960. 48 p. (Minn.; U of T)

Semchuk, Stepan

REFLIEKSII: POEZII, KNYZHKA PIATA. Winnipeg, 1965. 51 p. (U of T)

———.

ZHERELA: POEZII. KNYZHKA SHESTA. Winnipeg: Christian Press, 1966. 49 p. (Minn.; U of T)

———.

POEMY. Winnipeg, 1967. 67 p. (U of T)

———.

SOTVORENNIA: POEZII, KNYZHKA VOS'MA. Winnipeg, 1968. 75 p. (Minn.; U of T)

———.

POEZIIA I PROZA: KNYZHKA DEVIATA. Winnipeg, 1969. 79 p. (Minn.; U of T)

———.

SVITLIST' DUMKY: POEZII, KNYZHKA DESIATA. Winnipeg, 1970. 94 p. (Minn.; U of T)

———.

NAVKOLO SVITA: LIRYKA. Vol. 11. Winnipeg, 1971. 77 p. (Minn.; U of T)

Shankovs'kyi, Ihor

DYSONANSY. Philadelphia: Kyiv Publishing, 1960. 93 p. (UNO)

_______.

 KOROTKE LITO: POEZII. Edmonton: Ukrains'ka knyharnia, 1970.
114 p. (UNO; U of T)

Sharyk, Mykhailo

 ROZSYPANI PERLY: VIDHOMIN VYZVOL'NOI SURMY. Toronto: published
by the author, 1965. (Minn.)

Shcherbak, Mykola and Volodymyr Zhyla

 POLUM'IANE SLOVO: DO 50-RICHCHIA IARA SLAVUTYCHA. London, Ont.:
Ukrainian Publishing Company, 1969. 40 p. (Minn.)

Shevchuk, Tetiana

 NA PRESTIL MAIBUTNIKH DNIV. Winnipeg, 1964. 79 p. (U of T)

Shtohryn, Dmytro

 DOLIA UKRAINY. Philadelphia: Rus'kyi syrits'kyi dim, 1917.
(Minn.)

Skorups'kyi, Volodymyr

 AISTRY NEVIDTSVILI: POEZII. Toronto, 1972. 54 p. (U of T)

_______.

 BEZ RIDNOHO POROHA: POEMY. Edmonton: Ukrainian Riflemen's
Society,   1958. 62 p. (Metro; UNO; U of T)

_______.

 IZ DZHERELA: POEZII. Toronto: published by the author, 1961.
78 p. (Metro; UNO)

_______.

 MOIA OSELIA: POEZII. Edmonton: publ. by citizens of Edmonton,
1954. 96 p. (Metro; Minn.; UNO)

_______.

 U DOROZI: POEZII. Edmonton: Alberta Printing Co., 1957. 56 p.
(Minn.; UNO)

Slavutych, Iar

    MAIESTAT: SHOSTA ZBIRKA POEZII. Edmonton: Slavuta Publishing, 1942. 45 p. (Minn.; U of T)

_______.

    MUDROSHCHI MANDRIV: VOS'MA ZBIRKA POEZII. Edmonton: Slavuta Publishing, 1972. 89 p. (Metro; Minn.; St. Vlad.; U of T)

_______.

    TROFEI: 1938-1963. Edmonton: Slavuta Publishing, 1963. 320 p. (Metro; Minn.; St. Vlad.; U of T)

SLOVO. Vols. 1-3. New York: Association of Ukrainian Writers in Exile, 1962-68. (Minn.; U of T.)

Smotrych, Oleksander

    TYSIACHA DEVIATSOT TRYDTSIAT'TRY. Toronto: published by the author, 1975. 10 p. (U of T)

_______.

    VIRSHI. 3 vols. Toronto: published by the author, 1974-75. (U of T)

Stechyshyn, Mykhailo

    VIRSHI. n.p., n.d. (Minn.)

Struk, Danylo

    GAMMA SIGMA. Ed. by Bohdan Klymash. Cambridge, Mass.: Bohdan Klymash, 1963. 40 p. (U of T)

Suknaski, Andrew

    BLIND MAN'S HOUSE. Wood Mountain, Sask.: Anak Press, 1975. 8 p. (Metro)

_______.

    THE GHOSTS CALL YOU POOR. Toronto: Macmillan, 1978. 117 p. (Metro; St. Vlad.; U of T)

__________.

LEAVING. Seven Persons, Alta.: Repository Press, 1974. 78 p.
(Metro; U of T)

__________.

LEAVING WOOD MOUNTAIN. Wood Mountain, Sask.: Sundog Press,
1975. 41 p. (Metro)

__________.

THE NIGHTWATCHMAN. Wood Mountain, Sask.: Anak Press, 1972.
10 p. (Metro)

__________.

OCTOMI: POEMS. Drawings by William Johnson. Saskatoon:
Thistledown Press, 1976. 39 p. (Metro; U of T)

__________.

OLD MILL. Vancouver: Blewointment Press, 1972. 24 p. (Metro;
U of T)

__________.

ON FIRST LOOKING DOWN FROM LION'S GATE BRIDGE. Coatsworth, Ont.:
Black Mass Press, 1976. (Metro; U of T)

__________.

PHILLIP WELL. Caledonia Writing Series. Prince George, B.C.,
1973. 2 p. (Metro)

__________.

ROSEWAY IN THE EAST. Gronk Series 4, no. 7. Banff, Alta.,
1971. 10 p. (Metro)

__________.

SUICIDE NOTES, BOOK ONE. Wood Mountain, Sask.: Sundog Press,
1973. 32 p. (Metro)

————.

WOOD MOUNTAIN: POEMS. Comp. and introd. by Al Purdy. Toronto: Macmillan, 1976. 128 p. (Metro; St. Vlad.; U of T)

————.

WOOD MOUNTAIN POEMS. Wood Mountain, Sask.: Anak Press, 1973. 52 p. (Metro)

————.

WRITING ON STONE: POEM DRAWINGS, 1966-76. Wood Mountain, Sask.: Anak Press, 1976. 20 p. (Metro)

Sydor-Chartoryis'kyi, Mykola

INTER ARMA: POEZII. New York, 1949. (Minn.)

Sytnyk, Mykhailo

TSVIT PAPOROTI: POEZII. Toronto: Moloda Ukraina, 1975. 224 p. (U of T)

Tarasiuk, Ilarion

NA KRYLAKH VIRY: POEZII. Doroha pravdy, no. 24. Chicago-Toronto: Doroha pravdy, 1962. 183 p. (Minn.)

Tarnavs'ka, Marta

KHVALIU ILIUZIIU: POEZII. New York: Slovo, 1972. 47 p. (Minn.; U of T)

Tarnavs'kyi, Iurii O.

POEZII PRO NISHCHO. New York: New York Group, 1970. 384 p. (U of T)

————.

ZHYTTIA V MISTI. New York: Slovo, 1956. 64 p. (Minn.; U of T)

Tarnavs'kyi, Ostap

MOSTY: POEZII. New York: Slovo, 1956. 78 p. (Minn.; UNO; U of T)

_______.

SAMOTNIE DEREVO: POEZII. New York: Slovo, 1960. 96 p. (Minn.; UNO)

_______.

ZHYTTIA: VINOK SONETIV. Philadelphia: Kyiv Publishing, 1952. 21 p. (Minn.; St. Vlad.; U of T)

Tretiak, Ol'ha

PISEN' MOIKH UZORY: POEZII (DESHCHO Z RODYNNOHO AL'BOMA). Montreal, 1972. (U of T)

Veretenchenko, Oleksa

CHORNA DOLYNA: POEMA. Detroit: Literaturne bratstvo, 1953. 32 p. (Minn.)

_______.

DYM VICHNOSTY. Detroit: Prometheus, 1951. 60 p. (Metro; Minn.; U of T)

Vorsklo, Vira

LADA: POEZII. Toronto: published by the author, 1977. 469 p. (Metro)

_______.

LYSTY BEZ ADRESY: VYBRANI POEZII. Toronto: Homin Ukrainy, 1967. 65 p. (Metro; UNO)

Zakharchuk, Dmytro

NA CHUZHYNI: POEZII. Winnipeg: published by the author, 1934. (Minn.)

_______.

Z VESNIANYKH DNIV: POEZII. New York: Sichovyi bazar, 1923. (Minn.)

Children's Literature

Bilets'ka, Teklia

BABUNYNI KAZKY: DLIA DITEI KOZHNOHO VIKU. Toronto: Ob'iednannia pratsivnykiv literatury dlia ditei i molodi, 1973. 62 p. (Metro)

Bloch, Marie Halun

AUNT AMERICA. New York: Atheneum, 1963. 149 p. (UNO)

______.

BERN, SON OF MIKULA. Illus. by Edward Kozak. New York: Atheneum, 1972. 177 p. (Minn.)

______.

THE TWO WORLDS OF DAMYAN. Illus. by Robert Quackenbush. New York: Atheneum, 1966. (UNO)

Bodnarchuk, Ivan

KLADKA: DYTIACHI NOVEL'KY. Toronto: Ob'iednannia pratsivnykiv dytiachoi literatury, 1957. 41 p. (Minn.)

Cherin', Hanna

BRATIK I SESTRYCHKA. Chicago: Ukrainian-American Publishing and Printing Co., 1960. 91 p. (Minn.)

Dima

KIT-MUZYKA. Illus. by Edward Kozak. New York: Ukrainian National Women's League of America, 1971. (Metro)

Fedchuk, Bohdan

DLIA ROZVAHY I NAUKY. Toronto, 1965. (Minn.)

______.

DLIA ROZVAHY I NAUKY: P'IATA KNYZHECHKA ZAHADOK. Toronto: Association of Ukrainian Educators in Canada, 1964. 51 p. (Minn.)

______.

KHTO TSE? SHCHO TSE?: TRETIA KNYZHECHKA ZAHADOK. Toronto:
Association of Ukrainian Educators in Canada, 1963. 47 p.
(Minn.)

______.

KHTO VIDHADAIE?: PERSHA KNYZHECHKA ZAHADOK. Toronto:
Association of Ukrainian Educators in Canada, 1961. 60 p.
(Minn.)

______.

RIDNA KNYZHKA VSIM U RUKY DLIA ROZVAHY I NAUKY: SHOSTA
KNYZHECHKA ZAHADOK. Toronto: Association of Ukrainian
Educators in Canada, 1965. 61 p. (Minn.)

______.

STO ZAHADOK DLIA NASHYKH DITOK: DRUHA KNYZHECHKA. Toronto:
Association of Ukrainian Educators in Canada, 1961. 51 p.
(Minn.)

______.

STO I P'IATDESIAT: 1867-1967, 1917-1967: DESIATA KNYZHECHKA
ZAHADOK. Toronto: Homin Ukrainy, 1967. 64 p. (Minn.; UNO)

______.

ZAHADKY. Toronto: Association of Ukrainian Educators in
Canada, 1958. 47 p. (UNO)

______.

ZAHADKY: CHYTAI, DUMAI, VIDHADUI: SHISTNADTSIATA ZBIRKA
VIRSHOVANYKH ZAHADOK. Toronto: Association of Ukrainian
Educators in Canada, 1977. 74 p. (UNO)

______.

ZAHADKY: SIMNADTSIATA ZBIRKA VIRSHOVANYKH ZAHADOK. Toronto:
Association of Ukrainian Educators in Canada, 1978. 82 p.
(UNO)

Horishnyi, Mykola

  NA UKRAINS'KII FARMI: DITOCHA STSENICHNA KARTYNA. Jersey
  City, N.J.: Dnipro, 1956. (Minn.)

Khraplyva, Lesia

  ANTYPKOVI PRYHODY ABO U DEN' SV. MYKOLAIA: STSENICHNA KARTYNA.
  New York-Toronto: Ob'iednannia pratsivnykiv dytiachoi literatury,
  1965. 16 p. (UNO)

  ______.

  CHARODIINE AVTO: OPOVIDANNIA DLIA DITEI. Illus. by Petro
  Andrusiv. New York: Nashym ditiam, 1967. 95 p. (Metro; Minn.)

  ______.

  IARMAROK MYSHKY-HRYZYKNYZHKY: STSENICHNI KARTYNY-REVIIA DLIA
  DYTIACHOHO TEATRU NA "SVIATO KNYZHKY." Toronto: Ob'iednannia
  pratsivnykiv dytiachoi literatury, 1966. 36 p. (Metro)

  ______.

  ISKRY. Plastova biblioteka, no. 2. Cleveland: Ukrainian
  Printing and Publishing Co., 1955. 32 p. (Minn.; St. Vlad.)

  ______.

  KOZAK NEVMYRAKA: OPOVIDANNIA DLIA DITEI. New York, 1961.
  96 p. (Metro; Minn.; UNO)

  ______.

  NA VVES' BOZHYI RIK: DEKLIAMATOR DLIA DITEI. New York:
  Howerla, 1964. 94 p. (Metro; Minn.; UNO)

  ______.

  PYSANKA UKRAINS'KYM DITIAM. Illus. by Petro Andrusiv.
  Munich-New York: Ukrains'kym ditiam, 1965. 16 p. (Metro;
  UNO)

  ______.

  ROSTYKOVA KAZKA. Illus. by Nina Mudryk-Mryts. Cleveland-New
  York: Pershyi kurin' plastovoho senioratu im. S. Tysovs'koho,
  1962. (UNO)

_____.

VITER Z UKRAINY: DRUHA ZBIRKA OPOVIDAN' DLIA DITEI SHKIL'NOHO
VIKU. New York: Sentry Press, 1965. 143 p. (Metro; Minn.;
UNO)

_____.

ZABAVKY MARTUSI. Illus. by Nina Mudryk-Mryts. Munich-New York:
Ukrains'kym ditiam, 1960. (UNO)

Krokhmaliuk, Iurii

PRO LYTSARIA DOBRYNIU TA IOHO SESTRYCHKU ZABAVU. Toronto:
Ob'iednannia pratsivnykiv literatury dlia ditei i molodi,
1970. 30 p. (Metro)

Kumka, Mykhailo

DEKLIAMATSII NA DEN' MATERI. Winnipeg: Ukrainian Voice, 1937.
79 p. (St. Vlad.)

_____.

MONOL'OHY I DIIAL'OGY DLIA DITEI I MOLODI. Winnipeg: Ukrainian
Voice, 1935. 63 p. (St. Vlad.)

_____, comp.

NAIKRASHCHI ZAHADKY I ZABAVKY DLIA STARYKH I MALYKH.
Winnipeg: Ukrainian Voice, 1931. 91 p. (St. Vlad.)

Kuz'menko, Svitlana

IVASYK I IOHO ABETKA. New York-Toronto: Ob'iednannia pratsivnykiv
literatury dlia ditei i molodi, 1974. 48 p. (Metro; Minn.)

Kuz'movych-Holovins'ka, Mariia

HORBATEN'KA: OPOVIDANNIA. Illus. by B. Strebel's'kyi.
Dytiacha biblioteka, no. 1. Toronto: Dobra knyzhka, 1958.
48 p. (Metro; Minn.)

Levyts'kyi, Vasyl' Sofroniv

IUNYI SKOMOROKH: P'IESY DLIA DITEI I MOLODI. Teatral'na
biblioteka, no. 1. Toronto, 1972. 303 p. (Minn.; UNO)

Liaturyns'ka, Oksana

   BEDRYK: VIRSHI DLIA DITEI. Winnipeg: Trident Press, 1956.
   (Minn.)

   ______.

   KNIAZHA EMAL': POEZII. New York: Slovo, 1955. (Minn.)

Mel'nyk, Orysia and Nadiia Pip

   NAVKOLO NAS. Illus. by Ivan Pip. Winnipeg, 1967. 36 p. (Metro)

Mudryk-Mryts, Nina

   NA SVITANKU. Toronto: Ob'iednannia pratsivnykiv literatury
   dlia ditei i molodi, 1974. (Metro)

   ______.

   PRO IAHIDKY. Toronto: published by the author, 1965. 18 p.
   (Metro)

   ______.

   PRYHODY HORISHKA. Illus. by the author. Toronto: Ob'iednannia
   pratsivnykiv dytiachoi literatury, 1970. 15 p. (Metro)

   ______.

   SONIASHNI KAZKY. Illus. by the author. Toronto: Ob'iednannia
   pratsivnykiv literatury dlia ditei i molodi, 1975. 44 p.
   (Metro)

Parfanovych, Sofiia

   TAKYI VIN BUV ... ISTORIIA ODNOHO PSA: POVIST' DLIA MOLODI.
   Jersey City, N.J.: Svoboda, 1964. 198 p. (Minn.; UNO; U of T)

   ______.

   VIRNYI PRYIATEL': OPOVIDANNIA Z ZHYTTIA DOMASHN'OHO KOTA.
   Chicago: Mykola Denysiuk, 1961. 207 p. (Minn.; UNO; U of T)

Perelisna, Kateryna

KOTYKOVA PRYHODA: KAZOCHKA DLIA DITOK. Illus. by Nina Mudryk-Mryts. Toronto: Ob'iednannia pratsivnykiv literatury dlia ditei i molodi, 1973. 11 p. (Metro)

Savyts'ka, Ivanna

NASHA KHATKA: OPOVIDANNIA DLIA DITEI. Illus. by Petro Andrusiv. Philadelphia: Uchytel's'ka vydavnycha spilka, 1957. 44 p. (Minn.)

_______.

NEZABUD'KY: VIRSHI DLIA DITEI. 1 vol. Philadelphia, 1959. (Metro)

_______.

SERTSE: ZBIRKA DEKLAMATSII DLIA DITEI NA DEN' MATERI I INSHI UROCHYSTOSTI V ROTSI. Philadelphia: Ameryka, 1953. 30 p. (Minn.)

_______.

ZOLOTI DZVINOCHKY: KAZKY DLIA DITEI. Illus. by Petro Andrusiv. Philadelphia: Ukrainian National Women's League of America, 1958. (Metro; Minn.)

Surmach, Yaroslava

TUSYA AND THE POT OF GOLD. Winnipeg: Ukrainian Voice, 1972. (Minn.)

2nd ed.: New York, Atheneum, 1973. (St. Vlad.)

Sydor-Chartoryis'kyi, Mykola

BURCHYK, KHRYPCHYK, NIAVCHYK, HAVCHYK: KAZKA. New York: Howerla, 1957. (Minn.)

Symchych, Victoria and Olga Vesey, trans.

THE FLYING SHIP AND OTHER UKRAINIAN FOLK TALES. Illus. by Peter Kuch. Montreal-Toronto: Holt, Rinehart & Winston, 1975. 93 p. (Metro; St. Vlad.; UNO)

UKRAINS'KI NARODNI KOLYSKOVI I INSHI PISNI DLIA SHKOLY I DOMU.
Winnipeg: Ukrainian School Council, 1977. 31 p. (Metro)

Vynnyts'ka, Iryna

KAM'IANA SOKYRA. 2nd rev. and enl. ed. Biblioteka Samopomochi
dlia molodi, no. 1. New York: Samopomich, 1967. 71 p. (Metro)

Zavadovych, Roman

BOHUTA BAHATYR: ISTORYCHNA KAZKA V OBRAZKAKH. Book 1, pt. 1.
Biblioteka Veselky, no. 3. Jersey City-New York: UNA, 1956.
(Minn.)

————.

DIVA MARIIA DOPOMOHLA: STSENICHNA KARTYNA. Dytiacha biblioteka
"Moho pryiatelia," no. 1. Chicago-Winnipeg: Mii pryiatel', 1951.
(Minn.)

————.

IA PIDU!: OPOVIDANNIA Z KNIAZHYKH CHASIV V UKRAINI. Toronto:
Ob'iednannia pratsivnykiv literatury dlia ditei i molodi,
1970. 29 p. (Metro)

————.

KOBZAREVA HOSTYNA: STSENICHNA KARTYNA Z ZHYTTIA T. SHEVCHENKA
U 3 VIDSLONAKH. Biblioteka Veselky, no. 2. Jersey City, N.J.:
UNA, 1956. (Minn.)

————.

MEDIVNYI TELESYK: VIRSHOVANA KAZOCHKA DLIA MENSHYKH DITEI.
New York: Svoboda, 1953. 16 p. (Minn.; UNO)

————.

PEREPOLOKH. Biblioteka Ievshan zillia. Jersey City, N.J.:
Nashym ditiam, 1951. (Minn.)

————.

PERSHYI BII: OPOVIDANNIA DLIA DITEI I MOLODI. Toronto:
Ob'iednannia pratsivnykiv literatury dlia ditei i molodi,
1974. 27 p. (Metro; Minn.)

————.

SOIKA SHTUKARKA I INSHI OPOVIDANNIA Z PRYRODY DLIA DITEI I
MOLODI. New York: Iurii Tyshchenko, 1953. (Minn.)

Folklore

Gregorovich, Jennie, ed.

  UKRAINIAN CHRISTMAS EVE/SVIATYI VECHIR. Toronto: Library,
  Ukrainian National Federation, 1976. 9 p. (Metro)

Kimpins'ka-Tatsiun, Oleksandra

  VESIL'NI OBRIADY I ZVYCHAI V SOKAL'SHCHYNI. Winnipeg:
  published by the author, 1965. 47 p. (U of T)

Klymasz, Robert Bogdan

  A BIBLIOGRAPHY OF UKRAINIAN FOLKLORE IN CANADA, 1902-64.
  Anthropology Papers, no. 21. Ottawa: National Museum of
  Canada, 1969. 53 p. (Metro)

———.

  FOLK NARRATIVE AMONG UKRAINIAN-CANADIANS IN WESTERN CANADA.
  Mercury Series Publications, no. 4. Ottawa: Canadian Centre
  for Folk Culture Studies, 1973. 133 p. (Metro; St. Vlad.;
  U of T)

Onomyr, M.

  UKRAINS'KE VESILLIA: ETNOHRAFICHNYI NARYS. New York: Howerla,
  1971. 64 p. (St. Vlad.; U of T)

Rudnyts'kyi, Iaroslav Bohdan

  MATERIIALY DO UKRAINS'KO-KANADIIS'KOI FOLKL'ORYSTYKY I
  DIIALEKTOLOGII. Vols. 1-3. UVAN Zbirnik zakhodoznavstva.
  Winnipeg: UVAN, 1956- . (Metro: vol. 1; St. Vlad.: vols. 1, 3;
  UNO; U of T)

———.

  READINGS IN UKRAINIAN FOLKLORE. Winnipeg: University of
  Manitoba Press, 1951. 32 p. (U of T)

————.

UKRAINIAN-CANADIAN FOLKLORE: TEXTS IN ENGLISH TRANSLATION.
UVAN Ucrainica occidentalia Series, vol. 7. Winnipeg: UVAN,
1960. 232 p. (Metro)

Semenko, Iurii, comp.

NARODNIE SLOVO: ZBIRNYK SUCHASNOHO UKRAINS'KOHO FOLKL'ORU.
New York: Soiuz zemel' sobornoï Ukraïny, selians'koi partii,
1964. 128 p. (St. Vlad.; U of T)

UKRAINIAN-CANADIAN FOLK WISDOM. 2nd enl. ed. Trans. by T. Chimczuk.
    Windsor, Ont.: Sumner, 1976. 183 p. (UNO)

UKRAINS'KI PEREKAZY. 32 p. New York: Educational Council, UCCA.
    (U of T)

UKRAINS'KO-ANHLIIS'KYI FLIRT: TOVARYS'KA HRA. New York: Howerla,
    n.d. 30 p. (UNO)

VOROZHBYT. Ukrains'ka narodnia biblioteka, no. 16. New York,
    1965. 63 p. (UNO)

VI. THE ARTS

Visual and Decorative Arts

General Sources

Andrusiv, Petro

> LYTSEM DO UKRAINS'KOHO MYSTETSTVA. Philadelphia: Ameryka,
> 1971. (Minn.)

_____.

> MYSTETSTVO V ZHYTTIA NARODU. Philadelphia: Ob'iednannia
> Mysttsiv Ukraintsiv v Amerytsi, 1967. (Minn.)

Dmytriw, Olya, comp.

> UKRAINIAN ARTS. Ed. by Anne Mitz. New York: Ukrainian Youth
> League of North America, 1955. 217 p. (Metro; St. Vlad.)

Sichyns'kyi, Volodymyr

> ISTORIIA UKRAINS'KOHO MYSTETSTVA. 2 vols. New York: Shevchenko
> Scientific Society, 1956. (Metro; Minn.; UNO; U of T)

Iconography and Painting

Luciow, Johanna

> EGGS BEAUTIFUL: HOW TO MAKE UKRAINIAN EASTER EGGS. Minneapolis,
> 1976. 96 p. (St. Vlad.)

MYSTETS'KE OZDOBLENNIA UKRAINS'KOI PRAVOSLAVNOI KATEDRY SV.
VOLODYMYRA V TORONTO. Toronto, n.d. (St. Vlad.)

National Museum of Man

> MY SHCHE ZHYVEMO NASHYM MYSTETSTVOM. Trilingual edition.
> Ottawa: National Museums of Canada, n.d. (UNO)

St. Nicholas Ukrainian Catholic Parish, Toronto

> THE ICONOGRAPHY OF ST. NICHOLAS CHURCH. Toronto: St. Nicholas
> Parish, 1977. 174 p. (Metro; St. Vlad.)

Surmach, Yaroslava

   UKRAINIAN EASTER EGGS. New York: Surma, 1952. 32 p. (St. Vlad.;
   U of T)

Artists

Alexander Archipenko

ALEXANDER ARCHIPENKO: A MEMORIAL EXHIBITION, 1967-1969.
   Los Angeles: Ritchie Press, 1967. 80 p. (St. Vlad.; UNO;
   U of T)

ARCHIPENKO: INTERNATIONAL SOLIDARITY. Ed. by Donald H. Karshan.
   Pref. by S. Dillon Ripley. Foreword by David W. Scott. Essay
   by Guy Habasque. Washington, D.C.: Smithsonian Institute
   Press for the National Collection of Fine Arts, 1969. 116 p.
   (UNO; U of T)

ARCHIPENKO: THE AMERICAN YEARS, 1923-1963. Exhibition held
   July 23-August 15, 1970 at Bernard Danenberg Galleries.
   New York, n.d. 36 p. (UNO)

ARCHIPENKO: THE PARIS YEARS; ARCHIPENKO: THE AMERICAN YEARS.
   Toronto: Art Gallery of Ontario, 1971. (St. Vlad.; UNO)

THE ARCHIPENKO EXPOSITION OF SCULPTURE AND PAINTING. Ukrainian
   Pavilion, Chicago World's Fair, 1933. Chicago: Siege Printing
   and Publishing, 1933. (St. Vlad.)

Winnipeg Art Gallery

   ALEXANDER ARCHIPENKO EXHIBITION. Winnipeg: Winnipeg Art
   Gallery, 1962. (U of T)

Mykola Butovych

MYKOLA BUTOVYCH: MONOHRAFIIA. With an essay by V. Sichyns'kyi.
   New York: Slovo, 1956. (UNO; U of T)

Alexis Gritchenko

______.

MY ENCOUNTERS WITH FRENCH ARTISTS: MEMOIRS OF AN ARTIST.
Introd. by Matt Phillips. New York: Alexis Gritchenko
Foundation, 1968. 54 p. (St. Vlad.)

______.

ROKY BURI I NATYSKU: SPOHADY MYSTTSIA, 1908-1918. Introd.
by Sviatoslav Hordyns'kyi. New York: Slovo, 1967. 104 p.
(Metro; U of T)

______.

WORKS FROM THE 1920S: AN EXHIBITION. Held November 19-
December 31, 1976. Edmonton: Edmonton Art Gallery, 1976.
12 p. (Metro)

Jacques Hnizdovsky

De Wolf, Gordon

FLORA EXOTICA: A COLLECTION OF FLOWERING PLANTS. Woodcuts by
Jacques Hnizdovsky. Boston: David R. Godine, 1972. 60 p.
(St. Vlad.)

IAKIV HNIZDOVS'KYI. New York: Prolog, 1967. 178 p. (Metro;
U of T)

IAKIV HNIZDOVS'KYI: MALIUNKY, HRAFIKA, KERAMIKA, STATTI. New
York: Prolog, 1967. 178 p. (St. Vlad.; UNO)

Silverberg, Robert

THE AUK, THE DODO AND THE ORYX: VANISHED AND VANISHING SPECIES.
Illus. by Jacques Hnizdovsky. New York: Thomas Crowell, 1967.
246 p. (St. Vlad.)

Tahir, Abe M.

HNIZDOVSKY: WOODCUTS, 1944-1975: A CATALOGUE RAISONNÉ.
Foreword by Peter A. Wick. Gretna, La.: Pelican Publishing,
1976. 166 p. (St. Vlad.; U of T)

Vasyl' Hryhorovych Krychevs'kyi

Pavlovs'kyi, Vadym

VASYL' HRYHOROVYCH KRYCHEVS'KYI: ZHYTTIA I TVORCHIST'.
New York: UVAN in the U.S.,   1974. 222 p. (St. Vlad.;
U of T)

Michael Kuczer

KUCZER. Catalogue of an exhibition held at the Ukrainian
    Institute of Modern Art, Chicago, April 25-May 1975. Chicago:
    Ukrainian Institute of Modern Art, 1975. (Metro)

William Kurelek

________.

    FIELDS. Montreal-Plattsburgh, N.Y.: Tundra Books, 1976.
    (Metro; St. Vlad.)

________.

    KURELEK COUNTRY. Boston: Houghton Mifflin, 1975. 127 p.
    (U of T)

________.

    KURELEK'S CANADA. Toronto: Pagurian Press, 1975. 127 p.
    (Metro; St. Vlad.; UNO)

________.

    THE LAST OF THE ARCTIC. Toronto: McGraw Hill-Ryerson, 1976.
    94 p. (Metro; St. Vlad.; U of T)

________.

    LUMBERJACK: PAINTINGS AND STORY. Montreal: Tundra Books,
    1974. 48 p. (Metro; St. Vlad.; U of T)

________.

    NATURE, POOR STEPDAME: A SERIES OF SIXTEEN FARM PAINTINGS.
    Catalogue of the exhibition held at the Isaacs Gallery,
    November 11-30, 1970. Toronto, 1970. (Metro)

______.

A NORTHERN NATIVITY: CHRISTMAS DREAMS OF A PRAIRIE BOY.
Montreal: Tundra Books, 1976. 48 p. (Metro; U of T)

______.

O TORONTO. Introd. by James Bacque. Toronto: New Press,
1973. 43 p. (Metro; St. Vlad.; U of T)

______.

THE PASSION OF CHRIST ACCORDING TO ST. MATTHEW. Niagara
Falls, Ont.: Niagara Falls Art Gallery and Museum, 1975.
192 p. (Metro; St. Vlad.; UNO)

______.

A PRAIRIE BOY'S WINTER. Montreal: Tundra Books, 1973. 48 p.
(Metro; St. Vlad.; UNO; U of T)

______.

A PRAIRIE BOY'S SUMMER. Montreal: Tundra Books, 1975. 48 p.
(Metro; St. Vlad.; U of T)

______.

A PRAIRIE BOY'S WINTER AND SUMMER. Montreal: Tundra Books,
1978. 46 p. (St. Vlad.)

______.

SOMEONE WITH ME: THE AUTOBIOGRAPHY OF WILLIAM KURELEK.
Original unedited text with foreword by James Maas.
Ithaca, N.Y.: Center for Improvement of Undergraduate
Education, Cornell University, 1973. 523 p. (Metro; St. Vlad.;
UNO; U of T)

WILLIAM KURELEK: A RETROSPECTIVE. Catalogue of an exhibition
   held September 20-October 20, 1970 at the Edmonton Art
   Gallery in association with the Isaacs Gallery, Toronto.
   Toronto: Coach House Press, 1970. (Metro; U of T)

WILLIAM KURELEK: PAINTER, ILLUSTRATOR, AUTHOR. London: Canadian
   High Commission, 1978. 14 p. (Metro)

Arnold, Abraham

    JEWISH LIFE IN CANADA. Illus. by William Kurelek. Edmonton:
Hurtig, 1976. 91 p. (Metro; U of T)

Mitchell, William O.

    WHO HAS SEEN THE WIND. Illus. by William Kurelek. Toronto:
Macmillan, 1976. 33 p. (St. Vlad.)

Paximadis, Mary

    LOOK WHO'S COMING: THE WACHNA STORY. Illus. by William
Kurelek. Oshawa: Wachna Foundation, 1976. 124 p. (St. Vlad.)

Serhii Lytvynenko

Hordyns'kyi, S., ed.

    SERHII LYTVYNENKO: SKUL'PTOR. Essays by V. Sichyns'kyi,
M. Hotsii and M. Ostroverkha. New York: Knyhospilka, 1956.
36 p. (St. Vlad.)

Ia. Maidanyk

VUIKOVA KNYHA: RICHNYK VUIKA SHTIFA V RYSUNKAKH IA. MAIDANYKA.
    Saskatoon: Ukrainian Canadian Historical Publications, 1974.
90 p. (St. Vlad.; UNO)

Architecture

Sichyns'kyi, Volodymyr

    PAMIATKY UKRAINS'KOI ARKHITEKTURY. Vol. 1. Philadelphia,
1952. (St. Vlad.; UNO)

Ceramics

Sichyns'kyi, Volodymyr

    UKRAINS'KA PORTSELIANA. Philadelphia: Ameryka, 1952. 18 p.
(Minn.; St. Vlad.)

Embroidery and Costume

Antonovych, Kateryna Mykhailivna

UKRAINS'KYI NARODNYI ODIAH: PRAKTYCHNI PORADY, VZORY.
Winnipeg: Ukrainian Women's Organization of Canada, 1954.
(Minn.)

2nd ed.: Toronto, Zhinochyi svit, 1964. 40 p. (St. Vlad.)
3rd ed.: Toronto, Zhinochyi svit, 1976. (Metro)

Avramenko, Vasyl'

UKRAINIAN NATIONAL DANCES, MUSIC AND COSTUMES. Hollywood:
published by the author, 1947. 80 p. (U of T)

————.

UKRAINS'KI NATSIONAL'NI TANKY, MUZYKA, I STRII. Hollywood:
published by the author, 1947. (Minn.)

Kolbenheyer, Erich

UKRAINIAN BUKOVINIAN CROSS-STITCH EMBROIDERY. Windsor:
Eastern Executive of the Ukrainian Women's Association of
Canada, 1974. 32 p. 74 plates. (Metro; St. Vlad.; UNO; U of T)

Orshinsky, Peter

TRADITIONAL BUKOVYNIAN SHIRTS AND JEWELLERY FOR WOMEN AS FOUND
IN CANADA. Canadian Bukovynian Folklore Studies, no. 1.
Fenwick, Ont., 1974. 86 p. (UNO; U of T)

Ostapchuk, Emily, ed.

FOLK ART OF CARPATHO-UKRAINE. Foreword by Volodymyr Sichyns'kyi.
Trans. of foreword by Olga Prychodko. Toronto: Phillip
Ostapchuk, 1957. 42 p. 152 plates. (Metro; Minn.; St. Vlad.)

Ruryk, Nancy R., comp. and ed.

UKRAINIAN EMBROIDERY: DESIGNS AND STITCHES. 3rd ed. Winnipeg:
Ukrainian Women's Association of Canada, 1974. 130 p. (UNO)

Smolen, Gloria A.

KIEV AND HUTSUL COSTUMES. Vol. 1, no. 1. Ed. by Anne Hatfield.
New York: Ukrainian Youth League of North America Foundation,
1960- . 14 p. (Minn.; St. Vlad.)

Stechyshyn, Savelia

MYSTETS'KI SKARBY UKRAINS'KYKH VYSHYVOK. Winnipeg: Ukrainian
Women's Association of Canada, 1950. (Metro; Minn.)

Zacharczuk, Stella

THE UKRAINIAN COSTUME. New York: Ukrainian Youth League of
North America Foundation, 195(?). 12 p. (St. Vlad.)

Graphics

HRAFIKA V BUNKRAKH UPA: AL'BOM DEREVORYTIV VYKONANYKH V UKRAINI
   V ROKAKH 1947-1950 MYSTSIA UKRAINS'KOHO PIDPILLIA NILA
   KHASEVYCHA-"BEI-ZOTA"-TA IOHO UCHNIV. Philadelphia: Prolog,
   1952. 69 p. (Minn.; St. Vlad.; UNO)

Folk Dance and Ballet

AN AID IN READING CHOREOGRAPHY. Toronto (?), 196(?). 43 p.
   (U of T)

Association of United Ukrainian Canadians

   UKRAINIAN FOLK DANCES AND OTHERS. Toronto: AUUC, National
   Executive Committee, 196(?). 108 p. (Metro; U of T)

Avramenko, Vasyl'

   UKRAINIAN NATIONAL DANCES, MUSIC AND COSTUMES. Hollywood:
   published by the author, 1947. 80 p. (U of T)

   ______.

   UKRAINS'KI NATSIONAL'NI TANKY, MUZYKA I STRII. Hollywood:
   published by the author, 1947. (Minn.)

   ______.

   UKRAINS'KI NATSIONAL'NI TANKY. Winnipeg: Shkola ukrains'koho
   natsional'noho tanku, 1928. (U of T)

Joukowsky, Anatol M.

   THE TEACHING OF ETHNIC DANCE. Illus. by Serge Smirnoff. New
   Designs in Physical Education Series. New York: J.L. Pratt,
   1965. 190 p. (Metro)

Klymash, Bohdan, comp.

   THE UKRAINIAN FOLK DANCE: A SYMPOSIUM. Vol. 1. Toronto:
   Ukrainian National Youth Federation, 1961- . (Metro; UNO;
   U of T)

Knysh, Irena

   ZHYVA DUSHA NARODU: DO IUVILEIU UKRAINS'KOHO TANKU. Winnipeg:
   published by the author, 1966. 78 p. (Metro; Minn.; St. Vlad.;
   UNO)

Marchenko, Petro

   HAILKY V KHOREOHRAFICHNII INSTSENIZATSII OLENKY GERDAN-ZAKLYNS'KOI.
   New York: published by the author, 1963. 56 p. (Metro; Minn.)

———.

   VICHNE I NEVMIRUSHCHE: V MYSTETSTVI OLENKY GERDAN-ZALYNS'KOI.
   New York: published by the author, 1956. (Minn.)

Pasternakova, Mariia

   UKRAINS'KA ZHINKA V KHOREOHRAFII. Winnipeg: Nataliia
   Kobryns'ka Foundation of the Ukrainian Women's Association of
   Canada, 1963. 216 p. (Metro; Minn.; St. Vlad.; UNO; U of T)

———.

   UKRAINS'KA ZHINKA V KHOREOHRAFII. 2nd rev. ed. Winnipeg:
   Nataliia Kobryns'ka Foundation of the Ukrainian Women's
   Association of Canada, 1964. 238 p. (St. Vlad.)

UKRAINIAN FOLK DANCES AND OTHERS. Vol. 5. Toronto: Association
   of United Ukrainian Canadians, National Junior Council,
   1971. (St. Vlad.)

Music

Andriievs'kyi, Viktor

MYKOLA LYSENKO: BAT'KO UKRAINS'KOI MUZYKY. Biblioteka Vil'ne
slovo, no. 5. Toronto: Vil'ne slovo, 1962. (Minn.)

Demydchuk, Semen

KINTSEVYI VIDROBITOK. New York: Surma, 1958. (Minn.)

Havryliuk, M., ed.

UKRAINS'KI KOMPOZYTORY. Buenos Aires: Imprenta "Champion"
de Jose Kuzmyzc, 1970. (Minn.)

Hrinchenko, Mykola

ISTORIIA UKRAINS'KOI MUZYKY. 2nd ed. New York: Ukrainian Institute
of Music, 1961. 191 p. (Metro; Minn.; UNO)

Iemets', Vasyl

UKRAINI: IUVYLEINA PAMIATKA Z NAHODY 25-LITN'OI PRATSI
VASYLIA IEMTSIA DLIA UKRAINS'KOHO MUZYCHNOHO MYSTETSTVA.
n.p., 1936. (Minn.)

________.

VASYL' IEMETS': I. U ZOLOTE 50-RICHCHIA NA SLUZHBI UKRAINI.
II. PRO KOZAKIV-BANDURNYKIV. Hollywood: Basilian Press, 1961.
(Minn.)

Kohut, Iosyf, comp.

KOLIADY: ABO PISNI NA RIZDVO KHRYSTOVE, Z NOTAMY. Stewartburn,
Man., 1953. (Minn.)

KOLIADNYK: TSERKOVNI KOLIADY Z DODATKOM NARODNYKH KOLIADOK I
SHCHEDRIVOK. Based on the collection of O.M. Kinash. Winnipeg:
Ukrainian Booksellers and Publishers, n.d. 158 p. (St. Vlad.)

KOLIADY I SHCHEDRIVKY NA RIZDVO KHRYSTOVE I BOHOIAVLENNIA Z
  DODATKOM PISEN' STRASTNYKH, VOSKRESNYKH I YNSHYKH PISEN'
  TSERKOVNYKH. Jersey City, N.J.: Svoboda, 1927. (Minn.)

Koshyts', Oleksander Antonovych

  PRO UKRAINS'KU PISNIU I MUZYKU. 2nd ed. New York: Nasha
  bat'kivshchyna, 1970. 47 p. (U of T)

  ———.

  PRO UKRAINS'KU PISNIU I MUZYKU. From the Ukrainian Lecture
  Series held in 1941 by the Department of East European
  Languages, Columbia University and the Ukrainian National
  Association of America. Winnipeg: Orhanizatsiia kul'turno-
  osvitnykh pratsivnykiv im. O. Koshytsia, 1942. 40 p. (Minn.;
  UNO)

  ———.

  SPOHADY. 2 vols. Winnipeg: Ukrainian Cultural and Educational
  Centre, 1947-48. (Metro; Minn.; St. Vlad.; UNO; U of T)

  ———.

  VIDHUKY MYNULOHO: O. KOSHYTS' V LYSTAKH DO P. MATSENKA.
  Winnipeg: Ukrainian Cultural and Educational Centre, 1954.
  80 p. (Minn.; UNO)

  ———.

  Z PISNEIU CHEREZ SVIT: PODOROZH UKRAINS'KOI RESPUBLIKANS'KOI
  KAPELI. 2 vols. Winnipeg: Ukrainian Cultural and Educational
  Centre, 1952-70. (Minn.: vol. 1; UNO: vol. 1; U of T: vols. 1-2)

Kovaliv, Ivan

  VASYL' BARVINS'KYI: NARYS ZHYTTIA I TVORCHOSTY. Toronto:
  M. Lysenko Institute of Music, 1964. 14 p. (Minn.; UNO)

Kowalsky, Humphrey

  UKRAINIAN FOLK SONGS: A HISTORICAL TREATISE. Boston: Stratford,
  1925. (Minn.)

Krawchuk, Peter

>PISNIA I MUZYKA IOHO ZHYTTIA: ROZPOVID' PRO MYTTSIA DEM'IANA
>VYKHRYSTOVA. Toronto: Kobzar, 1973. 118 p. (U of T)

Levyts'ka, Liubov and Ivan Bodrevych

>LEV TURKEVYCH: ZHYTTIA I TVORCHIST'. Toronto: Liubov Levyts'ka,
>1965. 353 p. (Metro; UNO; U of T)

Levyts'kyi, Ivan

>POPULIARNA NAUKA HARMONII. New York: Howerla, 1966. 92 p.
>(UNO)

LIRA: SURMA: VELYKYI ZBIRNYK UKRAINS'KYKH PISEN'. New York:
>Surma, 1956. (Minn.)

Lys'ko, Zinovii, comp. and ed.

>UKRAINS'KI NARODNI MELODII. 5 vols. New York: UVAN in the
>U.S.,   1964- . (Minn.: vols. 1-5; U of T: vols. 1-3)

MALYI KOLIADNYK. Winnipeg: Ukrainian Orthodox Church in
>Canada, 1955. (Minn.)

Matsenko, Pavlo

>KONSPEKT ISTORII UKRAINS'KOI TSERKOVNOI MUZYKY. Winnipeg:
>St. Andrew's College, 1973. 101 p. (Metro; U of T)

__________.

>NARYSY DO ISTORII UKRAINS'KOI TSERKOVNOI MUZYKY. Roblin,
>Man., 1968. 151 p. (Minn.; U of T)

Mykhan'ko, M.

>IAHILKY: 51 UKRAINS'KYKH NARODNYKH PISEN' I ZABAV NA VELYKDEN'
>Z ROZVIDKOIU PRO GENEZU IAHILOK I IKH TEPERISHNYI VYHLIAD.
>New York: Howerla, 1966. 42 p. (UNO)

Navrots'kyi, Vasyl'

>SPIVANYK DLIA SHKIL NARODNYKH. New York: H.E. Smolen, n.d.
>(Minn.)

NOVYI ZBIRNYK NARODNYKH PISEN'. Winnipeg: Ukrainian Booksellers
   and Publishers, n.d. (Minn.)

Nyzhankovs'kyi, Ostap

   NASHA SLAVNA UKRAINA: UKRAINS'KYI PATRIOTYCHNYI SPIVANNYK Z
   NOTAMY Z POVNYM TEKSTOM PISEN'. Winnipeg: Ukrainian Booksellers
   and Publishers, n.d. (Minn.)

Opalinski, Christine

   MUSIC AND SONG OF UKRAINE. Mother Ambrose Series, no. 1.
   Weston, Ont.: St. Demetrius Ukrainian Catholic Church, 1976.
   36 p. (U of T)

REVOLIUTSIINI PISNI. Winnipeg: Ukrains'ki robitnychi visti, 1921.
   (Minn.)

ROBITNYCHI PISNI Z RADIANS'KOI UKRAINY, Z HALYCHYNY I POL'S'KOI
   NEVOLI. New York: Holos pravdy, 1921. (Minn.)

SAMOUCHOK: METODYCHNYI PIDRUCHNYK DLIA NAUKY NOTNOHO S'PIVU.
   2nd ed. n.p., n.d. (Minn.)

Shchypavka, Hryts'

   NOVI PISNI. With an appendix by D. Drapavka. Winnipeg:
   Ukrainian Printers, n.d. (Minn.)

Simpson, George Wilfrid

   ALEXANDER KOSHETZ IN UKRAINIAN MUSIC. Winnipeg: Ukrainian
   Cultural and Educational Centre, 1946.

Skrytyi, Marko

   PISNI SHCHYROI LIUBOVY. New York: Sichovyi bazar, 1920.
   (Minn.)

Sonevyts'kyi, Ihor

   ARTEM VEDEL' I IOHO MUZYCHNA SPADSHCHYNA. New York, 1966.
   177 p. (Metro; Minn.; U of T)

Tarnovs'kyi, Mykola, comp.

ROBITNYCHI PISNI. Biblioteka Soiuza ukrains'kykh robitnychykh
orhanizatsii. New York: Ukrains'ki shchodenni visti, 1928.
(Minn.)

TSERKOVNI KOLIADY Z DODATKOM KOLIADOK I SHCHEDRIVOK CHYSTO
NARODNYKH. 4th rev. ed. Yorkton, Sask.: Fathers of the Most
Holy Saviour, 1946. (Minn.)

TSERKOVNI PISNI Z NOTAMY: PRAVDYVYI PEREDRUK Z KRAIEVOHO VYDANIA.
Winnipeg: Rus'ka knyharnia, n.d. (Minn.)

"UKRAINS'KA MUZYKA" ANTONA RUDNYTS'KOHO: ISTORYCHNO-KRYTYCHNYI
OHLIAD CHY PASKVIL'? Chicago: Committee in Defense of Ukrainian
Culture, 1964. (Minn.)

UKRAINS'KA PISNIA ZA KORDONOM: SVITOVA KONTSERTOVA PODOROZH
UKRAINS'KOHO NATSIONAL'NOHO KHORU PID PROVODOM OLEKSANDRA
A. KOSHYTSIA. Paris: O.A. Koshyts' Ukrainian Music Society,
1929. (Minn.; U of T)

UKRAINS'KYI SPIVANNYK. Enl. ed. Winnipeg: Ukrainian Booksellers
and Publishers, n.d. (Minn.)

V DEN' MATERI: ZBIRNYK Z NAHODY "DNIA MATERI." Winnipeg:
Ukrainian Women's Association of Canada, 1931. (Minn.)

VESELA BANDURA: POVNYI ZBIRNYK VESELYKH I ZHARTIVLYVYKH PISEN'
I PRYSPIVIV DO MUZYCHNYKH INSTRUMENTIV I TANTSIV. Jersey
City, N.J.: Svoboda, n.d. (Minn.)

VOIENNI PISNI. 2nd ed. New York: Ukrainian Bookstore, n.d.
(Minn.)

Vytvyts'kyi, Vasyl'

MYKHAILO HAIVORONS'KYI: ZHYTIIA I TVORCHIST'. New York, 1954.
205 p. (UNO)

Zales'kyi, Ostap

KOROTKYI NARYS ISTORII UKRAINS'KOI MUZYKY. Populiarna
biblioteka "Ameryky," no. 3. Philadelphia: Ameryka, 1951.
20 p. (Minn.; U of T)

———.

    MYKOLA LYSENKO: 1842-1962. Winnipeg: Novyi shliakh, 1962.
(Minn.)

———.

    ZAHAL'NI OSNOVY MUZYCHNOHO ZNANNIA: TEORIIA MUZYKY. No. 125.
New York: Howerla, 1958. (Minn.)

Zavitnevych, Vasyl', comp.

    ANTOLOHIIA UKRAINS'KOI PISNI. Vol. 1. New York: Ukrainian
Orthodox Church of the U.S.A., 1967- . (Minn.)

———, comp. and ed.

    SPIVY IZ POSTOVOI TRIODY. New York: Ukrainian Orthodox
Church of the U.S.A., 1960. (Minn.)

———.

    SPIVY NA LITURHII. South Bound Brook, N.J.: Ukrainian
Orthodox Church of the U.S.A., 1963. (Minn.)

———.

    VELYKA SUBOTA I PASKHA. New York, 1964. (Minn.)

———.

    VSENOSHNA. Parts 1-2. New York: Scientific Theologic Institute
of the U.S.A., 1961. (Minn.)

ZHAIVORONOK: ZBIRNYK PISEN' Z NOTAMY DLIA UKRAINS'KOI MOLODI U
TROKH CHASTYNAKH Z DODATKOM: RUKHANKOVI VPRAVY. 2nd ed.
Winnipeg: Ukrainian Voice, 1952. 149 p. (Minn.; UNO)

DOMASHNIE MIASOVYROBNYTSTVO TA KONSERVUVANNIA OVOCHIV I IARYN:
ZBIRKA NAIKRASHCHYKH PRYPYSIV DLIA MIASNYKH VYROBIV DOMA,
KONSERVUVANNIA MIASA TA OVOCHIV TA IARYN. New enl. ed.
Winnipeg: Ukrainian Booksellers and Publishers, n.d. (Minn.)

Holy Ghost Ukrainian Catholic Parish, Sydney, N.S.

A BOOK OF UKRAINIAN TRADITIONAL AND MODERN RECIPES. Sydney:
Holy Ghost Parish, 1976. 164 leaves. (St. Vlad.)

Kostets'ka, Natalia

HORODYNA I OVOCHI: KUKHARS'KI PRYPYSY. Praktychna knyhozbirnia,
no. 2. Philadelphia: Ukrainian National Women's League of
America, 1955. (Minn.)

______.

KUKHOVARS'KI PRYPYSY: M'IASYVO, HORODYNA I OVOCHI. PECHYVO.
Philadelphia, 1969. (Minn.)

Sisterhood of St. John's Ukrainian Orthodox Church, Johnson City,
N.Y.

A BOOK OF FAVORITE RECIPES. Johnson City: Sisterhood of
St. John's, 1968. (St. Vlad.; UNO)

Stechyshyn, Savelia

TRADITIONAL UKRAINIAN COOKERY. Winnipeg: Trident Press, 1963.
(Minn.)

2nd ed.: 1959. 497 p. (Metro); 5th ed.: 1971 (Metro);
6th ed.: 1973 (St. Vlad.; UNO)

Terlets'ka, Zenoviia

UKRAINS'KI STRAVY: DAVNI PRYPYSY Z HALYTS'KOI UKRAINY.
Praktychna knyhozbirnia, no. 4. Philadelphia: Ukrainian
National Women's League of America, 1971. 210 p. (Metro;
Minn.)

Ukrainian Catholic Women's League, Yorkton, Sask.

UCWL COOKBOOK: UKRAINIAN TRADITIONAL AND FAVOURITE RECIPES.
2nd ed. Yorkton: UCWL, 1970. 112 p. (St. Vlad.)

Ukrainian Catholic Women's League, St. George's Cathedral, Saskatoon

    FOR BETTER COOKING. 2nd ed. Saskatoon: St. George's UCWL,
1970. 117 p. (St. Vlad.)

———.

    UKRAINIAN TRADITIONAL AND FAVOURITE RECIPES: TO MARK THE
FIFTIETH ANNIVERSARY OF THE UKRAINIAN WOMEN'S ASSOCIATION OF
CANADA: DAUGHTERS OF UKRAINE, MONTREAL, QUEBEC, 1926-1976.
Montreal: UWAC, Daughters of Ukraine branch, 1976. 136 p.
(St. Vlad.)

Ukrainian Women's Association of Canada, Montreal

    UKRAINIAN TRADITIONAL AND FAVOURITE RECIPES. Montreal: UWAC,
Daughters of Ukraine branch, 1975. 136 p. (St. Vlad.)

————, North Battleford, Sask.

    CENTENNIAL COOKBOOK: UKRAINIAN AND MODERN FAVOURITES DEDICATED
TO THE PIONEERS BY THE UKRAINIAN WOMEN'S ASSOCIATION OF
CANADA, O. PCHILKA BRANCH, NORTH BATTLEFORD, SASK. North
Battleford: UWAC, O. Pchilka branch, 1976. 86 p. (St. Vlad.)

————, Vancouver

    A BOOK OF RECIPES: UKRAINIAN TRADITIONAL AND MODERN FAVOURITES
TO MARK THE THIRTIETH ANNIVERSARY OF THE LESIA UKRAINKA BRANCH
OF THE UKRAINIAN WOMEN'S ASSOCIATION OF CANADA, 1933-1963.
Vancouver: UWAC, Lesia Ukrainka branch, 1965. 106 p. (St. Vlad.)

UKRAINS'KO-ANGLIIS'KA KUKHARKA: PRAKTYCHNI PORADY I POIASNENNIA
    V UKRAINS'KII MOVI IAK VARYTY I PECHY NA ANGLIIS'KYI SPOSIB.
    Trans. and comp. by E. Hykava, et al. Winnipeg: Ukrainian Booksellers
    and Publishers, n.d. 178 p. (UNO)

UKRAINS'KO-ANGLIIS'KA KUKHARKA: PRAKTYCHNI PORADY I POIASNENNIA
    V UKRAINS'KII MOVI IAK VARYTY I PECHY NA ANGLIIS'KYI SPOSIB.
    II. STAROKRAIEVA DOMASHNIA KUKHNIA. III. VKAZIVKY DLIA
    ZDOROVLIA. Winnipeg: Ukrainian Booksellers and Publishers,
    n.d. 220 p. (UNO)

UKRAINS'KO-ANGLIIS'KA KUKHARKA. Pt. 2. 3rd ed. Winnipeg:
    Ukrainian Booksellers and Publishers, n.d. (Minn.)

    4th ed.: Winnipeg, Ukrainian Booksellers and Publishers,
    n.d. (Minn.)

INDEXES

* Publishers have not been included.

ORGANIZATIONS:

Academies; Cultural, Government and Religious Institutions;
Learned Societies, Museums

Canadian Association for Adult Education, 22
Canadian Centre for Folk Culture Studies, 216
Canadian High Commission (London, England), 223
Canadian Historical Association, 21
Canadian Institute of Onomastic Sciences, 19, 20, 141, 142, 143, 145
Canadian Institute of Ukrainian Studies, 15, 21
Canadian-Ukrainian Educational Association, 16, 148
Canadian Ukrainian Immigrant Aid Society, 10
Canadian-Ukrainian Institute "Prosvita." See Prosvita
Carpathian Sich Brotherhood, 141
Cathedral of Ss. Vladimir and Olga, Winnipeg, Man., 46
Catholic Truth Society of Canada, 47
Chornomors'ka Sich, 102
Committee for Defense of Rites and Traditions of the Ukrainian
    Catholic Church in Canada, 44
Committee in Defense of Soviet Political Prisoners, 113
Committee in Defense of Ukrainian Culture, 233
Congress of Ukrainian Canadians. See Ukrainian Canadian Committee,
    Congresses
Cooperatives. Winnipeg, 34
Council of Eastern Orthodox Youth Leaders of the Americas, 37, 91
Cyrillo-Methodian Brotherhood, 163, 193

Edmonton Art Gallery, 221

Federation of Ukrainian Social Democracy in Canada (FUSD), 59
Federation of Ukrainian Student Organizations of America. See Soiuz
    ukrains'kykh students'kykh tovarystv Ameryky
Federation of Ukrainians in the U.S., 102
Federatsiia amerykans'kykh ukraintsiv v Mishigen. See Ukrainian-
    American Federation of Michigan
Federatsiia ukrains'koi sotsiial-demokratii v Kanadi. See Federation
    of Ukrainian Social Democracy in Canada
Federatsiia Ukraintsiv v Zluchenykh Derzhavakh (FUZD). See Federation
    of Ukrainians in the U.S.
Fond dopomohy ukraintsiv Kanady. See Ukrainian Canadian Relief Fund
Fundatsiia im. T. Shevchenka. See Ukrainian Canadian Foundation of
    Taras Shevchenko

Government of Canada. Ministry of Mines and Natural Resources, 22;
    Ministry of the Secretary of State, Citizenship Branch, 18
Government of Ontario. Department of the Provincial Secretary and
    Citizenship, 3; Ministry of Community and Social Services, 121

"Haidamaky" Ukrainian Progressive Workers Organization of America, 102
Harvard Ukrainian Research Institute, 77

Ob'iednannia pratsivnykiv dytiachoi literatury (OPDL), 139, 209, 211,
   213
Ob'iednannia pratsivnykiv literatury dlia ditei i molodi (OPLDM),
   135, 209, 212, 213, 214, 215
Ob'iednannia ukrains'kykh lisnykiv i derevnykiv (OBULID), 102
Ob'iednannia ukrains'kykh pedahohiv u Kanadi. See Association of
   Ukrainian Educators in Canada
Ob'iednannia ukrains'kykh pys'mennykiv "Slovo." See Association of
   Ukrainian Writers "Slovo"
Ob'iednannia ukrains'kykh pys'mennykiv v ekzyli. See Association of
   Ukrainian Writers in Exile
Ontario Modern Language Teachers' Association. Ukrainian Teacher's
   Committee, 134
OPLDM. See Ob'iednannia pratsivnykiv literatury dlia ditei i molodi
Organization for the Defense of Four Freedoms of Ukraine (OOChSU),
   165, 175, 194
Organization for the Defense of the Lemkian Region, 146, 191
Organization for the Defense of Ukraine. See Orhanizatsiia oborony
   Ukrainy
Organization for the Rebirth of Ukraine (ODVU), 59, 103
Organization of Ukrainian Nationalists (OUN), 59, 103
Organizatsiia kul'turno-osvitnykh pratsivnykiv im. O. Koshytsia v
   Kanadi, 230
Orhanizatsiia derzhavnoho vidrodzhennia Ukrainy. See Organization
   for the Rebirth of Ukraine
Orhanizatsiia oborony chotyr'okh svobid Ukrainy. See Organization
   for the Defense of Four Freedoms of Ukraine
Orhanizatsiia oborony Lemkivshchyny. See Organization for the Defense
   of the Lemkian Region
Orhanizatsiia oborony Ukrainy (OOU), 103
Orhanizatsiia ukrainok Kanady im. Ol'hy Basarab. See Ukrainian
   Women's Organization of Canada
Orhanizatsiia ukrains'kykh natsionalistiv. See Organization of
   Ukrainian Nationalists
Orhanizatsiia "Za voliu Ukrainy," 103
Oseredok ukrains'koi kul'tury i osvity. See Ukrainian Cultural and
   Educational Centre

Plast. Canada, 59-60; U.S., 104, 148
Progressive Labour Party, 8, 25
Prohresyvna partiia pratsi. See Progressive Labour Party
Prosvita, 34, 51, 52, 53, 54, 58, 98, 145

Rada ukrains'koi shkoly Kanady, 135
Redemptorist Fathers of the Eastern Rite, Yorkton, Sask., 47

Scientific Theologic Institute of the USA, 234
Shevchenko Foundation. See Ukrainian Canadian Foundation of Taras
  Shevchenko
Shevchenko Scientific Society, 11, 21, 22, 54, 88, 93, 96, 97, 98,
  122, 123, 124, 126, 127, 128, 132, 149, 158, 177, 178, 198, 219
Shkil'na rada UKKA. See Ukrainian Congress Committee of America,
  Educational Council
Shkola ukrains'koho natsional'noho tanku, 227
Sisters Servants of Mary Immaculate, 44, 46, 47
Hryhorii Skovoroda Ukrainian School, 50
Slavia Library, 85
Slovo. See Association of Ukrainian Writers "Slovo"
Society of Volyn in Toronto, 49, 96
Soiuz het'mantsiv derzhavnykiv Ameryky i Kanady, 60, 104
Soiuz trudovoi demokratii v Amerytsi (STDA), 104
Soiuz uchasnykiv ukrains'koi vyzvol'noi borot'by (SUUVB), 104
Soiuz ukrainok Ameryky. See Ukrainian National Women's League of
  America
Soiuz ukrainok Kanady. See Ukrainian Women's Association of Canada
Soiuz ukrains'koi molodi Kanady (SUMK), 60
Soiuz ukrains'kykh robitnychykh orhanizatsii (SURO), 82, 105
Soiuz ukrains'kykh students'kykh tovarystv Ameryky (SUSTA), 105
Soiuz ukraintsiv samostiinykiv (SUS). See Ukrainian Self-Reliance
  League of Canada
Soiuz vyzvolennia Ukrainy, 15, 105
Soiuz zemel' sobornoi Ukrainy, selians'koi partii (SZSU), 105, 217
Spilka ukrains'koi molodi Ameryky. See Ukrainian Youth Association
  in America (SUMA)
Spilka ukrains'koi molodi Kanady. See Ukrainian Youth Association
  (SUM) of Canada
Spilka ukrains'kykh zhurnalistiv Ameryky (SUZhA). See Association of
  Ukrainian Journalists of America
Spilka ukrains'kykh zhurnalistiv Kanady. See Association of Ukrainian
  Journalists of Canada
Spilka vyzvolennia Ukrainy (SVU), 105, 116, 145
Svitova federatsiia ukrains'kykh orhanizatsii, 82
Svitovyi kongres ukrains'koho zhinotstva. See World Congress of
  Ukrainian Women
Svitovyi kongres ukrains'koi vil'noi nauky. See World Congress of
  Free Ukrainian Scholarship
Svitovyi kongres vil'nykh ukraintsiv (SKVU). See World Congress of
  Free Ukrainians

Tantalus Research, 10
T.H. Shevchenko Museum in Palermo. Oakville, Ont., 52
Toronto Department of Education, Community Programs Branch, 17

Ukrains'kyi kongresovyi komitet Ameryky (UKKA). See Ukrainian Congress
    Committee of America
Ukrains'kyi muzei-arkhiv u Klivlendi. See Ukrainian Museum-Archives,
    Cleveland
Ukrains'kyi muzychnyi instytut. See Ukrainian Institute of Music
Ukrains'kyi narodnyi dim. See Ukrainian National Home
Ukrains'kyi narodnyi dim v Vinnipegu. See Ukrainian National Home
    Association in Winnipeg
Ukrains'kyi narodnyi fond, 116
Ukrains'kyi narodnyi soiuz (UNS). See Ukrainian National Association
Ukrains'kyi pravoslavnyi sobor sv. Pokrovy, Winnipeg, Man., 43
Ukrains'kyi publitsystychno-naukovyi instytut. See Ukrainian Research
    and Information Institute
Ukrains'kyi robitnychyi soiuz. See Ukrainian Workingmen's Association
Ukrains'kyi sotsiolohichnyi instytut (Ukrainian Sociological Institute),
    12, 79
Ukrains'kyi tekhnichno-hospodars'kyi instytut. See Ukrainian Husbandry
    Academy
Ukrains'kyi vil'nyi universytet. See Ukrainian Free University
Ukrains'kyi vyzvol'nyi fond Kanady. See Ukrainian Liberation Fund
    of Canada
Ukrains'kyi zolotyi khrest. See Ukrainian Gold Cross
Union for the Liberation of Ukraine. See Soiuz vyzvolennia Ukrainy.
Union of All Ukrainian Lands, Ukrainian Peasant Party. See Soiuz
    zemel' sobornoi Ukrainy, selians'koi partii
United American Ukrainian Organizations Committee of New York, 84
United Ukrainian-American Relief Committee (UUARC), 82, 116-17
U.S. Army Language School, Monterey, Cal., 140
U.S. Congress, House Committee on the Judiciary, 84

Volhynian Research Institute, 27
Vzaimna pomich. See Ukrainian Fraternal Society of Canada

Wachna Foundation, 18, 224
Winnipeg Art Gallery, 220
Winnipeg Credit Union, 30
Workers' Benevolent Association of Canada (WBA), 22
World Congress of Free Ukrainian Scholarship, 100, 118
World Congress of Free Ukrainians (WCFU), 50, 74, 117-18
World Congress of Ukrainian Women, 118
World Federation of Ukrainian Organizations. See Svitova federatsiia
    ukrains'kykh orhanizatsii

Zhromadzhennia sester sluzhebnyts'. See Sisters Servants of Mary
    Immaculate
Zluchenyi ukrains'kyi amerykans'kyi dopomohovyi komitet (ZUADK). See
    United Ukrainian-American Relief Committee